—— Praise for *The First Fleet* ——

'Alan Frost is the myth-buster of Australian history ... should be studied by ... anyone interested in the nation's beginnings.'—*The Saturday Age*

'It is almost certain that Frost knows more than anybody else about the early maritime history of this land ... This book will surely alter the way Sydney sees its history.'—GEOFFREY BLAINEY, *The Weekend Australian*

'This book has rewritten the rules of First Fleet scholarship.'—*The Sydney Morning Herald*

'Frost positively rampages through the pronouncements of earlier scholars, smiting conventional wisdoms left and right ... We need more Frosts.'
—*The Canberra Times*

'This is revisionist history at its best, immaculately researched and written.'
—*Bookseller & Publisher*

'Highly readable, Frost's work will be enjoyed by anyone with an interest in early Australia.'—*The Sunday Herald Sun*

'An exciting reassessment of the origins of the British colony in Terra Australis.'—*The Courier Mail*

—— Praise for *Botany Bay: The Real Story* ——

'Iconoclastic and refreshing ... an exhilarating read'
—*The Sydney Morning Herald*

'Fascinating and compelling'—*The Weekend Australian*

'[An] amazing work ... Frost has presented a powerful and compelling case.'
—*The Canberra Times*

'A nuanced, complex story'—*The Sunday Age*

'Frost's evidence is compelling, making the book essential reading for anyone interested in Australia's European settlement.'—*The Herald Sun*

The First Fleet

The First Fleet: The Real Story

ALAN FROST

Published by Black Inc.,
an imprint of Schwartz Media Pty Ltd
37–39 Langridge Street
Collingwood VIC 3066 Australia
email: enquiries@blackincbooks.com
http://www.blackincbooks.com

Copyright © Alan Frost 2012
First published 2011

ALL RIGHTS RESERVED.
No part of this publication may be reproduced, stored in a retrieval system, or transmitted in any form by any means electronic, mechanical, photocopying, recording or otherwise without the prior consent of the publishers.

The National Library of Australia Cataloguing-in-Publication entry:

Frost, Alan, 1943-

The First Fleet : the real story / Alan Frost.

2nd ed.

ISBN: 9781863955614 (pbk.)

Includes bibliographical references and index.

Great Britain. Royal Navy. Fleet, First.
First Fleet, 1787-1788.
Australia--History--1788-1851.

994.02

Cover image: A Two-Decker and a Frigate Running into the Thames off Gravesend (detail). By Charles Brooking, date unknown. Reproduced courtesy of the National Maritime Museum, Greenwich, London.

Cover design by Thomas Deverall and Peter Long
Book design by Thomas Deverall
Typeset by Duncan Blachford
Index by Michael Ramsden

Printed in Australia by Griffin Press an Accredited ISO AS/ NZS 14001:2004 Environmental Management System printer.

The paper this book is printed on is certified against the Forest Stewardship Council® Standards. Griffin Press holds FSC chain of custody certification SGS-COC-005088. FSC promotes environmentally responsible, socially beneficial and economically viable management of the world's forests.

Contents

Preface ... xi
Introduction ... 1

Part One: Planning a Convict Colony
1. *Announcing the Decision* ... 17
2. *The Colony: Society, Law and Governance* ... 27

Part Two: Assembling the Fleet
3. *The People 1: Officials and Officers* ... 49
4. *People 2: Ships' Crews, Marines, Convicts, Wives and Children* ... 64
5. *The Ships* ... 81
6. *Equipping the Colonists* ... 95
7. *Loading the Ships and Embarking the People* ... 114

Part Three: Preparing to Sail
8. *At Portsmouth* ... 129
9. *Preparing Bodies for the Voyage* ... 140

Part Four: The Voyage
10. *Leaving the World* ... 159

Part Five: The Cost
11. *No Cheaper Mode?* ... 181

Conclusion ... 198

Acknowledgments ... 217
Endnotes ... 219
Select Bibliography ... 250
Index ... 253

Thus, under the blessing of God, was happily completed, in eight months and one week, a voyage which, before it was undertaken, the mind hardly dared venture to contemplate, and on which it was impossible to reflect without some apprehensions as to its termination. This fortunate completion of it, however, afforded even to ourselves as much matter of surprise as of general satisfaction; for in the above space of time we had sailed five thousand and twenty-one leagues; had touched at the American and African continents; and had at last rested within a few days' sail of the antipodes of our native country, without meeting any accident in a fleet of eleven sail, nine of which were merchantmen that had never before sailed in that distant and imperfectly explored ocean: and when it is considered, that there was on board a large body of convicts, many of whom were embarked in a very sickly state, we might be deemed peculiarly fortunate, that of the whole number of all descriptions of persons coming to form the new settlement, only thirty-two had died since their leaving England, among whom were to be included one or two deaths by accident; although previous to our departure it was generally conjectured, that before we should have been a month at sea one of the transports would have been converted into a hospital ship.

—DAVID COLLINS,
An Account of the English Colony in New South Wales, 1798

The Voyage of the First Fleet

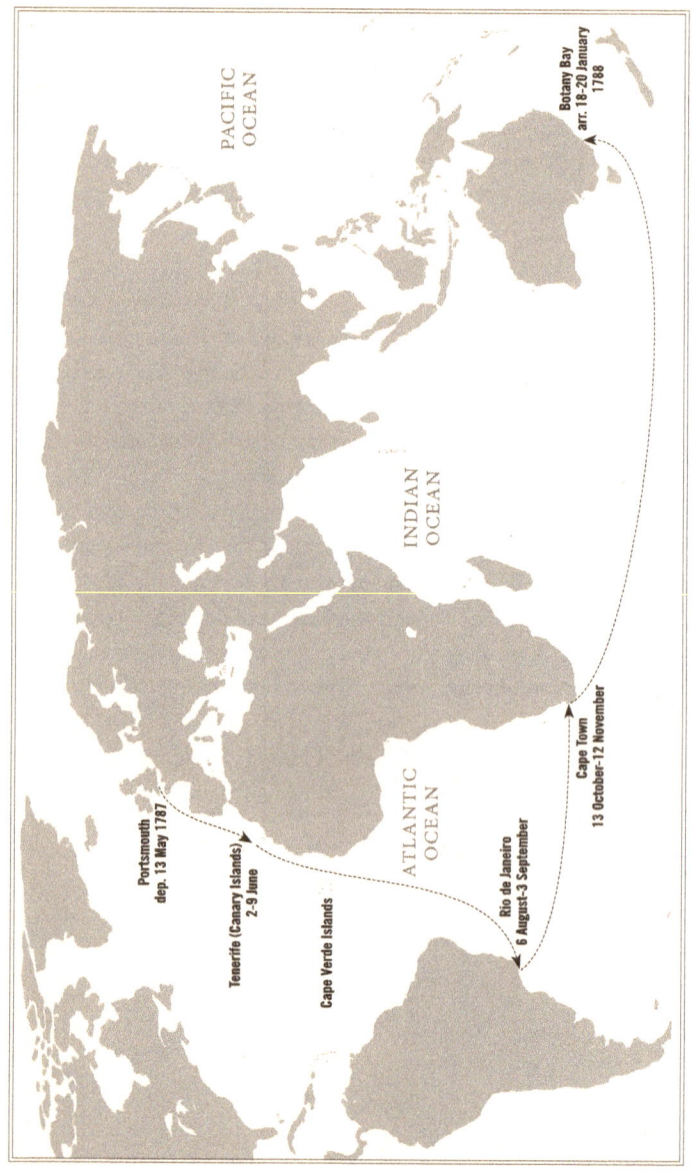

Preface

SURPRISING AS IT IS, THIS IS the first extended study of the mounting of the First Fleet that carried the officials, marines and convicts who began the British colonization of New South Wales in 1788.

It is based on some 2000 documents that I have collected over the past thirty-five years, and that Dr Natasha Campo and I have transcribed and edited. I have told the story of this gathering in *Botany Bay: The Real Story* (Black Inc., Melbourne, 2011). While this long process may reflect no particular merit except persistence, it is also true that such a study as this could not properly have been undertaken without a detailed knowledge of the extended documentary record.

Despite its being so extensive, it is clear that even this record is not complete. Much of the planning was undertaken in conversations among officials at the Home Office, Treasury, Admiralty and Navy Board, and First Fleet officers such as Arthur Phillip (governor) and John White (chief surgeon). Also, numbers of the documents that were created are now lost to history. But while some aspects of the venture remain obscure (e.g. Phillip's appointment), most can now be elucidated in considerable detail.

Editorial practices

In editing the documents we have mostly modernized spelling, capitalization and punctuation. (The principal exception is that we have left in their original form legal documents, such as Letters-Patent and Acts of Parliament.) Sometimes, in the interest of readier comprehension, we have also broken up very long passages into shorter paragraphs. While misspellings have been silently corrected, we have indicated where we have corrected obviously wrong words. We have standardized the spelling of personal and geographical names.

To avoid repetition, I have throughout referred to the Treasury and Admiralty Boards simply as Treasury and Admiralty, but retain the full titles for the Navy Board and Board of Trade.

Introduction

THE FIRST FLEET CARRYING the Botany Bay colony's officials, marines, convicts, animals, plants and supplies set out from Portsmouth harbour in the early morning of Sunday, 13 May 1787.

Comprising eleven ships – two Royal Navy ships, six convict transports and three storeships – it wasn't really a 'fleet'. A more accurate characterization would be 'squadron' or, better, 'convoy'. Still, 'fleet' is how it is known in Australian history, so that is the term I shall continue to use.

The First Fleet has had possibly a worse press than the decision to establish a convict colony at Botany Bay. Manning Clark wrote that 'an indescribable hopelessness and confusion dominated the scene' as the ships gathered at Portsmouth.[1] A.G.L. Shaw thought that the government 'did not seriously consider the needs of a new settlement, penal or otherwise'.[2] Jonathan King wrote that 'bureaucratic sloth, poor communications, faulty equipment and bad conditions' delayed the departure of the Fleet.[3] David Mackay held that 'the despatch of the First Fleet to Botany Bay was a reckless act on the part of a desperate ministry ... The expedition itself was poorly organized and badly equipped'.[4] Robert Hughes found that the planning of the expedition was marked by 'muddle and lack of foresight'.[5] John Molony spoke extravagantly of 'criminal negligence'.[6] Mollie Gillen first pointed to 'muddled' preparations and 'real deficiencies in preparing for the settlement', then reached a crescendo with the view that the very colonization was a 'monstrous crime'.[7] Charles Wilson strained to equal her in hyperbole:

> The execution of everything essential ... to the satisfactory despatch of the Fleet and its successful transportation of its passengers and their settlement on arrival in New South Wales rested more [than with Phillip] with an ill-chosen, ill-organized, contentious and unwilling body of what passed for public servants in a dozen ministries and institutions, and a venal and corrupt body of private contractors.[8]

*

Underlying such comments are the same instinctive assumptions and lack of attention to detail that characterized the historians' treatment of the decision to colonize New South Wales.

There is also a myriad mistakes. Clark wrote luridly that, at Portsmouth, 'the women convicts lolled on the decks in indescribable filth and their all too scanty clothing'.[9] This false assertion is based on something Governor Arthur Phillip wrote: 'the situation in which the magistrates sent the women on board the *Lady Penrhyn* stamps them with infamy – though almost naked, and so very filthy, that nothing but clothing them could have prevented them from perishing'.[10] But Phillip was commenting on the condition of the women as they arrived from regional jails to the holding one in London before being put on board the *Lady Penrhyn* in the Thames. It is not a description of how they were neglected at Portsmouth. Once under the supervision of the First Fleet officers and surgeons at Plymouth and Portsmouth, the women were bathed, clothed, fed properly and had their ailments treated. Clark grossly misrepresented the real situation.

Mind you, he has some distinguished company. Hughes thundered that 'the Fleet was under-victualled by its crooked contractor, Duncan Campbell'.[11] He was wrong on three counts here. As I show in *Botany Bay: The Real Story*, Campbell was not 'crooked'.[12] Neither was he the contractor for the First Fleet: William Richards Jr was; and he did not

2

stint the rations. William Bowes Smyth, the surgeon on the *Lady Penrhyn*, wrote that 'few marines or soldiers going out on a foreign service under government were ever better, if so well provided for as these convicts are'. The marine officer Watkin Tench recorded that 'the provisions served on board were good, and of a much superior quality to those usually supplied by contract'. When the colonists were at last on land at Sydney, David Collins, the deputy judge-advocate, wrote: 'the high health which was apparent in every countenance was to be attributed not only to the refreshments we met with at Rio de Janeiro and the Cape of Good Hope, but to the excellent quality of the provisions with which we were supplied by Mr Richards Jr, the contractor'.[13] Whom should we rather believe – the art critic whose historical research was inadequate; or people on the spot who knew what they were taking about?

Shaw, too, comprehensively panned the organization of the venture: 'No farmers were sent out, no skilled craftsmen or mechanics, no person "knowledgeable in flax-dressing" ... no anti-scorbutics ... insufficient surgical supplies, even for the marines ... overcrowding on the ships'.[14] The trouble is, none of these charges is true, as I shall show.

There's an obvious way of showing up the falseness of these views and assertions. Altogether, the people on the First Fleet numbered at least 1420 on embarkation; and with deaths and births *en route*, about 1373 reached Sydney.[15] David Collins wrote:

Thus, under the blessing of God, was happily completed, in eight months and one week, a voyage which, before it was undertaken, the mind hardly dared venture to contemplate, and on which it was impossible to reflect without some apprehensions as to its termination. This fortunate completion of it, however, afforded even to ourselves as much matter of surprise as of general satisfaction; for in the above space of time we had sailed five thousand and twenty-one leagues;[16] had touched at the American and African continents; and had at last rested within a few days sail of the antipodes of our native country, without meeting any accident in a fleet of eleven sail, nine of which were merchantmen that had never before sailed in that distant and imperfectly explored ocean: and when it is considered, that there was on board a large body of convicts, many of whom were embarked in a very sickly state, we might be deemed peculiarly fortunate, that of the whole number of all descriptions of persons coming to form the new settlement, only thirty-two had died since their leaving England, among whom were to be included one or two deaths by accident; although previous to our departure it was generally conjectured, that before we should have been a month at sea one of the transports would have been converted into a hospital ship.[17]

Now, Duncan Campbell said that a good result for a convict voyage across the Atlantic Ocean was a 10 per cent death rate, but that the average over an extended period was about 14 per cent.[18] Yet, during a much longer and more difficult voyage, the First Fleet death rate was about 2 per cent. It would have been impossible for Phillip and his officers to have achieved this success if the ships were as poorly equipped and provisioned as the historians have claimed.

Behind such individual errors lies an abiding fault in the writing of history in and of Australia. All too often, later writers have simply accepted what earlier ones have said without ascertaining its accuracy, so that mistakes have been passed from one generation to the next.

The identification of the *Sirius* as an East Indiaman offers one good example of this habit. This characterization was evidently first made by M. Barnard Eldershaw (the *nom-de-plume* of Marjorie Barnard and Flora Eldershaw) in *Phillip of Australia* in 1938.[19] It was thereafter frequently repeated, including by me, when I simply followed what those before me had said.[20] Graeme Henderson and Myra Stanbury corrected it in 1988, when they pointed out that Philip King's description of it as an 'East country man' meant that it was built for the Baltic rather than the East India trade, a point confirmed by details of its construction. Yet still the mistaken characterization goes on, most recently by David Hill in *1788*.[21]

Let me give a more serious example of this persistent failure to assess evidence rigorously. In 1935, W.S. Campbell published a very short article, in which he announced confidently that he had 'solved' the puzzle of why Arthur Phillip was appointed governor of the Botany Bay colony: he felt 'sure that Phillip's appointments were due to the influence of Sir George Rose', for the pair had been neighbours near Lyndhurst in the New Forest.[22]

Showing all the enthusiasm of the amateur, and none of the discrimination of the professional, and also showing no awareness of the ironies of his story, Campbell related how he had recently travelled to Lyndhurst; and that he had 'failed altogether to obtain any information respecting Phillip, or whereabouts his farm was situated. 'The whole place has been altered,' he reported, 'and the fine mansion once occupied by Sir George Rose at Chuffnells [actually, Cuffnells] has been converted into a hotel'.

Nonetheless, Campbell pressed his case. Rose, he said, had been 'Head' of the Navy. (Wrong. Lord Howe was the First Lord of the Admiralty, and Philip Stephens Secretary of the Admiralty Board. Rose was Secretary of the Treasury.) After citing Howe's unfavourable response to Sydney's advice that Phillip was to be appointed, Campbell quoted a supposed reply from Sydney (which I don't believe is in fact by Sydney; but as Campbell gave no source, it is impossible to verify this); and he then identified Rose as the 'Minister'. (Wrong again. William Pitt was the Prime Minister.)

Campbell then told how he went to the Admiralty and the Public Record Office in search of information about Phillip's appointment, only to draw a complete blank. Mystifyingly, he therefore concluded, 'This all tends to show ... that Sir George Rose appointed Phillip, but that he made no record of the appointment'.

Well! So we have an explanation of an historical 'puzzle', but one entirely lacking in evidence, except *perhaps* the circumstantialities that Phillip and Rose were neighbours in the New Forest, and that Phillip named the area to the west of Sydney that we know as Parramatta 'Rose Hill'.

It was routine for eighteenth-century explorers to name geographical features of a new country after prominent public figures, who may or may not have been patrons. Phillip named Sydney Cove (after Lord Sydney);

the Carmarthen Hills (after the Marquess of Carmarthen, the Foreign Secretary of State); the Lansdowne Hills (after the Marquess of Lansdowne, the former Prime Minister); the Nepean River (after Evan Nepean); and Pitt Water, an expanse in the mouth of the Hawkesbury River (respectively, after William Pitt, the Prime Minister, and Lord Hawkesbury, the President of the Board of Trade). His naming Rose Hill might be evidence of a connection to George Rose, were it supported by some documentation, such as letters between them. However, while Phillip wrote many letters from New South Wales to Sydney, Nepean and Banks, and at least one to Lansdowne, none is known to Pitt, Carmarthen, Hawkesbury or Rose. Campbell's idea was a will-o'-the-wisp, which should never have been pursued nor publicized.

But it was, and it developed a corporeality it simply didn't deserve. In 1938, Barnard Eldershaw repeated it. True, they were circumspect, saying that 'nothing definite is known', and that it was only 'possible' that Rose was Phillip's patron;[23] but their very mentioning the idea gave it legs. Then, in 1962, Manning Clark gave it a gee-up when he said that Phillip 'was again farming at Lyndhurst when Lord Sydney offered him the position of governor of New South Wales', an assertion for which, once more, there is not the thinnest shred of evidence. J.J. Auchmuty heeled it along in his edition of *The Voyage of Governor Phillip to Botany Bay* in 1970; and John Moore set it going again in 1987.[24]

The currency of this idea now extends through more than seventy years, with David Hill repeating it in 2008: 'There is some indication that Sir George Rose, the Under-Secretary of the Treasury, was the minister responsible for making the decision. Rose's estates were at Cuffnels [sic] near Lyndhurst, so he was a near neighbour of Phillip, who was then a gentleman farmer in the same district'; and by Tom Keneally in 2009: 'A neighbour of Phillip's in the New Forest, Sir George Rose, Secretary of the Treasury, was involved in the costing of the enterprize, and he supported Phillip's appointment'.[25]

But consider. So far as we know, Phillip, with his wife, was on the Vernals farm at Lyndhurst only from 1766–68. The parish register shows that he became an overseer of the poor in April 1766; that he paid another to undertake this duty in April 1768; and that he ceased to hold the office at the end of July 1768.[26] In 1769 he and his wife concluded a formal separation.

Rose did not purchase the Cuffnells estate until 1784; and how frequently and for how long he was in residence thereafter is unknown, although clearly his duties at the Treasury kept him in London for much of the year. In the first half of 1784, Phillip was sailing back from India, reaching England again in late April. From October 1784 into 1785, Nepean had Phillip spying in France. In October 1785, he again obtained leave to travel in France – i.e., to spy – for another twelve months. Precisely when he returned to England again is unknown, but presumably he was there by the beginning of October 1786. Whether he returned of his own accord, or was summoned back by Nepean to prepare for Botany Bay, is also unknown.[27]

On the face of things, then, it is extremely unlikely – look, given the sixteen-year gap, let me say impossible! – that Phillip and Rose were ever 'neighbours' near Lyndhurst; and therefore, in the sheer absence of any other evidence, it is also most unlikely that Rose had any hand in Phillip's appointment.

There is in fact one piece of evidence that confirms conclusively that George Rose had nothing to do with Arthur Phillip's appointment as governor, and therefore that my criticism of the historians is valid.

In late November 1786, after first approaching Rose about the business, Newton Fowell's mother wrote to Evan Nepean, asking that the young man, who had just obtained his lieutenant's passing certificate, be appointed to one of the Royal Navy ships going out to New South Wales. Nepean replied:

> Captain Phillip, who is to command on the expedition to Botany Bay, offered to take with him any young gentleman I might think fit to recommend, as a midshipman, and conceiving himself under some obligation to me, for what I know not, he promised, that if the young man behaved well, he would make him an officer, if a vacancy offered during his command.

Mr Rose, knowing my intimacy with Captain Phillip, desired me to ask him to take out a young man who had been recommended by Mr Justice Buller, which Captain Phillip refused to do, declaring that his complement of persons of that class had been completed long before. I met Mr Buller soon after, and finding that he was particularly interested in the success of his application, I offered to give him the vacancy which had been reserved for my nomination and [I] can assure you that I was particularly glad to find it was in favour of your son, Newton.[28]

Nepean's letter tells us two things. First, if Rose had engineered Phillip's appointment, he would not have had to ask the favour via Nepean; and second, Phillip would not have refused it. Nepean's having employed Phillip as a spy, and the resulting close connection between them, is an infinitely better explanation of Phillip's appointment. But like a worn-out old nag, the idea that George Rose was involved keeps limping around the Australian historical farm.

*

The desire to avoid such errors was one of my principal motivations in my long quest to recover original documents. The historiography of the First Fleet has been based on a very incomplete documentary record. True, as well as those documents published in *Historical Records of New South Wales*, historians have made use of many more – e.g., those published in *Historical Records of Australia* and in Owen Rutter's *The First Fleet*. They have used, too, many of the journals and letters of those who went on the voyage, and numbers of the unpublished sources in the British National Archives, the British Library and elsewhere.

However, even when taken together, these records still constitute an inadequate basis for making judgments about the mounting of the First Fleet and the equipping of the colonists. In 1980, I remarked: 'No one has yet described adequately the mounting of the First Fleet ... A comprehensive description of this mounting would lay to rest the myths that the Pitt administration was generally indolent in assembling the Fleet, that it equipped the colonizing party poorly, and that these features reflect its callous disregard of the convicts' welfare'.[29] Now, another thirty years on, this present work fills this wide gap.

As before remarked, this is the first full-scale analysis of the *mounting* of the First Fleet. Most of the earlier works which might from their titles seem to deal with the subject, such as those by Victor Crittenden and Jonathan King, are narrative collations of original records rather than analytical studies, and are in any case concerned more with the voyage than the equipping of the expedition. They are also far from comprehensive or accurate. The relevant chapter in David Hill's *1788* is replete with error, and wildly wrong in its general conclusions. A.K. Cavanagh's account of the return of the ships is precise, but deals only with that aspect.

Only two previous studies have been soundly based. The first is that by Charles Bateson (1959, 2nd ed. 1969), but his concern was solely with the ships that constituted the fleet, which he dealt with in a few pages. The other is that by Roger Knight, which is based on an extensive knowledge of relevant records and Navy Board procedures, but which was never intended to be more than a conference paper.

In essence, the documents I have gathered have allowed me largely to reconstitute original series which have become scattered over more than two hundred years. Sometimes, original papers sent from one government department to another were returned, without copies having been taken. Attachments became separated from their covering letters. It was by no means uncommon for senior administrators in the eighteenth century to consider state papers as their own, and to take them when they left office. Later, when these private collections were dispersed, the migration of individual pieces was often widespread.[30]

Nonetheless, by the later eighteenth century, the British bureaucracy had developed firm record-keeping procedures. While it is always possible to find earlier foreshadowings of such practices, let me locate their substantial beginnings in the second half of the seventeenth century, when the two revenue-collecting departments of Customs (tax on imported and exported goods) and Excise (generally, tax on domestic produce and goods, either at the point of production or of sale) were gradually placed on a secure footing. By the turn of the eighteenth century, these branches of government were showing many of the features that we associate with a modern, professional civil service: senior officials' tenure was independent of whichever party held political power; these officials were paid a salary rather than given fees based on the revenue collected; lesser posts were no longer in the gift of politicians; those holding them were examined to ensure they had the requisite skills, particularly in mathematics; continuity of employment meant the accumulation of a broad body of experience; the collection of revenue proceeded in accordance with the law; and meticulous records were kept of goods produced or imported, and of the taxes paid on them.[31]

During the course of the eighteenth century, other government departments adopted these practices. Senior administrators held their positions for extended periods. (In the 1780s, for example, George Rose and Thomas Steele at the Treasury, Evan Nepean at the Home Office, William Fraser at the Foreign Office, Philip Stephens at the Admiralty, and Sir Charles Middleton at the Navy Board served under a series of administrations.) Again, as the sphere of operations of the Royal Navy progressively enlarged, the Admiralty and Navy Board needed to have to hand details of ships, men, supplies and finance, not only in Britain but also in North America, the West Indies, the Mediterranean and India. So the Admiralty needed to collect and file all the logs kept by the admirals, captains, commanders and lieutenants who served on its hundreds of ships, and all the correspondence to and from these officers.

The Navy Board needed to know where the ships were, what was their state of repair, who comprised their crews and when these crews were paid. As a result, there are tens of thousands each of reports, musterbooks and paybooks. The Board needed to know how many masts were in the dockyard ponds; and what were the quantities of cables, cordage, canvas and hemp in the warehouses. It needed to maintain annual contracts for the delivery of English oak, American and Baltic masts and spars and Russian hemp; and to let a myriad specific contracts for the provision of equipment, food and clothing. It needed to have details of the 'warrant' officers – masters, carpenters, gunners, cooks, surgeons – whom it appointed to the hundreds of ships; and to maintain an army of workmen, not only at the major home yards of the Thames, Portsmouth and Plymouth, but also those at New York and Charleston, Jamaica and Antigua, and Gibraltar.

The meeting of all these needs gave rise to another vast body of records. For example, the Deptford yard in the Thames was the main place for the inspection, repair and fitting out of Royal Navy ships in Britain. There are thousands of folio-sized letterbooks, each with hundreds of pages, recording the Deptford officers' correspondence with the Navy Board in the eighteenth century.

The situation was similar in other government departments. Let me give only one particular example now. After the reorganization of the old Southern and Northern Departments of State into the Home and Foreign Offices in 1782, one of Evan Nepean's tasks was to run the secret service in France, Spain and elsewhere in southern Europe. This espionage had a number of aspects. There were informers in the government departments and armed forces of the European countries, who passed information to local spies, who sent it on, directly or indirectly, to Nepean. Embassy officials and patriotic private citizens also reported back – as in mid-1785, when the ambassador to France (the Earl of Dorset) and Lord Dalrymple, who was in Paris on private affairs, sent details of a secret purpose to Lapérouse's coming voyage.[32] Nepean also often received information about the movement of enemy shipping from naval officers serving at sea, masters of merchant vessels, and smugglers. And, at moments of need, he sent agents fluent in European languages into these countries to obtain particular information – as in 1784–85, when he had Arthur Phillip report on activity in the French dockyards.[33]

In 1790, after news reached Europe that Spanish officers had seized British trading ships at distant Nootka Sound, on Vancouver Island, relations between Britain and Spain reached flash point. At the height of this crisis, Nepean was receiving, from a variety of sources, weekly reports of the number of ships in the Spanish fleet and the disposition of these ships, information which he carefully collated and entered into the registers that he controlled, information which was then available to the politicians who were contemplating ending the crisis by destroying the enemy's fleet.[34]

The growth of this administrative competence means that the records of British government departments in the 1780s are voluminous. Indeed, even a comparatively minor matter might generate a lengthy sequence of correspondence. (For example, from mid-October to mid-December 1786, the Admiralty, Navy Board, Deptford officers and its commander gave extended consideration of what size cannon the *Supply* should carry, which has left a sequence of twenty-two documents.) Even when a particular document has been lost or was not copied, given the mode of minuting then (which involved summarizing the contents of the document being responded to before recording the decision), it is often possible to know what was in the missing one.

*

It is a curious thought that the records I have gathered now allow us to know more about the mounting of the First Fleet than all but three people knew at the time. Two of these were Sir Charles Middleton, the Comptroller (Head) of the Navy Board, and Evan Nepean, the Under-Secretary of State at the Home Office. For reasons which will become clear, Nepean's view of the business was significantly broader than was Middleton's. Nonetheless, both these men knew a great deal about it; and they often took steps ahead of the necessary formalities. For example, in December 1786, somewhat irritated that Nepean had questioned his proposed disposition of people and stores on the ships, Middleton told him, 'I trust and hope that when any business of this kind is agitated again, that I may have some notice of it before it is sent officially'; and in March 1787, when Phillip was insistent, both that the convicts on board the ships at Portsmouth should be fed fresh food while they waited to depart, and that the expedition should receive more medical supplies, Middleton advised Nepean that he had 'given directions agreeable to [your] letter concerning provisions, essence of malt, wine etc., trusting

Introduction

to official authority in due time'. And each sympathized with the other concerning 'this disagreeable and troublesome business'.[35]

Arthur Phillip was the third person possessed of a comprehensive knowledge of the mounting of the First Fleet. Sometimes to the annoyance of other officials, he had a hand in just about every aspect of it; and, as I shall show, it was largely due to his efforts that it was as well-equipped as it was.

In general, the various lesser officials involved in the business had no significant overview of it. For example, Joshua Thomas and George Teer, the Navy Board officials most concerned with the fitting and provisioning of the ships, were not involved in the making of the legal arrangements for the colony. This was the work of the Law Officers and the Privy Council. Conversely, the personnel of these departments had no idea of the trouble the Navy Board was at in gathering the ships and fitting them out. Similarly, the marine officers who sailed on the ships had no notion of Phillip's instructions, nor of private understandings he had been given about the colony's purposes.

The documentary record I have assembled allows a much more comprehensive understanding of the venture than any previous one. It forms the basis of the story I tell here of the First Fleet – the real story.

PART ONE:
PLANNING A CONVICT COLONY

1.

Announcing the Decision

As I explain in *Botany Bay: The Real Story*, William Pitt's Cabinet met on Saturday, 19 August, and decided to establish a convict colony at Botany Bay, on the eastern coast of New South Wales. No minutes of this decision, so momentous in its consequences, are known. However, the administrative steps that followed immediately afterwards confirm the fact of it.

As Home Secretary, Lord Sydney was responsible for calling Cabinet meetings. In practice, this meant that it was Evan Nepean, the Under-Secretary (or, in our terms, permanent head) of the Home Office, who summoned other Cabinet ministers and drew up agendas. While he certainly was at some, whether Nepean was present at all Cabinet meetings is unknown. However, it was not necessary for him to attend these meetings to know what the ministers were thinking. Inevitably, he was in close contact with Sydney, and, as we shall see, also with William Pitt, the Prime Minister.

Then as now, government departments could not undertake new initiatives without knowing that there was money to pay for them. On Monday, 21 August, Nepean went into the office and drafted a letter to the Treasury formally announcing the Botany Bay decision, and giving details of the scheme for colonization.[1]

When Lord Sydney had signed this letter, it went to the Treasury together with a copy of the Heads of a Plan, the three enclosures to that plan, and another two enclosures, as outlined in Sydney's letter:

- Estimate of provisions to be provided for the intended settlement on the coast of New South Wales
- Staff establishment for the settlement at New South Wales
- Messrs Turnbull, Macaulay and T. Gregory's letter of 21 August 1786 (offering to contract for the venture)[2]
- List of the tools, utensils etc. for the convicts and marines intended to proceed to New South Wales
- Estimate of clothing to serve a male convict for one year[3]

George Rose and Thomas Steele, the Treasury Secretaries,[4] received these items the same day, and entered them in the minute book as though the Board had considered them on 18 August. The reason for this subterfuge was that, by Monday, the Treasury Board had actually adjourned for the summer recess. The Secretaries also recorded that Pitt and two other Board members had on 19 August 'read and approved the minutes of yesterday'; and that the Board would next meet on 10 October. Until this date, they proceeded 'by the direction of Mr Pitt', who held the two financial portfolios of First Lord Commissioner of the Treasury and Chancellor of the Exchequer.[5]

The nature of the administrative procedure and range of the business are best conveyed by the minute itself. After summarizing the contents of Sydney's letter, the Treasury Secretaries listed the following points:

My Lords, impressed with the necessity of sending a number of convicts out of the kingdom immediately, are pleased to direct a letter to be written to the Commissioners of the Navy to take measures for providing a proper number of vessels for the conveyance of 680 male and 70 female convicts to Botany Bay in New South Wales, together with the provisions, necessaries and implements for husbandry which are judged requisite for the use of them and the marines who are to go to the same place on duty, giving notice that one of the ships must be fitted up for the accommodation of the above-mentioned number of women so as to keep them separate from the men.

Acquaint the Commissioners that the marine corps will be supplied during their passage out by the Victualling Department, but that provisions must be sent for their use after their landing, and that the daily rations for them, for the convicts, and for some women who it is expected may be prevailed upon to come to the new settlement from the neighbourhood will amount to one thousand, and that a quantity equal to two years consumption must be provided for them over and above the provisions for the convicts during the voyage.

Acquaint the Commissioners of the Navy that my Lords are of opinion it will be most advisable to give notice that they are ready to receive proposals for the passage, and the victualling the convicts during the same, and for a stock of provisions to be landed equal to two years consumption at the rate of one thousand rations a day.

Transmit to the Commissioners a list of the tools and utensils of husbandry to be provided for the marines and the convicts, and a list of the clothing and bedding, and acquaint them that my Lords will approve of their directing the person who shall take the contract on terms the most advantageous to the public, to purchase the same on the commission usually allowed. When my Lords have the particulars of the surgeon's instruments, medicines and necessaries for the sick, they will direct the same to be provided under the inspection of the Commissioners for the Sick and Hurt.

Acquaint Mr Nepean for the information of Lord Sydney that if the commanding officer who shall be entrusted with the care of the service shall draw bills from the Cape Verde Islands or from the Cape of Good Hope for the purchase of cattle, seed grain or other necessaries, my Lords will order the same to be paid, representing to his Lordship however the necessity of the commanding officer's transmitting vouchers of such expenditure.

Acquaint Mr Nepean also that when my Lords are informed of the particulars of the quantities and kinds of merchandize which it will be necessary to put on board the ship of war or tender previous to their sailing, my Lords will order the same to be provided, and that my Lords have already given directions for taking up the ships, and for providing the provisions, tools and other necessaries for the marines going out and for the convicts, and that they wait only to be acquainted with the particulars of the surgeon's instruments, medicines and necessaries for the sick, to order them also.

On 31 August, Nepean drafted a similar letter for Sydney to sign to the Admiralty, informing it of the decision and enclosing a copy of Heads of a Plan.[6] This letter advised that the Treasury had been asked to arrange for a number of vessels to convey the convicts to Botany Bay, 'together with provisions and other supplies for their subsistence, as well as tools to enable them to erect habitations, and also implements for agriculture'. It requested that the Admiralty provide 'a ship of war of a proper class' and a tender of about 200 tons burden*, both to escort the convoy and 'for other purposes after their arrival'. It further advised that three companies of marines should be sent to preserve order and to guard the settlement. (Attached to this request was the advice that these would 'be properly victualled by a commissary immediately after their landing', a proviso which was to cause considerable trouble before the Fleet sailed.) The marines' term of service was to be three years, and volunteers were to be given first preference. They were to be provided with the necessary tools and equipment. As their service while on land would be 'entirely unconnected with maritime affairs', they were then to be responsible to the Home Office.

The East India Company also needed to be told of the decision, as its royal charter gave it the exclusive monopoly of all British trade in the vast region between the Cape of Good Hope and the coasts of the Americas. Nepean drafted and Sydney signed a letter to the Company giving details of the proposed colony and asking for its agreement on 15 September, with which went the Heads of a Plan (without the attachments). The letter pointed out that the Court of Directors' 'concurrence' would not

---

* 'Tons burden' is not the weight of the ship; rather, it is a mathematical estimate of its carrying capacity.

only please His Majesty, 'but will be a means of preventing the emigration of our European neighbours to that quarter, which might be attended with infinite prejudice to the Company's affairs'. The Chairmen referred the request to the Court of Directors, which agreed on 21 September.[7]

Despite this quick agreement, there may well have been considerable opposition to the venture among the shareholders of the Company. In early October, William Richards, who was supplying the transports, told Pitt that 'the whole interest of a certain set of gentlemen that are materially affected by its adoption, have been employed to thwart every means of its being obtained'; and a few days later, the *Daily Universal Register* advised that the Company's directors were unhappy that, while the government was paying Richards £7 per ton for his ships on the outward voyage, they were paying £10 per ton for the homeward one.[8]

*

By this time, the public had also been made aware of the Botany Bay decision.[9] On 19 September, for example, the *Public Advertiser* announced that it was 'the design of government to form a settlement at Botany, on the east side of New Holland, in the Indian seas, for the reception of male and female felons sentenced by the laws of this country to transportation'; and it offered a very detailed description of the Botany Bay area taken from Hawkesworth's compilation of Cook's and Banks's journals.[10] Other London and country newspapers did likewise, often simply repeating one another's words.[11]

In the next weeks, more details of the planned expedition came out. Towards the end of the month, the *Daily Universal Register* informed readers that Captain Arthur Phillip was to be the colony's governor, with a salary of £500 per annum; and that 700 male and 150 female convicts were to be transported.[12]

The public's attention was also drawn to other motives for the decision. On 25 September, the *Birmingham Daily Gazette* reported that there were some who thought that 'besides providing a place for our convicts, from which all escape will be impracticable, the settlement may be otherwise highly beneficial to our Asiatic commerce'.[13] In the middle of October, the *Morning Chronicle* announced that the government was pursuing James Matra's scheme, then quoted two paragraphs from it, those dealing with the centrality of New South Wales to future naval operation against the Dutch and Spanish empires in the Indian and Pacific oceans. It also pointed to the prospect of obtaining masts from New Zealand. Also quoting from Matra, the *London Chronicle* told readers about 'that very valuable article of New Zealand hemp or flax plant'.[14] In December, the *London Chronicle* announced that 'the Botany Bay expedition may in the end keep in this island much of the money now sent to Holland for spices', which resonated both with Matra's scheme and the second last paragraph of Heads of a Plan.[15]

In December, there were a number of reports that the principal site of settlement was to be Norfolk Island rather than Botany Bay. The *St James's Chronicle* was the first to say so, followed by the *Daily Universal Register*. The latter paper also subsequently reported that one ship would sail ahead to the island 'to find the properest station for the first landing of the convicts'. Administration records make clear that this was never the case; but the fact that it was reported indicates that there was some knowledge abroad of official interest in the island's potential as a source of supply of naval materials. And, indeed, the *Daily Universal Register* advised the correct situation early in January 1787, when it said that the governor had 'discretionary power to land the convicts at Botany Bay, or Norfolk Island, or elsewhere, as he shall think proper. He is not particularly bound to Botany Bay; on the contrary, his command on that head is not limited'.[16]

Some of the papers were supportive of the decision. After pointing out the inconvenience of continuing to keep the convicts at home, and the impossibility of sending them to America or Africa, the *Morning Chronicle* praised Botany Bay as a site, saying that, since the convicts 'may become useful to the empire', it was reasonable to spend some public money establishing them there.[17] The *Public Advertiser* held that 'the banishment of the convicts to Botany Bay is an instance of modern humanity, for it will be little else than freedom in a new country, and a plentiful store of implements to till the land, and labour for a sustenance'.[18]

In January 1787, a number of papers advised readers that

> the expedition to Botany Bay comprehends in it more than the mere banishment of our felons. It is an undertaking of humanity, for in all the islands of the South Seas, there is not a four-footed animal to be found but the hog, the dog and the rat, nor any of the grain of the other quarters of the world ... By the number of cattle now sending over of various sorts, and all the different seeds for vegetation, a capital improvement will be made in the southern part of the New World; and our ships, which may hereafter sail in that quarter of the globe, must receive refreshment in greater plenty that from the exhausted soil of Europe, considering that all New South Wales is formed of a virgin mould, undisturbed since the creation.[19]

However, public approval of the venture was certainly not general. Some reporting of it was doubtful, if respectful. In November, for example, the *Daily Universal Register* said that there was some question of the expedition's being abandoned, on the grounds of cost; then, a few days later, it gave readers figures that it must have received from Nepean, demonstrating that the difference in cost between keeping a male convict on a hulk and sending him to New South Wales was only £4 (£28 as against £32).[20] In December, however, this paper came out against the decision, on the grounds, first, that the colony would shortly become a nest of pirates, who would ravage Britain's eastern trade; and second, that the colonists would soon demand independence in the manner of the ungrateful Americans.[21]

Other notices heaped scorn upon the decision. The *Gentleman's Magazine* said that 'this plan is so wild and extravagant, that we can hardly believe it could be countenanced by any professional man after a moment's reflection'; and it pointed out that 'it is notorious that the Dutch East India ships lose more than half the recruits they take on board for their settlement in India in crossing the Line'.[22] The *Bath Chronicle* was particularly scathing:

Botany Bay still continues to be a subject of town talk, without anybody seeming to know anything about the matter. First, it is Botany Bay where the convicts are to be transported to; then it is not Botany Bay in that huge island New Holland, but the small rock called New Norfolk in the South Sea! Then it is both Botany Bay and Norfolk! Then it is neither of them, but the commodore may conveniently dispose of them at Botany Bay, or New Norfolk, or the Lord knows where! Wherever he can shoot his rubbish!

If we could really believe such folly reigns among statesmen, as to adopt any of the schemes above alluded to, we should say, it is very little difference to the bulk of the destined wretches which of those remote places they are bound for. We believe the first land that two-thirds of them will reach will be the bottom of the sea, there to make their final deposit in the bosom of the great deep; and probably there will be but a dark account of the remaining third part.[23]

*

News of the decision was soon abroad in Europe. On 19 September the Portuguese ambassador in London informed his Court of the expedition, and that Captain Arthur Phillip, who had served in the Portuguese Navy, had been given command of it.[24] In mid-October, the Spanish ambassador sent a selection of newspaper reports of the business to his Court.[25] There were persistent rumours that the Dutch government was opposed to the venture. For example, in early October one correspondent told the *Public Advertiser* that from his conversations during a recent trip to France and Holland, he thought it likely that both nations would oppose the venture, perhaps even by arming the Aborigines. Ten days later, the *Hampshire Chronicle* reported that 'the East India companies in Holland pretend to have a property in [New South Wales], though they were ill-used by the inhabitants when they attempted to settle themselves there'. There was one report that the Dutch government intended to object formally, on the grounds that Dutch navigators had been the first Europeans to discover New Holland. A number of other papers repeated this claim. At the beginning of 1787, the *Hampshire Chronicle* followed up with:

> Private letters from Holland mention that the Dutch have at this instant, either in Botany Bay, or within a few leagues of that place, several transports and two men of war, with troops, to preserve their prior claim to that part of the world. Government must certainly have heard of this, as the matter of sending out the troops last spring was notorious, although their destination was not generally known. Spain means to support Holland in this scheme; and therefore the probable consequence of our Minister's inexperience, and juvenile obstinacy, may involve this country in a war.[26]

I have never found any official correspondence to confirm this claim of Dutch opposition; however, it is by no means impossible, even though some of the details in these reports were fantastical. No diplomatic record of any such protest has ever been found, however.

*

After the ministers had drafted it and Pitt had read it at the Cockpit the evening before, the King delivered his address to open the new session of parliament on 23 January 1787. His Majesty assured members of both Houses that 'the tranquillity of *Europe* has remained uninterrupted, and that all foreign powers continue to express their friendly disposition to this country'. He announced that Britain had concluded a commercial treaty with France; that such negotiations were continuing with other nations; and that agreement had been reached with Spain concerning a disputed article in the peace treaty. He introduced budget estimates, and asked that they be voted; and that revenue and administrative reform continue. He also announced: 'My Lords and Gentlemen: A plan has been formed, by my direction, for transporting a number of convicts, in order to remove the inconvenience which arose from the crowded state of the jails in different parts of the kingdom; and you will, I doubt not, take such farther measures as may be necessary for this purpose.' In their addresses-in-reply, both Houses assured His Majesty that they would adopt this plan.[27]

Historians holding to the traditional view of the reasons for founding the Botany Bay colony have made much of the fact that at this time the King mentioned only the convict motive.[28] But this is a naïve view of what to expect in such a public address. Were the King and Cabinet really going to announce: 'We are establishing a naval base at Botany Bay, the better to conduct offensive operations against the Dutch and Spanish colonies'? To do so would have mightily alarmed Britain's recent Continental adversaries. Were they really going to say: 'We are establishing a base at Botany Bay in order to expand British trade throughout the Pacific Ocean'? To do so would have further aroused the ire of the East India Company. Much more politic was the bland commonplace that the convicts had to be shipped out because the jails were full, which was a sentiment the members of parliament could readily agree with. As Earl Camden, the Lord President of the Privy Council, remarked in advising that he would be unable to attend the meeting on Friday 12 January 1787 when Cabinet was to discuss the draft of the King's address, apart from that dealing with the unrest in Ireland, all its advices were 'no more than communications'; that is, they were announcements of decisions to parliament, not discussions of the reasons for them.[29]

2.

The Colony: Society, Law and Governance

THE BOTANY BAY COLONY WAS A very peculiar creation – as the Lord President of the Privy Council observed as it was forming, he was unable to regard this 'embryo' as either a 'settlement or colony'.[1]

Certainly, there was no precedent elsewhere in the British empire at the time. It was not founded, with the Crown's permission, either by religious separatists (as some New England colonies had been), or by merchant adventurers (Virginia). It was not a Crown colony, ruled by a vice-regal representative in conjunction with a nominated council and/or an elected assembly (Jamaica). It was not a conquered colony (New York, Quebec). It was not a commercial enclave within a foreign territory (the East India Company's 'factories' at Bombay, Madras and Calcutta). It was not even a random cluster of Britons employed in gathering raw materials (the 'logwood' settlement in Honduras).

No, Botany Bay was *sui generis*. It was a colony of convicts, administered by a handful of civil officials, and guarded by marines and two small warships. In the beginning, there were no free settlers. And, for the first time in the history of British convict transportation, it was government officials, rather than private merchants and free settlers, who were responsible for organizing the shipping out of the convicts, and their upkeep and employment on the other side of the world.

As I have explained in *Botany Bay: The Real Story* and elsewhere, there was a purpose to this colony quite unrelated to convicts. According to

European notions of international law prevailing at the time, by transferring some of their population and at least a portion of their laws to New South Wales, the British made *actual* the *preliminary* right to possess this territory that they had acquired as a consequence of Cook's having been its first discoverer, and of his having claimed it on behalf of the King.[2]

Rather than examining this situation again, however, let me now consider contemporary ideas of how this colony composed of men and women banished from their homeland for criminal activity might develop.

Society

There is no purposeful statement from August 1786 of how the Pitt administration envisaged the Botany Bay colony developing. The Heads of a Plan and Sydney's letter to the Treasury are concerned only with the symbiotic purposes of ridding the kingdom of felons and making their labour useful to the state, and with mechanisms for establishing the colony. However, there are four other documents that do cast a considerable amount of light on the administration's expectations for it.

The first of these documents is James Matra's addendum to his August 1783 proposal for a free settlement in New South Wales, which he presented to the Home Office in April 1784. Matra considered that sending the convicts thither would combine 'good policy and humanity'. 'Give them a few acres of ground, as soon as they arrive in New South Wales, in *absolute property*,' he urged,

> with what assistance they may want to till them. Let it be here remarked, that they cannot fly from the country; that they have no temptations to theft; and that they must work or starve. I likewise suppose that they are not by any means to be reproached for their former conduct. If these premises be granted me, I may reasonably conclude that it is highly probable they will be useful, [and] that it is very possible they will be moral subjects of society.
>
> Do you wish either by private prudence, or by civil policy, to reclaim offenders? Show by your treatment of them, that you think

their reformation extremely practicable, and do not hold out every moment before their eyes, the hideous and mortifying deformity of their own vices and crimes. A man's intimate and hourly acquaintance with his guilt, and the frowns and severities of the world tend more powerfully even than the immediate effects of his bad habits to make him a determined and incorrigible villain.

By the plan which I have now proposed, a necessity to continue in the place of his destination, and to be industrious is imposed on the criminal. The expense to the nation is absolutely imperceptible, comparatively with what criminals have hitherto cost government; and thus two objects, of most desirable and beautiful union, will be permanently blended: economy to the public and humanity to the individual.[3]

There are indications that this idea that transportation to the distant colony might prove the means of the convicts' redeeming themselves was a significant factor in the administration's thinking. On 23 September 1786, William Pitt reminded his friend William Wilberforce of his offer to find a suitable person to minister to the convicts. On this same day – and it cannot be coincidental – Wilberforce or one of his evangelical friends asked the Reverend Richard Johnson if he were interested in going out. Johnson later stated that the good he might do had been uppermost in his mind when he accepted the position as the colony's chaplain:

From my first hearing that a colony was about to be established ... I always understood that it was the intention of government to see whether some reformation might not be affected amongst these unfortunate and abandoned people. [These] motives appear very strong and sufficient reasons for the convicts being carefully instructed in the various and important duties of morality and religion. But, when it is further considered, that convicts, as well as others, are possessed of souls that are immortal and that they must ere long appear before the solemn tribunal of God, there and then to answer for their actions – whoever considers this ... must ... see and allow, that all possible means should be made use of, to reclaim them from their former wicked course of life.

And Arthur Phillip wrote from the colony that he was 'serving the cause of humanity'.[4]

*

The second document is perhaps the most interesting and informative. This is a long memorandum in which Arthur Phillip presented his views of how he might conduct the voyage, and of the social policies he might pursue in the colony. Partly because it was implicitly mis-dated to March 1787 when published in *Historical Records of New South Wales*,[5] and partly because the 'dumping of convicts' view, which has dominated the historiography for so long, has obliterated all other insights, this memorandum has only rarely received the consideration it deserves. In fact, Phillip wrote it in 1786, soon after he was offered the governorship of the colony – that is, in the period between the end of September and 11 October.[6] My surmise is that he did so at the request of the administration, and after he had been briefed – certainly by Lord Sydney and Evan Nepean, very probably by Sir Joseph Banks, perhaps even by William Pitt himself. If anything is the 'blueprint' for the colony's development, this memorandum is it.

I shall discuss in another chapter what this document tells us about how Phillip thought to manage the voyage out to New South Wales and the necessary first steps in physically establishing the colony. Let me now concentrate on what it and a couple of related ones show of his ideas about the colony's possible social development.

First, Phillip wanted to establish good relations with the 'natives'. Indeed, he hoped to persuade the Aborigines 'to settle near us', giving them 'everything that can tend to civilize them, and to give them a high opinion of their new guests'. To this end, he intended to prohibit the crews of the transports from having any contact with the Aborigines while the ships remained in New South Wales. And he intended to locate the convicts within the settlement so as to prevent their having contact also, 'for if they have, the arms of the natives will be very formidable in their hands, the women abused, and the natives disgusted'. However, Phillip was realistic enough to understand that this ban might not be maintained forever: 'The natives may, it is probable, permit their women to marry and live with the men [i.e., convict men] after a certain time, in which case I should think it necessary to punish with severity the man who used the woman ill.'[7]

It would be necessary to organize and supervise the work of the convicts. Phillip's ideas here were to divide them into gangs according to their skills, and to have the marine officers oversee them, by 'occasionally encourag[ing] such as they observed diligent, and point[ing] out for punishment such as they saw idle or straggling in the woods'.[8]

Considering that some of the women sentenced for theft might retain some personal dignity and sexual morality, Phillip also wanted to isolate them from the men. However, he thought that they should be able to receive male visitors at certain hours, and that when couples wished to marry, 'they should be encouraged if they are industrious, by [being allowed] one day in the week more than the unmarried on their own lots of ground'. As for the rest (the 'most abandoned') of the convict women, he admitted the realities of human nature and suggested that they be allowed to 'receive the visits of the convicts in the limits allotted them at certain hours, and under certain restrictions' – that is, he was willing to sanction prostitution, in the belief that this might reduce social tension.[9]

Phillip had some general strictures. Given that the colony was to be ruled according to British law, he thought slavery should be banned from its very beginning. (What he had seen during his years in Brazil and at the Cape of Good Hope presumably influenced his aversion to slavery as a social institution.) And, 'as I would not wish convicts to lay the foundations of an empire, I think they should ever remain separated from the garrison, and other settlers that may come from Europe, and not be allowed to mix with them, even after the seven years or fourteen years for which they are transported may be expired'.[10] This idea of permanent exclusion seems to sit ill with his opposition to slavery; and in the event, he found it impossible to maintain. Indeed, his five years in New South Wales are marked by an astonishing social inclusion.

Beyond this, Phillip envisaged the emergence of a class of yeoman-farmers. He thought that those convicts 'who behave well' should be rewarded 'by being allowed to work occasionally on the small lots of land set apart for them, and which they will be put in possession of at the expiration of the time for which they are transported'. And he wanted to know 'how far I may permit the seamen and marines of the garrison to cultivate spots of land when the duty of the day is over, and how far I can give them hopes that the grounds they cultivate will be secured to them hereafter; likewise, how far I may permit any of the garrison to remain, when they are ordered home'.[11]

There is in Phillip's memorandum an interesting extension of this idea of a yeoman class. This concerned the women the administration proposed bringing from the Friendly Islands (now Tonga), not only to augment the number of women, but also, I think, to introduce the gathering and gardening skills that had so impressed navigators who had called at these islands. Phillip thought that these women should be 'supported', but also be kept separately, and be given land when they chose to marry 'the soldiers of the garrison'. His distinction between convict women for convict men and Polynesian women for marines is curious, although it does correlate with his more general one between convicts and free people. Presumably, he hoped to encourage the development of a creole class in the colony, something else which would have been familiar to him from Brazil.[12]

The third and fourth documents that convey Phillip's and the administration's ideas about the colony are the draft of his instructions, which the Home Office produced at the beginning of March, and his comments on this draft. The instructions said that he was to 'endeavour by every possible means to open an intercourse with the natives, and to conciliate their affections, enjoining all our subjects to live in amity and kindness with them; and if any of our subjects shall wantonly destroy them, or give them any unnecessary interruption in the exercise of their several occupations, it is our will and pleasure that you do cause such offenders to be brought to punishment according to the degree of the offence'. Phillip went further: 'any man who takes the life of a native will put on his trial the same as if he had killed one of the garrison'.[13]

He was instructed to emancipate convicts who behaved well and showed a willingness to work, and to grant them lands in the following amounts: thirty acres to a single male; twenty more acres if married; and ten acres for each of a couple's children in the colony. These grants were to be free of rents and other charges for ten years. And he might supply such individuals or families with food for twelve months, together with agricultural implements, seeds and animals, if the general stock permitted this.

In case any of the marines should wish to settle in the colony at the end of their term or any private settlers should arrive, he was to report on the colony's soils, and suggest how free settlers might be given land.

He was, as opportunity arose, to bring women from the Pacific Islands, but he was to see that the officers in charge of this 'do not upon any account exercise any compulsive measures, or make use of fallacious pretences'. Excised from the draft of the instructions was the proviso, which Phillip must have known about, that he was 'to exert every means to prevent their living in common with the convicts, but to hold out every indulgence ... to promote matrimonial connection'.

There was another excision from these draft instructions, which is both curious and interesting. In the England of the 1780s, the Church of England was the state religion, and while some 'dissenting' groups were tolerated (e.g. Methodists and Baptists), there were severe restrictions on others. Roman Catholics could not openly practise their religion, and were banned from holding public offices and positions in universities. Even in Ireland, Catholics were banned from holding office and from voting, and were forced to pay tithes to the hated English church. Indeed, after the King had forbidden him to grant the Irish some relief from these onerous restrictions, Pitt resigned as Prime Minister in 1801.

The draft of Phillip's instructions contained the proviso that all persons who may hereafter inhabit our said territory of New South Wales, or the islands adjacent within your government, should have full liberty of conscience and the free exercise of all such modes of religious worship as are not prohibited by law, we do therefore hereby require you to permit all persons within your said government to have such liberty, and to exercise such modes of religious worship as are not prohibited by law, provided they be content with a quiet and peaceable enjoyment of the same, not giving offence or scandal to government.

Excised this passage may have been, but it shows how the administration contemplated giving a great degree of religious toleration to the New South Wales colony than then existed in England.[14]

*

These, then, were Phillip's and the administration's ideas about how the Botany Bay colony might develop as the venture was beginning. We should not suppose that the politicians who took the decision to found it and the civil servants whose task it was to implement this decision thought exactly as the first governor did. However, it is worth reiterating the point I make in *Botany Bay: The Real Story*, that Phillip could not have advanced these ideas if they had differed radically from those held by senior administrators and their advisers – that is, to put it bluntly, he could not have seen the colony as an imperial venture and envisaged the development of a free population in it if he had been told that the government's only intention was to dump the convicts.[15]

Law

When James Matra was asked by a member of the Beauchamp Committee in May 1785 if he thought 'the use of martial law and prompt justice to be necessary' for a colony of convicts, he replied: 'So essentially so that without them they could not be governed'.[16]

Arthur Phillip also suggested that he should at first govern according to military law. He had a particular reason. In order to build up breeding stocks, persons bringing animals to the colony should be allowed to slaughter them only with the governor's express permission: 'This order would only be necessary for a certain time, and I mention it here only to show the necessity of a military government'.[17]

This seems also to have been the Pitt administration's view initially, for in informing the Irish government of the venture towards the end of October 1786, Evan Nepean remarked, 'The form of government is not yet settled, though I rather think it will be a military one, at least whilst the settlement is in an infant state'.[18] In keeping with this intention, the first commissions of the governor and the colony's other officials (lieutenant-governor, deputy judge-advocate, clergyman, surgeon and assistant surgeon), issued on 12 and 24 October 1786, enjoined them to obey orders 'according to the rules and discipline of war'.[19]

But then, a serious complication arose, for the Law Officers pointed out that persons sentenced under one form of law in one jurisdiction were not amenable to being governed under another form of law elsewhere – i.e., since the convicts had been sentenced under civil law in Britain, they could not be subjected to military law in New South Wales. This advice has seemingly not survived; however, there can be no doubt that it was given, for on 9 November Nepean related to Sydney a conversation he had had with Howe:

> I told him that a deputy judge-advocate would be wanted, and that it was probable that he would be appointed also to control the criminal and civil courts for the trial of matters which might pass between the convicts ... When I mentioned a civil and criminal court his Lordship seemed rather surprised, as he had understood that the whole was to have been under military law, *convicts* as well as *soldiers*; and though I attempted to convince his Lordship that the former were not amenable to military discipline, he did not appear satisfied, but seemed to think (perhaps without considering well the importance of the subject) that they should be punished according to the discretion and judgment of the governor, even in capital part. How far his Lordship's opinion upon this matter may

be proper to be adopted I will not pretend to say, but I should think that such a discretion would occasion infinite clamour at home.

Nepean concluded this letter to Sydney with the observation: 'However, the matter will be talked over when the Cabinet next meet, and I suppose something conclusive will be done'.[20]

The business was considered further, with Sydney looking at possible analogies. One was what had been done in the former province of Senegal, where: 'Five officers sufficient for a court-martial. Five must concur in this bill to put a man to death. All other sentences [by] a majority. Fixed jury necessary. Rotation impossible'. Another was the practice in Gibraltar, where 'till [1752] everything judged by military law. Since that a jury taking in the military'.[21] One of the Law Officers quickly ruled both these possibilities out:

> I do not conceive that the authority given by the commission and instructions to the governor of Senegambia will apply to the settlement at Botany Bay, and the charter for erecting a court of criminal jurisdiction at Gibraltar appears exceptionable, though perhaps not so much so as the former. Lord Thurlow's idea is that it is within the prerogative of the Crown to direct summary 'convictions in capital cases'. The *particular circumstances* that attend this settlement may perhaps make such a regulation the more necessary, and I cannot see, when *those* are considered, any objection can possibly be made against it. It will, however, be necessary to consider what those proceedings in capital cases are to be – who is to preside in the court to be established? whom the person presiding is to call in to his assistance? the mode of proceeding at the trial? how the defence of the criminal is to be made? and what controlling power the governor is to have in cases of punishment, which do not affect the life of the culprit? It may also be proper to consider, whether in the latter case the governor should not have a power of absolute pardon instead of reprieving (supposing that to be in his commission), as otherwise the prisoner must remain in custody till the King's pleasure is known.[22]

While there is no primary record of Cabinet's consideration of this matter, there is an illuminating newspaper report. On 27 November, the *Daily Universal Register* informed readers that the Attorney-General and Solicitor-General had 'attended the [Privy] Council at St James's for the purpose of laying before His Majesty and the Cabinet the new code of laws which they have been drawing up by order of the Cabinet, for the future government of the new intended settlement at Botany Bay, New South Wales'. In an apparent reference to the *mode* of administering the law that would be adopted – i.e., a panel of civil and military or naval officers hearing cases under criminal and civil law according to a summary procedure – the report went on: 'This code is in part military, and in part civil'.[23]

Criminal and civil courts

At the end of January 1787, the administration prepared a bill to provide for a criminal court in the Botany Bay colony, with the Lord President remarking that 'I believe [a summary] jurisdiction in the present state of that embryo (for I can't call it either settlement or colony) is necessary, as the component parts of it are not of the proper stuff to make juries, in capital cases especially'.[24] Earl Camden here alluded to a difficulty which was to beset the colony into the 1820s. It was a fundamental right in British law that accused persons be tried by a jury of their peers; however, with the vast majority of the European population of early New South Wales convicted felons (who strictly had no rights at law), it was not possible to convene juries of free men.

The administration introduced the bill 'to establish a Court of Criminal Judicature on the East Coast of *New South Wales*, and the Parts adjacent' into the House of Commons on 1 February. Among other things, this provided for the governor to convene a court to try all those crimes recognized in Britain, which was to consist of a 'judge-advocate to be appointed in and for such place, together with six officers of His Majesty's forces by sea or land'. It was 'to proceed in a more summary way that is used within this realm' – that is, by calling such offenders respectively before that court, and causing the charge against him, her or them respectively to be read over; which charge shall always be reduced into writing, and shall be exhibited to the said court by the judge-advocate, and by examining witnesses upon oath ... , as well for as against such offenders respectively, and afterwards adjudging, by the opinion of the major part of the persons composing such court, that the party accused is or is not ... guilty of the charge, and by pronouncing judgement therein (as upon a conviction by verdict) of death, if the offence be capital, or of such corporal punishment, not extending to capital punishment, as to the said court shall seem meet.

It required that five members of the courts concur in a death sentence. And it was to be 'a Court of Record, and shall have all such Powers as by the Laws of *England* are incident and belonging to a Court of Record'. After some amendments, this bill passed through parliament and received royal assent on 23 February as 27 Geo. III, c.2.[25]

The civil court established for New South Wales derived its authority from the monarch's personal tribunal, the Court of King's Bench. Originally created to hear both criminal and civil matters, by the late eighteenth century, with the Lord Chief Justice at its head, this court was dealing mostly with a broad range of civil causes. For this reason, it seems, the New South Wales civil court did not need to be established by legislation. It was to comprise the judge-advocate and 'two fit and proper persons' to be appointed by the governor or lieutenant-governor. It was 'to hold plea of, and to hear and determine in a summary way all pleas concerning lands, houses, tenements, and hereditaments, and all manner of interests therein, and all pleas of debt, account, or other contracts, trespasses, and all manner of other personal pleas whatsoever'. It had the power to 'grant probates of wills and administration of the personal estates of intestates dying within the place or settlement'; and to issue summonses and to imprison in civil causes. There was to be appeal from the decision of this court to the governor; and when there was a sum of more that £300 in question, from the governor's decision to the Privy Council. The Privy Council issued Letters-Patent providing for the operation of both the civil and criminal courts on 2 April 1787.[26]

The vice-admiralty court and commission for the trial of pirates

On 26 March 1787, clearly mindful of the potential for escaped convicts to turn pirates, the Home Office advised the Admiralty that the governor of the Botany Bay colony should be given 'such powers as have been usually granted to the governors of His Majesty's colonies in America'. However, as the Lord Commissioners of the Admiralty quickly pointed out, they were empowered to appoint a vice-admiral and 'a judge and other officers requisite for a court of vice-admiralty' only at places where this had previously been done, so that this matter, too, required an explicit decision by the Privy Council.[27]

This the Privy Council gave on 4 April. The Council sent a copy of the requisite commission to the Admiralty on 12 April, and on 18 April, the Admiralty resolved to appoint the colony's governor also vice-admiral of New South Wales, with the commandant of marines one of the vice-admiralty court's judges, the commissary its registrar, and the governor's clerk its marshal. On 30 April, the High Court of Admiralty issued Letters-Patent appointing these officers; and on 5 May it issued a revised charter, now naming the colony's surveyor and the officers of the two Royal Navy ships being sent also as members of the court, along with 'all other captains and commanders of our ships who are or shall be within the Admiralty jurisdiction of the said territory called New South Wales'.[28]

A commission 'for the trial of persons committing offences upon the high seas' – i.e., for the trial of pirates – was a necessary accompaniment to that for a vice-admiralty court. Sydney wrote to the Lord President of the Privy Council requesting this on 26 March. On 4 April, the Council referred it to the Board of Trade, which reported on 13 April that the Law Officers should draw it up; and that the court should be comprised of the officials listed above. The Privy Council accepted this recommendation on 20 April, and issued the commission on 5 May. Phillip acknowledged receipt of it on 10 May.[29]

The governor's civil commission

Once the decision to provide the colony with civil rather than military law had been taken, a different commission for its governor was required. The Privy Council drafted this on 26 March, and it passed the Great Seal on 2 April.[30] It was based on those given to the governors of British colonies in North America, specifically on that for Lord Dorchester as governor-general of the Canadian provinces in 1786.[31] It was, however, necessary to depart from this precedent in one notable way. Whereas Dorchester's commission required him to frame regulations for the provinces in consultation with a nominated council and an elected assembly, as there would be no substantial group of free men in New South Wales to provide the membership of such bodies, Phillip's second commission was silent about them. Indeed, some of the First Fleet officers were taken aback when they learned of the extent of his powers. For example, Arthur Bowes Smyth, the surgeon of the *Lady Penrhyn,* commented that his commission was 'a more unlimited one than was ever before granted to any governor under the British Crown'.[32]

Otherwise, Phillip's commission followed Dorchester's closely. He was enjoined to swear allegiance to, and to maintain, the Protestant succession; to administer civil justice impartially; to enforce the laws relating to trade and plantations; to appoint 'justices of the peace, coroners, constables and other necessary officers and ministers in our said territory and its dependencies for the better administration of justice and putting the law into execution'; to care for idiots and lunatics and administer their estates. He was given the power to pardon, either absolutely or conditionally, according to the seriousness of the crime. He had 'full power and authority to levy, arm, muster and command and employ all persons whatsoever residing within our said territory and its dependencies under your government and as occasion shall serve, to march from one place to another or to embark them for the resisting and withstanding of all enemies, pirates and rebels, both at sea and land'. He might proclaim martial law in war or other emergencies, and 'erect, raise and build ... such and so many forts and platforms, castles, cities, boroughs, towns and fortifications' as he should judge necessary. In wartime, he might appoint and promote naval officers, and exercise his powers as vice-admiral through the court of that office. He might assign lands and establish 'fairs, marts and markets'. His subordinates were to obey him, or those to whom he delegated his authority. He was to pass all legal instruments under the colony's Great Seal.

Subsequent commissions and instructions

It was some years before the Pitt administration issued all the ancillary commissions and instruments needed to underwrite the wide-ranging powers it gave to the Botany Bay colony's first governor. Clearly, officials considered it necessary to complete only those relating to its immediate establishment before the ships sailed. Nonetheless, it is appropriate to describe the later instruments now, so as to indicate the full extent of the colony's governance.

Explicit power for the governor to grant land and details of how he was to do so were conveyed in a set of additional instructions which passed the Privy Council in mid-1789, when the time was approaching for the marines who had sailed out in 1787 to return home. Wishing to encourage numbers of them to settle in the colony, so as to boost its free population and its capacity to defend itself, non-commissioned officers were to be offered one hundred acres and privates fifty acres, 'free of all fees, taxes, quit-rents and other acknowledgements for the space of ten years'. If they were to enrol in the corps that would replace the marines, after five years they would be offered double the amount of land, and be given goods and clothing, seeds and agricultural implements besides. Free persons migrating to the colony were to be given similar grants of land, and convict servants might be assigned to both classes. In allocating land, though, the governor was to reserve areas for towns and the Crown's future needs.[33]

Another commission was needed to permit the governor to remit the convicts' sentences if he saw fit. The administration dealt with this in 1790. I presume it delayed issuing this on the assumption that the convicts in New South Wales remained under sentence. This was generally true, but the terms of some who had been sentenced in the early 1780s had in fact expired by this time. In March 1790, the Solicitor-General advised Evan Nepean that there was a legal problem concerning the pardoning of convicts in New South Wales, as that was not the jurisdiction in which they had been sentenced. But he drafted a bill to provide for this, which conveyed the power to pardon to the governors of all colonies to which felons had been or would be sent. This bill passed through parliament in May and June 1790, and received royal assent on 9 June as 30 Geo. III, c. 47. In November, the Privy Council issued a commission to Phillip conveying this power. Grenville sent this commission, together with additional instructions based upon it, to Phillip a week later.[34]

Similarly, once the governor of New South Wales had been empowered to grant lands and to remit sentences, a Great Seal was needed to give legal effect to the instruments by which he did so. The Privy Council ordered this to be produced in May 1790 and instructed the King's engraver about the design. When finalized, the colony's seal comprised:

> *One one side:* Convicts landed at Botany Bay, their fetters taken off and received by Industry sitting on a bale of goods, with her attributes, the distaff, bee-hive, pick axe and spade, pointing to oxen ploughing, to rising habitations, and a church on a hill at a distance, with a fort for their defence. Motto, *Sic fortis Etruria crevit*; with this inscription round the circumference, *Sigillum Nov. Camb. Aust.**
>
> *On the reverse:* Your Majesty's arms in a shield, with the supporters, garter and imperial crown with the motto, and round the circumference Your Majesty's titles.

The King gave the seal his final approval in January 1791.[35]

The lack of a currency

One thing that was conspicuously lacking from the arrangements for the Botany Bay colony was money – its governor remarked wistfully in 1788,

---

* 'Thus Etruria grew strong'; 'Seal of New South Wales'.

'this country has no Treasury'.[36] In all the documents, there is simply no mention of its needing a currency. Phillip's being supplied with ducats for purchasing goods in the East Indies indicates that this absence cannot have been an oversight, but what it indicates about official thinking is unclear.

I think there were probably three underlying assumptions, two of which were bluntly practical. If there were money in the colony, the convicts, many of whom were thieves by inclination, would expend their energies in stealing – that is, one of the principal evils that transportation was intended to remove would be perpetuated, with all its attendant violence and social discord. And then, convicts in possession of money would be able to purchase goods from calling ships, or, indeed, passages away from New South Wales, which would negate another purpose of transportation.

More abstractly, the third assumption presumably was that money was unnecessary in a peasant economy. The government would feed and clothe the convicts, who in return would labour in the nation's interest. They would raise herds and crops, which would at first lessen the cost of the colony, then produce a surplus for ships proceeding into or returning from the Pacific Ocean. They would build houses and harbour facilities, so as to consolidate the settlement and increase its role as a place of transportation. They would erect fortifications and harvest naval materials, which, together with its growing population, would make the colony a greater resource in time of war.

Although they did not have a currency available, the colony's officials were not entirely without the means of purchasing goods. The governor and the commissary of stores were authorized to issue bills of exchange (a modern equivalent might be a cross between an open cheque and a bond). Offered to the masters of ships with needed cargoes, or to merchants in foreign ports, these might pass from one person to another before being presented for payment (sometimes years later) to the Treasury in London. (Given the length of time the holder might have to wait before obtaining their sterling value, these bills were usually discounted as they changed hands.)

The paymaster of the marines was the third colonial official able to issue bills of exchange, returnable to the regimental paymaster in England. In the 1790s, the opportunity to have their salaries paid in this way enabled the officers of the New South Wales Corps to band together to import goods from the Cape of Good Hope, India and the East Indies, thus beginning the notorious trade in rum.

The colony

Clearly, all this apparatus of governance far exceeded what was needed for a stark penal outpost. And although the administration initially thought to put the colony under military law, there was always an understanding that it would become a civil settlement. Both Phillip and Nepean indicated that any period of military law would be limited. Once legal imperatives had dictated that it should have civil law, the administration gave it structures of governance which, while truncated, laid a basis for eventual growth in the manner of Crown colonies elsewhere.

Then again, Phillip's conception of how the colony might develop turned on the growth of a body of free settlers who would expand on the beginnings made by the convicts. If he did not share Matra's view that, once reformed, the convicts should be able to return fully to society, neither did he completely reject the idea of their regaining some social ease. His notion of fostering the development of a class of farmers and gardeners – convict, free, and mixed-race – meant not only that the colony would in time become self-supporting, but also that it would be able to offer supplies to calling ships, so that it might become that base south of the equator desired by the Prime Minister as part of the nation's strategic and commercial policies.

Again and again, Phillip alluded to this underlying purpose. He told Nepean that, at the end of his envisaged three-year term, he hoped the colony would not only be self-supporting, but also have become 'of the greatest consequence to this country'. When he had found that splendid waterway – 'the finest harbour in the world, in which a thousand sail-of-the-line may ride in the most perfect security' – and settled his charges about Sydney Cove, he told Lansdowne that 'this country will hereafter be a most valuable acquisition to Great Britain from its situation'. And his design for the permanent township, with its main streets to be 200 feet wide, and with its strategic placement of government buildings so as to offer views down to the North and South Heads, was such as to befit a colony that would become a 'seat of empire', to which 'ships of all nations' would resort.[37]

These were not the meanderings of an impractical visionary. Phillip was an accomplished and hard-headed naval officer. He had participated in the gruesome business of hunting and rendering whales in the Arctic Ocean. He had seen men shorn apart in battle. He had seen them die of scurvy. He had seen the brutality of slavery in Brazil and at the Cape of Good Hope. He had ordered men flogged. In New South Wales he presided over executions. Rather, these were expectations based on what those who decided to establish the colony had said to him. Together, these expectations and the mode of govenance tell us a good deal about the Pitt administration's intentions for the convict colony.

PART TWO:
ASSEMBLING THE FLEET

3.

The People 1: Officials and Officers

IT IS NOT MY INTENTION HERE to give a comprehensive account of the First Fleet colonists. Rather, what I wish to do is to convey a sense of the composition of the various groups; to indicate the roles of and to offer short biographies of some of the more prominent officials; and to indicate those who were sent because they had relevant skills. In this, as in other major aspects of the mounting of the First Fleet, we see both broad and detailed planning, and therefore other signs that the Pitt administration took the business seriously.

The civil establishment
In the sketch of the colony's civil establishment, prepared in mid-August 1786 as an attachment to Heads of a Plan, Nepean allowed for the following appointments and specified their annual salaries:[1]

	£
The naval commander to be appointed governor or superintendent-general	500
The commanding officer of the marines, to be appointed lieutenant-governor or deputy superintendent	250
The commissary of stores and provisions for himself and assistants (to be appointed or named by the contractors for the provisions)	200

Pay of a surgeon	182.10
Ditto of two mates	182.10
Chaplain	182.10
Total	£1497.10

By 10 October, which is the date by which we may consider the civil establishment to have been largely (but not entirely) finalized, he had expanded this list to include:[2]

	£
Allowance to the governor	1000
Lieutenant-governor	250
Deputy judge-advocate	182.10
Commissary	182.10
Provost marshal	91.5
Chaplain	182.10
Surgeon	182.10
Three mates, at £91.5.0 each	273.15
Agent (i.e., for transports)	150
Payment of fees upon the receipt and audit	200
To be paid in advance:	2695

A surveyor was later added to this list.

The governor

The person appointed as the colony's first governor was Captain Arthur Phillip (1738–1814). As a boy, Phillip was educated at Greenwich Hospital School for the sons of poor seamen, and in his youth sailed on whaling voyages to the Arctic Ocean and on trading voyages to the Mediterranean. He joined the Royal Navy in 1755, and in the Seven Years' War (1756–63) saw battle in the Mediterranean and the West Indies.[3]

He married in 1763, to Charlott Denison, a rich widow who was significantly older than he. For a brief period, the couple seem to have resided at Hampton, just to the west of London. By 1766 they had acquired Vernals Farm, on the outskirts of Lyndhurst, in the New Forest. Phillip's enjoyment of the life of a country gentlemen was brief. He seems to have left the district in mid-1768; and in April 1769, after they had lived apart for some time, he and Charlott concluded a formal separation agreement.

In September 1769, Phillip obtained permission from the Admiralty to go to St Omers, in northern France, 'for the benefit of his health'.[4] Given that he and the Home Office later used this reason as a blind, it is probable that this marks the beginning of his career as a spy. In November 1770, at the time of the Falklands Islands crisis, occasioned by Britain's establishing a settlement on these remote islands claimed by Spain, he joined the *Egmont* as 4th lieutenant, but saw only routine service. He left this ship in July 1771, and remained on half-pay until January 1775. In these years, however, he spent two more extended periods in France.

At the end of 1774, with the encouragement of superiors, together with a number of other junior British officers, Phillip joined the Portuguese Navy, serving in Brazilian waters for four years. Portugal was Britain's oldest ally in Europe, and from time to time the Admiralty helped out the much smaller Portuguese Navy. This also gave British officers the opportunity to gather information about harbours and fortifications, particularly in the Spanish colonies.

Britain's American colonies having rebelled in 1776, and France having taken their side, Phillip returned to England at the beginning of October 1778 and was immediately appointed 1st lieutenant of the *Alexander*, a 74-gun line-of-battle ship. In September 1779 he was given the command of the fireship *Basilisk*. Promotion to post-captain of the 24-gun frigate *Ariadne* followed in November 1781. In early 1783, just as the war was ending, in command of the 64-gun *Europe* he sailed as part of a small squadron intended to attack the Spanish settlements in South America. A storm ravaged the ships in the Bay of Biscay and all the captains but Phillip were forced to turn back. Phillip made his way via Rio de Janeiro to India, where he joined the squadron under Admiral Hughes and Sir Richard King, returning to England via the Cape of Good Hope in late April 1784.

There is a considerable mystery concerning some of Phillip's activities in these years. In January 1781, he supplied Lord Sandwich, the First Lord of the Admiralty, with charts of the South American coastline, which showed 'three good harbours, where ships that wanted to wood and water would find only a few settlers'.[5] Then, his name disappears from the records from February to mid-October 1781, with the exception that it continues in the list of half-pay officers – i.e., those who were not presently on active service, but whom the Admiralty wished to retain. If this were really the situation, we should expect that he would have written repeatedly to offer his services, which he did not.

As he was negotiating the terms of his appointment in New South Wales, Phillip made two comments which presumably bear on this silence. The first, to Evan Nepean, was: 'you recollect that in the late war I was deprived of the chance of those advantages every other officer enjoyed, and put to no small expense'. The second, to Lord Sydney, was that 'every officer must naturally wish to meet with some recompense for his labours, and I have hitherto paid for having been anxious to render an essential service to my country'.[6]

Arthur Phillip spoke five European languages: English, German, French, Spanish and Portuguese. The Home Office repeatedly employed him to spy on naval preparations on the Continent; and in the mid-1770s, the Admiralty placed him in the Portuguese Navy so that he might obtain information about coastlines and harbours, ports and their defences in South America. I suspect that the government sent him back to South America in 1781 to prepare the way for a secret expedition it was planning against Spanish settlements there. And if I am right, it is presumably to this hidden period that the following curious story belongs, about which I have been unable to obtain any further details, whether in English archives, or those of Portugal and Brazil:

> Captain Phillip, the commander-in-chief of the expedition to Botany Bay, was several years in the Portuguese service, and obtained no small degree of reputation from the following incident. Being employed about five years since to carry out with him near 400

52

criminals from Lisbon to the Brazils, during the course of the voyage an epidemical disorder broke out on board his ship, which made such havoc that he had not hands sufficient to navigate her. In this dilemma he called up the most spirited of the transports [i.e., convicts], and told them in a few words his situation, and that if they would assist in conducting the vessel and keep their companions in order, he would represent their behaviour to the Court of Lisbon, and, in short, do all in his power to get their sentence mitigated. This speech had the desired effect. The prisoners acted with fidelity, and brought the ship safe to [Rio de Janeiro][7], where they were delivered into the custody of the garrison; and on Captain Phillip's return to Lisbon, and representing the meritorious conduct of the transports, they were not only emancipated from their servitude, but had small portions of land allotted them in that delightful country.[8]

In October 1784, Nepean sent Phillip to spy in France again; and then once more in October 1785. When Phillip returned to England is unknown, but presumably it was about the end of September 1786, for the *Daily Universal Register* announced his appointment on 27 September. When precisely he was first thought of for the governorship of the Botany Bay colony is also unknown. The earliest evidence of this is Howe's dismal comment to Sydney on 3 September 1786, that 'I cannot say the little knowledge I have of Captain Phillip would have led me to select him for a service of this complicated nature'.[9]

But consider. Already by the mid-1780s, Phillip had wide experience of the Atlantic and Indian oceans and of a number of the countries that border them. He had charted coastlines and harbours, and noted their resources. He had made the long voyage out to India, which was the nearest analogy to that to New South Wales. In his espionage, he had shown himself to be just that 'discreet' officer that Nepean had pointed out would be needed in the Heads of a Plan.

And if the story of his having transported convicts to Brazil is true, then he was also qualified for the business in a way in which no other British naval officer was.

There is an additional tantalizing possibility. While it is something about Phillip's life I was never able to elucidate properly, it seems that he had strong connections with the cloth trade. His first wife was previously married to John Denison, a wealthy London cloth and wine merchant. His second wife was Isabella Whitehead, the daughter of Richard Whitehead and Elizabeth Sudell, both of whose families were much involved in the cotton and linen weaving industry.[10] Then, there is the report that one of his midshipmen on the *Europe* in 1783–84 was 'the son of a merchant in the calico printing business in Old Street road, London, at whose table the captain had been kindly entertained'.[11] Phillip's attempts to breed cochineal insects are another indication of this connection, as is his prompting Nepean to obtain cotton seed for New South Wales. So too is Philip Gidley King's advising Nepean in 1791 that he could 'write to a friend of Governor Phillip' to procure cotton seed for Norfolk Island.[12] Given that the Botany Bay colony was part of the Pitt administration's Bounty scheme, an understanding of the business of cotton would have been an additional attribute in the person chosen to govern it.

The lieutenant-governor

Robert Ross (c. 1740–94) joined the marines as a 2nd lieutenant in June 1757; and was reportedly at the siege of Quebec in 1759. He was promoted to captain in March 1773, and may have been at the battle of Bunker Hill in 1775. In 1778 and 1779 he recruited in Ireland, and he served as major on guardships at Plymouth in 1783–84. He was offered the command of the marine companies going to New South Wales in October 1786, and issued with a military commission as lieutenant-governor at the same time. What precisely the everyday duties envisaged for Ross in this second role were is most unclear. His commission is silent about them, and the Admiralty's subsequent directives to him are concerned only with his military duties. Before he sailed, he was also made one of the members of the colony's vice-admiralty court.[13]

Ross gave Phillip no end of trouble in New South Wales. Cantankerous and opinionated, he refused to let the marine officers supervise the convicts in their labour, tried to shield marines who committed crimes from punishment, and insisted on strict adherence to military protocols. He also resented the egalitarian social policies which Phillip pursued, writing at one point: 'Could I have possibly imagined that I was to be served with ... no more butter than any one of the convicts (nearly 6 ozs per week), I most certainly would not have left England without supplying myself with that article ... or oil for my own use'.[14]

He was soon off-side, not only with Phillip, but also with his officers, whom he wanted to court-martial as a group. In March 1790, so as to have some respite from his complaints and obstinacy, Phillip sent him to Norfolk Island, where, true to form, he administered three different kinds of law – civil, military and a hybrid of his own devising.

In view of Ross's recalcitrant behaviour in New South Wales, it is tempting to think that the administration may have had an inkling of this, and therefore preferred John Hunter (see below) as 'governor-in-waiting'. However, this would be anachronistic. Whereas another naval officer might command the warships, and also appropriately fill the role of governor on a temporary basis, a marine officer might serve as acting governor but not exercise any authority over Royal Navy ships and their officers. Hunter was the appropriate choice to act as governor in Phillip's absence or death.

The deputy judge-advocate

David Collins (1756–1810) sailed with a civil as well as military appointment, for in addition to that he received from the Admiralty to adjudicate at courts-martial, on 24 October 1786 the administration appointed him to head the colony's civil and criminal courts. It is unclear whether Collins's first commission in military form as deputy judge-advocate was ever superseded by one in civil form. In asking for a supply of stationery on 7 February 1787, he referred to his commission 'from His Majesty', but no second commission has ever been found.[15] In the colony, he also served as the governor's official secretary.

The commissary of stores

Andrew Miller (c. 1759–90) had been on the *Basilisk* with Phillip, first as a seaman and then as purser's steward in August 1779. In December 1782 he followed Phillip into the *Europe*. He was offered the position of the colony's commissary (i.e., keeper of the government's stores) before the end of December, when his name appeared in the list published by the *Daily Universal Register*.[16]

The provost marshall

George Alexander was first appointed to this position, but he was not on board when the ships sailed in May 1787; and, indeed, according to Phillip, he 'had not been seen for a considerable time before we sailed'.[17] In his absence, Phillip gave it to his loyal follower Henry Brewer, who had served as his clerk on the *Basilisk*, *Ariadne* and *Europe*, and who joined the *Sirius* in December 1786 as a midshipman. Brewer was also appointed marshal of the vice-admiralty court. One shipmate described him as a person 'of coarse, harsh features, a contracted brow which bespoke him a man soured by disappointment, a forbidding countenance, always muttering as if talking to himself'; but this writer also said that 'if honesty merits heaven, Harry is there'.[18]

The chaplain

At the end of September 1786, a number of people asked the Reverend Richard Johnson if he were interested in going out to New South Wales. Conscious of the inevitable long separation from his extended family and friends that this would involve, of 'the dangers of the sea', and of the disadvantages of life in 'a country wild and uncultivated', where he and his immediate family might be 'exposed to savages, and perhaps to various wild beasts of prey', he was initially very uncertain of the wisdom of doing so. However, he fasted and prayed, and God showed him that he should say yes.[19]

Johnson was recommended by John Newton, former master of slaving ships who had come to detest the trade, and who was the author of 'Amazing Grace'. Newton described Johnson as 'humble and spiritual [... with] no taste or desire for the extensive mode of life so generally prevalent ... a simple man'. He was appointed at the urging of Pitt's friend

William Wilberforce and of Sir Charles Middleton, members of the influential Clapham 'sect', an evangelical group within the Church of England.[20] His commission, in military form, was issued on 24 October 1786. It is also unclear whether this was later superseded by a civilian one.

Two days earlier, on Sunday 22 October, Johnson went down to the hulks to begin his acquaintance with the convicts. Although the Society for the Propagation of the Gospel equipped him lavishly for the daunting task of saving their souls, he had a very hard time of it in New South Wales. Many of his charges showed themselves quite uninterested in religion; the authorities did not hasten to build him a church; and when at last he had one some malicious person burned it down.

Otherwise, Johnson's time in the colony was notable for three things: he fed sick convicts out of his own rations; at the time of the smallpox epidemic in mid-1789, he and his wife took in a young Aboriginal girl; and he proved himself to be one of the best farmers.

The surgeons

John White (c. 1756–1832) was the colony's chief surgeon. Between 1778 and 1786, he served on various Royal Navy ships as surgeon's mate and then as surgeon, before being recommended for Botany Bay by Sir Andrew Snape Hamond.[21] Like other subsidiary officials, he was issued with a military commission on 24 October 1786. Again, it is unclear that this was ever superseded.

White displayed some of the ignorance of his time. He believed, for example, that foul air caused scurvy. However, in general he showed himself to be a very competent medical officer, and the excellent health record of the First Fleet is in large part due to his skill and to his insistence on having proper medical supplies.

White was keenly interested in natural history, and kept an informative journal of his time in New South Wales. He otherwise did not enjoy the colony, though, describing it as 'a country and place so forbidding and so hateful as only to merit execration and curses'.[22]

The assistant surgeons ('surgeon's mates') were Dennis Considen (?–1815); Thomas Arndell (1753–1821); and William Balmain (1762–1803), who had sailed on the *Nautilus* when it explored the southwest coast of Africa.

The agent (for transports)

John Shortland (c. 1739–1803) joined the Navy in 1755, aged fifteen, and was promoted to lieutenant in 1763. Thereafter, he made a career in the Transport Service, taking a convoy to relieve Gibraltar in 1782 and bringing another from North America in 1786. The Navy Board appointed him agent for the First Fleet transports in September 1786. Together with Phillip and White, he was responsible for the success of the voyage. He returned to England in May 1789.

The surveyor

August Alt (1734–1815) trained as an engineer, and was present at the siege of Gibraltar in 1779. In times of peace, he recruited for the army and built roads.

The position of surveyor to the colony was not originally thought of, but it became necessary once the governor was given authority to grant lands. It was included, without the name of the person to hold it, in the list of those to provide members of the panel to try pirates dated 13 April 1787. Alt's name appears in the commissions for this and for the vice-admiralty court issued on 5 May 1787.[23]

The botanist

One of the most persistent criticisms of the Pitt administration's mounting of the First Fleet has been that no botanist was sent. This is true, but things were not exactly as this makes it seem.

The presence of an expert botanist in the colony would have been, if perhaps not quite necessary, certainly advantageous in locating the best soils and in advising on the progress of plantings. He might also have extended that beginning made by Banks and Solander in 1770 in the collection and classification of the unique flora of New South Wales. And the First Fleet officers did sail with the expectation that they would have one, for Tench recorded, 'we flattered ourselves ... that Masson, the

King's botanical gardener, who was employed [at the Cape of Good Hope] in collecting for the royal nursery at Kew, would have joined us'.[24]

Born in 1741 in Aberdeen, Scotland, Francis Masson worked at Kew Gardens as a gardener in the 1760s. When Banks ordered him to collect in southern Africa, James Cook left him at Cape Town in October 1772, where he remained until 1775, in this time sending back some 500 species. In 1776, he collected in the Atlantic islands, but war and a hurricane destroyed his harvests. In 1783 he was in Portugal.

He returned to south Africa in January 1786, and thereafter figured in Banks's plans for the new colony. How strongly in 1786–87 is unclear. In mid-1789, however, as the *Lady Juliana* was preparing, Banks wrote to him that 'I intended about this time to have asked leave of His Majesty to order you to Botany Bay; but, finding from your letter to Mr Aiton that you had an aversion to the place, I have made interest that another person should be sent there, and I hope I shall succeed'.[25] The botanist, gardener and surveyor David Burton sailed out to New South Wales in the *Gorgon*, arriving in September 1791, where he supervised agriculture at Parramatta and collected for Banks.

The second captain of the Sirius

The *Sirius* carried two captains. As the senior naval officer, Phillip would command the Royal Navy ships and conduct the convoy on the way out; but then, since his presence would be required on land, he could not command the ships when they were again at sea. A second officer was needed, but one who must remain under the governor's general direction. The solution that the administration arrived at was to appoint a *second* captain to the *Sirius*, one junior to the governor in naval rank, but senior to the lieutenants of the *Sirius* and *Supply*. Such an arrangement was by no means unknown in the Royal Navy. For example, it was common with the small squadron on the Newfoundland station, which was evidently the model for that in New South Wales;[26] but it had seldom, if ever, been applied to a ship as small as the *Sirius*.

Before the end of October, Phillip had approached Lord Sydney about giving this appointment to John Hunter, who was then assisting him to prepare the *Sirius*.[27] Hunter (1732–1821) was a Scot who joined the Navy in 1754, being promoted to lieutenant in 1760 after service in North American waters, where he served again during the American war. He was appointed second captain in mid-December. Later, he became the colony's second governor, from 1795–1800. Like the other naval officers, Hunter kept a detailed journal, which he published in 1793 as *An Historical Journal of the Transactions at Port Jackson and Norfolk Island ... in New South Wales*.

Partly because of Phillip's pride, and partly because of Lord Howe's obduracy, this arrangement caused real trouble. Phillip considered that the appointment of a second captain should entitle him to fly the broad pennant while at sea and when in foreign ports. This pennant indicated the presence of a commodore of a detached squadron sailing on a particular mission, and therefore a status superior to a captain's. Nepean evidently promised Phillip that on this point he would 'go away satisfied', but Howe was opposed to it.[28] I am surmising here, but I think the basis of the First Lord's opposition was that, because as soon as he arrived at New South Wales his business would become 'entirely unconnected with maritime affairs', Phillip would cease to be under the control of the Admiralty, and instead be answerable only to the Secretary of State.[29] In Howe's view, he would not then be entitled to the broad pennant, as he would not be on sea service.

Technically, Howe was in the right. However, I think there may have been other considerations involved. One was that the Admiralty did not have control of the expedition; another was that Phillip had not been Howe's choice to lead it; and a likely third was that Howe suspected that Phillip was seeking this arrangement so that he might obtain status and emoluments he was not genuinely entitled to. Howe could not but have been made more determined in his opposition by a newspaper report on 31 October – that is, while the business was still under discussion and well before anything had been finalized – that Hunter was to be appointed second captain of the *Sirius*, and that Phillip would 'hoist a broad pennant, as soon as his ship comes within sight of [New] South Wales'.[30]

Phillip persisted with his request to this point, but then, in the face of Howe's continuing opposition, backed off, asking Sydney not to pursue the matter: 'My situation would be still more disagreeable if [Hunter] was to be removed, *for somebody must command the ship when I am on shore.* It might, I think, be better if Lord Howe was left to act as he pleases, my dependence being on your office'.[31] But the matter continued to rankle with Phillip, and he did ask again, only for Sydney to tell him in April, as his instructions were being finalized, that 'it is not thought advisable under the present circumstances of the service which you are to perform, that you should be authorized to wear any distinguishing pennant'; but that any officer junior to him arriving in New South Wales would be instructed to follow his orders.[32] In the end, Phillip sailed only with this understanding.

Still, puzzles about this business remain. One of the officers who made the voyage recorded that Phillip 'immediately hoisted his broad pennant as commodore of the squadron'; and midshipman George Raper's painting of the First Fleet ships entering the harbour at Rio de Janeiro shows the red, swallow-tailed pennant flying from the *Sirius*'s mainmast.[33] I do not know what to make of this. Phillip can scarcely have flown this pennant without some approval. It may be that he had a quiet understanding that he might 'wear' it at Rio de Janeiro, as he had served in the Portuguese Navy and a superior naval status would help him in his dealings with the viceroy.

Despite being disappointed in the matter of the broad pennant, Phillip did leave England with Hunter as second captain of the *Sirius*. Because it was unprecedented to have two captains on a 6th-rate (i.e., a warship carrying up to 32 guns, and commanded by a post-captain), the arrangement required Privy Council approval. The Admiralty wrote to the Council on 14 December, which approved the arrangement the next day. The Admiralty informed Phillip on 18 December, and the Navy Board on 22 December. Before the ships sailed, the Privy Council issued Hunter with a dormant commission, empowering him to act as governor in the event of Phillip's absence or death.[34]

Junior naval officers

Among the middle-ranking officers on the *Sirius* were Lieutenants William Bradley (1758–1833) and Phillip Gidley King (1758–1808), one of Phillip's followers, who was to become the colony's third governor (1800–06). Both of these kept detailed and informative journals, with Bradley adding charts and watercolours. So too did George Raper, one of the midshipmen, whose drawings are particularly striking (see the cover). Newton Fowell, another of the midshipmen, described the venture in a long series of letters home.

Lieutenant Henry Lidgbird Ball (1758–1818) commanded the *Supply*.

Marine officers

The commandant of marines was Lieutenant-Governor Ross, who was introduced above. Each of the companies of marines that went out to New South Wales was commanded by one captain and three lieutenants. A number of these fulfilled associated duties: e.g., Lieutenant John Long the adjutant (i.e., administrative assistant to the commandant); and Lieutenant James Furzer the companies' quartermaster.

Three other marine officers deserve more detailed consideration. Watkin Tench (c. 1758–1833) joined the service as 2nd lieutenant in 1776, and volunteered for New South Wales on 25 October 1786.[35] The most literate of the colony's chroniclers, Tench was genuinely interested in the experiment taking place around him, and his two accounts of its early years offer details of agricultural and social development not found elsewhere.

William Dawes (1762–1836) joined the marines as 2nd lieutenant in September 1779, then served on ships in North American waters. He was evidently something of a Renaissance man. One patron recommended him in this way: 'He understands the Spanish and Portuguese languages, as also French and Italian; he has studied botany some considerable time together, with mineralogy; he is a tolerable good astronomer and draws very well'. This recommendation was successful, for on 25 October the Admiralty agreed to his having three weeks leave 'on his private affairs' – i.e., to travel to London to have his scientific expertise assessed.[36]

Dawes attended the Home Office with a recommendation to Brook Watson, the naval stores dealer and friend to the administration, that 'whatever you desire him to do respecting the flax from New Zealand, or any other important article of commerce which that country may produce, his future conduct will prove that his abilities, and application, are worthy your protection'. His major purpose in coming to town, however, was to present himself to Neville Maskelyne, the Astronomer-Royal, in the hope of being appointed astronomer to the expedition. In this he succeeded, for in November the Board of Longitude agreed to supply him with a long list of relevant instruments and books.[37]

Dawes was an upright young man, but an inflexible one. In the colony, he was put in charge of artillery and fortifications; he built an observatory at Dawes Point; and he helped lay out Sydney and Parramatta. However, he and Phillip quarrelled, and he chose to return to England rather than serve another term in the colony. He took with him a notable vocabulary of a local Aboriginal language.

David Collins joined the marines in February 1771. In June 1775 he fought at Bunker Hill, and then afterwards served in Nova Scotia. He was promoted to captain in August 1779, and went on half-pay at the end of the war. On 1 January 1787 the Admiralty appointed him to oversee courts-martial in the colony. He wrote a long account of its beginnings, and subsequently became lieutenant-governor of Van Diemen's Land (Tasmania).

4.

People 2: Ships' Crews, Marines, Convicts, Wives and Children

LET US NOW CONSIDER THOSE who made up the majority of the First Fleet's people: the crews of the various vessels, the marines, the convicts, and the wives and children who travelled with them.

Ships' crews: the Royal Navy

In October 1786, the Admiralty fixed the complement of the *Sirius* at 160, and that of the *Supply* at fifty-five. These complements included marines – twenty-two and twelve respectively.

It was usual for senior naval officers to take boys intending to become officers to sea, so as to begin their training in mathematics, navigation and drawing. These trainees were known as 'Captain's servants'; and post-captains were entitled to bear four on a ship's book. In view of the length of the voyage and nature of the business these ships were embarked on, however, the Admiralty decided not to permit their commanders to take servants with them, decreeing that only 'able seamen' [i.e., those rated 'Able-bodied' or AB] should go. The Admiralty paid the commanders an allowance instead.[1] Reflecting the fact that the Navy was a young man's occupation, most of these crewmen were in their twenties or thirties.

However, some who were not trained sailors also joined the crews. Henry Dodd, who sailed as an AB on the *Sirius*, had reportedly been a farm-hand for Phillip in England. He supervised the labour of the convicts and the establishment of agriculture in the colony. Roger Murley (sometimes spelt Morley) also went out as AB on the *Sirius*. Described by King as 'an adventurer [who] had been a master weaver', he was in the first party sent to Norfolk Island in February 1788. The *Sirius*'s blacksmith also settled in the colony.[2]

Ships' crews: the transports

There is considerable doubt about the number of crewmen on the six convict transports and three storeships, as various sources do not agree about the numbers. In the following table, I give those stated in the passes (certificates) required by the Navigation Act, and those from Philip Gidley King.[3]

	Pass	King
Alexander	19 British, 6 foreign (total 25)	30
Borrowdale	13 British, 4 foreign (total 17)	22
Charlotte	23 British, 7 foreign (total 30)	30
Fishburn	17 British (total 17)	22
Friendship	13 British, 4 foreign (total 17)	25
Golden Grove	15 British, 5 foreign (total 20)	22
Lady Penrhyn	19 British, 6 foreign (total 25)	30
Prince of Wales	17 British, 5 foreign (total 22)	Not recorded
Scarborough	27 British, 8 foreign (total 35)	30
Total	208	211+

Even these totals might be quite inaccurate, however, for the ships may have carried more crew, together perhaps as many as 100.

Marines

The four marine companies sent to New South Wales each comprised one captain, three lieutenants, three sergeants, three corporals, two drummers and forty privates – a total of 208, which became 212 with the addition of the commandant, deputy judge-advocate, adjutant and quartermaster.[4] In view of Botany Bay's distance from England, and of the unusual nature of the service to be undertaken, the Admiralty stressed to the commanding officers of the Portsmouth and Plymouth barracks that in the first instance those enlisted should be volunteers on full pay. Offers of service poured into the Admiralty, many more than were needed. In the end, Tench tells us, all but two of the 212 men in the four companies were volunteers.[5] It is unclear whether the additional thirty-four marines posted to the *Sirius* and *Supply* were also volunteers.

The marine enlistment had naturally been wound back at the end of the war in 1783, so that it was adequate only to 'the requisite demands of parties for [the King's] ships employed in time of peace, and the ordinary duties on shore at the several headquarters'. The decision to send four companies to New South Wales inevitably strained the force's capacity. Accordingly, on 21 November, the Admiralty requested permission to raise four more companies, each to comprise one captain, two 1st and one 2nd lieutenants, three sergeants, three corporals, two drummers and forty-eight privates – a total of sixty personnel each.[6] The Privy Council issued an Order for doing so three days later, which Stephens then conveyed to the Ordnance Board; and the Admiralty instructed the commanders at the Portsmouth and Plymouth barracks each to recruit two new companies.[7]

As subsequent events showed, the private marines who went out to New South Wales were no better and no worse that their peers in society. Some behaved well, others very badly. One was exiled to Norfolk Island for the rape of a little girl. Six were executed for the theft of the precious stores.[8] Indeed, we may suppose that, given education and class, it was probably only luck that many of them travelled free rather than in chains. It is one of the ironies of the colony's first years, and an indication of the strange reversals that occurred there, that, with the governor's approval, the convicts formed a night-watch to prevent assaults and robbery of huts and gardens, and Major Ross argued that errant marines should be immune to arrest by these amateur constables.

Marines' wives and children

In the course of preparations, the Admiralty advised the Home Office that it was usual for some wives to accompany their marine husbands on overseas postings.[9] We may suppose that the basic criterion was that the couples had young, dependent families, though the women would also have fulfilled certain useful domestic duties, such as mending clothes. In all, twenty-eight wives of marines seem to have gone out to New South Wales, together with some twenty-four children. These women were victualled at half the ration of the men, and their children at a quarter.[10]

Convicts

In August 1786, at the time of the decision, the administration intended to send 750 convicts to Botany Bay – 680 men and seventy women. Home Office correspondence with county officials makes clear that the men were to be taken from the hulks in the Thames and at Plymouth. In the weeks before the Fleet sailed, there was some relaxation of this policy, with some convicts being sent also from country jails.

In mid-October, Sir Charles Middleton received a strange letter from an anonymous correspondent, urging him to increase the number of women:

> There appears not now more than *one woman* to five or six men. This can never be right, either as to policy or humanity. *Without* women no colony can thrive. And a *deficient* number will certainly occasion *contentions* and at length *bloodshed*, not to mention *more odious consequences.*

The solution that this writer proposed was that some of the numerous prostitutes who frequented the taverns at Portsmouth should also be shipped out, and once in New South Wales married by lot to the male convicts. Citing as a precedent the method the French Crown had evidently used to populate New Orleans, he observed: 'we do not find that these predetermined weddings turned out worst than the run of marriages commonly do'.[11]

About this time a decision was made to increase the number of women; but precisely when is difficult to establish. Sydney told the Treasury on 22 December that it was 'upon many accounts ... advisable' to do so.[12] However, the decision does seem to have been taken significantly earlier, at least informally, for while the *Hampshire Chronicle* reported on 18 September that 'there are 680 men felons and 70 women felons to go' (which is correct in terms of the Home Office's August advice to the Treasury and Admiralty), two weeks later the *Reading Mercury* announced that 'about 700 men and 150 women' were being sent (which is much closer to the final number).[13]

In October and November, the Home Office wrote to the sheriffs of Hampshire, Bristol, Derby, Kent, Worcester, Gloucester, Devon, Wiltshire and other counties, asking for details of any women transports being held in their jails, and directing that they be sent either to the *Dunkirk* hulk at Plymouth or to the Southwark jail in London, to await embarkation. And arrive the women did – one from Chester, one from Liverpool, one from Durham, two from Brecon, two from Worcester, two from Derby, one from Suffolk, one from Norfolk, one from Reading, three from Norwich, four from Lancaster, one from Durham, four from Bristol, one from Cardiff, three from Salisbury, one from York, two from Worcester. The process continued into 1787.

Alhough the figures are not quite precise, it seems that in the period of embarkation, 586 men and 192 women convicts and wives were taken on board. Seventeen of these died and two were pardoned before the ships sailed on 13 May, so that the actual number who sailed was 568 men and 191 women, for a total of 759.

The ages in 1787 of a sample group of 280 of the convicts were:

Age	No.
1–9	0
10–19	37
20–29	153
30–39	66
40–49	15

50–59	5
60+	4

That is, 68 per cent of the group were aged under thirty, 91 per cent under forty.

The ages of the youngest convicts were (on arrival) thirteen and fourteen, the oldest sixty-seven and sixty-eight, with the great majority aged between twenty and thirty-nine.

Convicts' wives and children

There was a curious group who were supposed to go out with the convicts: relations who asked the administration to send them with their menfolk. As the *London Chronicle* reported in October,

> On Monday applications were made at the Treasury by some females to accompany the convicts to Botany Bay, among whom were the wife and mother of one of the felons now under sentence of transportation. The clerks of the Treasury were for some time at a loss how to act, but on Mr Nepean's coming, and the affair being stated to him, the petitioners were dismissed, with orders to call again in a few days, and a promise that the nature and propriety of their request should be seriously taken into consideration.[14]

These women's plea was successful. The administration made provision for some twenty-five of them to go, clothed and victualled in the same manner as the women convicts.[15] They were to take with them a small number of children. In April, William Richards was still expecting them to come to Portsmouth to be embarked on the *Prince of Wales*, but it seems they never arrived.

Selecting the people

There are two questions to be asked about the First Fleet personnel, which bear on the central one of whether the Pitt administration wished simply to dump the convicts as far away as possible, or whether it also wished to establish a viable colony capable of realizing other purposes. In other words, did it mount the First Fleet in a willy-nilly fashion, or purposefully? These questions are: Was there any selection of those sent? If so, what were the criteria used in selection?

Clearly, as I have indicated in the previous chapter, numbers of the officers were chosen for the particular skills they had – but what of the men and women convicts, and the merchant and Royal Navy seamen and marines?

As a consequence of demographic analysis undertaken in conjunction with Ezra Zebrow,[16] I can now offer the following conclusions, some of which remain tentative:

1. There was no selection of convict women, by age or any other criteria. Particularly once the decision had been taken to increase their number, these women were simply taken from metropolitan and county jails and assembled at Plymouth and London.

2. There was no selection of convict men by age. The age profiles of those sent correlate with those of males in the general population.

3. There may have been a selection of male convicts according to skills. In February 1787, Nepean sent Campbell a list of 120 convicts, asking him to 'select 100' to be put on board the *Scarborough*.[17] Tench said that 'the major part of the prisoners were mechanics and husbandmen, selected on purpose by order of Government'.[18] Ralph Clark says that of the seventy-six men on the *Friendship*, forty-four had 'trades'. His list includes six weavers, two carpenters, three farmers or gardeners, four brickmakers or bricklayers, and one blacksmith.[19] Gillen was able to establish that at least 163 men and sixty-seven women convicts had a trade[20] – but whether these were higher proportions than in the English population at large is unclear.

4. There may have been some selection according to fitness. I know that Phillip's comment in January 1787 that there were several men embarked who 'cannot help themselves' seems to contradict this.[21] However, when delivering convicts for transportation, Duncan Campbell did not include those who were sick or injured. In sending his deputy

lists of the convicts to be put on board the *Alexander* and *Scarborough*, Campbell asked to be informed of their health and whether any had died. In late February, when despatching convicts to the *Scarborough*, Campbell did not send seven from the list of 191 nominated.[22] Subsequently, he asked Erskine to inform him which of the convicts 'who from sickness and other causes were thought unfit to be removed with the other prisoners' were now well enough to follow their confreres.[23]

There is also subsequent vindication of this point. Phillip later reported to Sydney that twenty-six of the seventy-two convict deaths in the colony between January 1788 and February 1790 had been due to 'disorders of long-standing'. However, after the arrival of the Second Fleet in June 1790 he wrote, 'The sending out the disordered and helpless clears the jails, and may ease the parishes from which they are sent; but, Sir, it is obvious that this settlement, instead of being a colony which is to support itself, will, if the practice is continued, remain for years a burden to the mother country'.[24] Together, these comments indicate that there was a selection according to health of the male convicts sent on the First Fleet.

5. Interestingly, there was at least a partial selection according to the seriousness of the crime committed. In nominating in March 1785 first 150, and then 200, men for transportation to Africa, Evan Nepean pointed out to Sir Charles Middleton that these were 'the most abandoned scoundrels in the country selected for this purpose'.[25] It was these men, their numbers altered somewhat by death or release, who formed the bulk of those put on board the *Alexander* in the Thames in December 1786.

6. There evidently was some selection of Navy personnel according to skills that would be useful in the colony. Jacob Nagle, the American sailor on the *Sirius*, recorded that Phillip had 'the privilege of taking any men that turned out from the men-of-war, there was great number turned out, but the captain took his pick, all young men that were called seamen, 160 in number'.[26] This is confirmed by Admiralty correspondence, for as the *Sirius* waited at Portsmouth, and sick sailors were discharged from it, the official in charge asked for volunteers from the guardships, noting their names and trades, and 'as the returns were very numerous and many

handicrafts among them, I had foreborne to complete her complement till Captain Phillip came down, that he might furnish himself with those who occupations he might stand most in need of'.[27]

7. There also seems to have been some selection of the enlisted marines according to relevant skills. Certainly, Nepean called for this in the Heads of a Plan: 'as many ... as possible should be artificers, such as carpenters, sawyers, smiths, potters (if possible) and some husbandmen'.[28] And in October 1786 Colonel John Hughes advised that from the 200 volunteers at the Plymouth barracks he had chosen 'many of all trades'.[29]

In his return of marines engaged in building works in 1788 Ross listed five masons, ten carpenters, five sawyers, seven shinglers, one miner and one file cutter.[30] The presence in the colony of the representatives of the last two categories may have been haphazard, but it seems unlikely that that of those in the first four was.

8. There is also one report that Phillip 'had the peculiar indulgence from government to choose all his own officers'.[31] There does seem to be some truth to this, for there is evidence that, of the commissioned officers, Phillip personally chose at least Hunter and King; and of the warrant officers at least James Lochart (purser), Thomas Brooks (boatswain) and Peter White (sailmaker); and as well he took his clerk Henry Brewer with him (as midshipman).

9. Finally, the administration may have encouraged tradesmen to join the crews of the transport ships, as another means of providing the colony with the skills it needed. While firm evidence for this is lacking, the *Daily Universal Register* reported at the end of November:

> Almost daily applications have been made at Lord Sydney's office by artificers in different branches, to accompany the felons [to Botany Bay], in order to assist in forming and bringing to maturity the intended new settlement ... How far it may be sound policy in government to permit as many as are willing to embark, we will not say, but a limited number of several different professions, we suppose, will of necessity have leave to go.[32]

As well as from the *Sirius* and *Supply*, Phillip did hire some men from the transport ships while they remained at Sydney. It is not impossible that these were men who had come out to work in the colony, but who chose not to stay when they saw the prevailing conditions.[33]

*

Let me end this chapter with two stories which exemplify aspects of the society from which the First Fleet sailed.

James Lochart

James Lochart had been purser on the *Europe* during its voyage to India and back; and he followed Phillip into the *Sirius*. A purser's life was often an uneasy one. He was responsible for dispensing the ship's provisions and clothing ('slops'), for which he did not pay directly, but whose value was charged against his account, to be reconciled at the end of a voyage. To this end, he was required to keep precise records of what he dispensed daily to each officer and man. He was also required himself to pay for 'necessaries' for the ship – such things as wood and coal, oil, candles, hammocks and beds, again for later reconciliation. When in foreign ports, he was able to purchase items, but had to keep strict records, including evidence that he had bought at prevailing market prices. If it happened that these prices were above those in the Navy Board's schedules, he was not compensated for the difference. Likewise, if items were lost through shipwreck or enemy action, he was not compensated.

In order for him to have some profit, the purser was entitled to serve food at 14 ounces to the pound rather than 16 ounces, a practice that the seamen naturally resented, as they saw themselves being deprived of proper amounts. And there was always the suspicion that the purser might be further injuring them by dispensing even shorter rations, since the more rations he had left over at the end of a voyage, the more money he could make by selling them back. It was also usual for him to buy stocks of tobacco for private sale to the men. The Navy Board required him to give large sureties, and he was frequently obliged to borrow money from friends and merchants in order to get his business started, with his financial returns being months and even years away. Pursers were thus prime candidates for bankruptcy.

Lochart had ended the *Europe*'s voyage in April 1784 without all of his documentation in order; but on Phillip's testifying on his behalf, on 6 December 1786 the Victualling Board agreed to pass his accounts so that he might go on the *Sirius*.[34]

Then, two weeks later, disaster overwhelmed James Lochart. His two letters to Phillip tell the wrenching story of this demise much more eloquently than I might.

[c. 21 December 1786]

I intended to have seen you yesterday to have thanked you for your good intentions towards me and to have relinquished the *Sirius*. Before you receive this I am left town, therefore apply for a new purser when you think fit. I should think Mr Miller very proper to be recommended. Let me be forgotten. Tomorrow you shall have the particulars relative to the fitting, what I have paid, and what remains due to tradesmen.

The horror of my situation is not to be described and never can be felt by you.

22 December 1786

In my confusion yesterday, I know not what I wrote. Was it possible, I would make every apology for the inconveniences I have put you to, but alas that is as much out of my power as my return to my native country which I am now quitting forever.

Mr Addington, Erle Street, Blackfriars, furnished the *Sirius* with twenty-one cauldrons of coals, for which the purser must pay him. I paid for wood £22, some odd shillings. There is due to Mr Bernard at Deptford £6 for more wood. I paid for candles £7.5.0. And for greens etc. daily expense about £3.3.0. There is due to Mr Eade, ironmonger, Wood Street, Cheapside, for lamps, lanterns etc. an account which I never got from him, but the purser must pay him or return the things. Mr Thomas, coppersmith, King Street, Deptford, has a claim for sundry articles supplied by him. Mr Fisher, tallow chandler, King Street, Deptford, has supplied a box or two of candles and some loose dozens, without being paid and has shipped on board the *Charlotte* three puncheons of tallow, and has all the other candles ready. I have paid him nothing. The purser must settle this.

The steward has distinct accounts of receipts of provisions. The master knows everything has been faithfully stowed away, the three puncheons for the tallow above-mentioned excepted, which return to the ship when she can stow them. When the money that I laid out is recovered from the purser I request that £20 thereof may be given to Lieutenant Maxwell for the honest purpose I have wrote him and the remainder to Mr William Crees, Plymouth.

And now, Sir, I take farewell forever. I was my own master at fourteen years of age, and have experienced wonderful vicissitudes of fortune; have formed some attachments to friends; and have in the end met with disgust and disappointment in them all, yourself, my uncle and two friends in the City excepted. I have had no happiness yet, and now expect none. A miserable existence I shall not long support, and the sneer of mine enemies, or the sympathy of my well-wishers will soon be matter of indifference to me. But I beg pardon for intruding upon your time with reflections that relate only to myself.

Phillip passed on these letters to the Admiralty without comment. It was a hard world, and he needed another purser.[35]

Susanna Holmes and Henry Cabell

There is a very curious story told by John Simpson, the jailor at Norwich, concerning the convicts Susanna Holmes and Henry Cabell (known in the colony as Kable), and their son Henry.

The following narrative, which I believe to be strictly true, having escaped notice though published three weeks ago in the *Norwich Mercury*, I trust will be acceptable to your readers, as it is really a very interesting relation.

In consequence of the late determination of government to send some convicts to Botany Bay, with a design of establishing a colony in New South Wales, an order lately came down to the keeper of Norwich jail to send such female convicts as were then in prison to Plymouth, to be in readiness to go upon that expedition. Three unhappy women, who had been a long while in the castle under sentence of transportation, were accordingly sent, and were committed to the care of Mr Simpson, turnkey of the prison. One of these unfortunate females was the mother of an infant about five months old, a very fine babe, whom she had suckled from its birth. The father of the child was likewise a felon under a similar sentence, and has been in prison more than three years. He had repeatedly expressed a wish to be married to this woman, and though seldom permitted to see the child, he discovered a remarkable fondness for it; and that the mother's only comfort was derived from its smiles, was evident from her peculiarly tender manner of nursing it. When the order came down for her removal the man was much distressed, and very importunate to attend the woman, and application was made to the minister to permit him to go, but so many similar applications having been made, this could not be complied with. The miserable woman was therefore obliged to go without the man, who offered to be her husband, that he might be her companion and protector during a long and melancholy voyage, and in a distant and unknown land. The child, however, was still her property, as the laws of England, which are distinguished by the spirit of humanity which framed them, forbid so cruel an act as that of separating an infant from its mother's breast.

When Mr Simpson arrived at Plymouth with his party, he found that they were to be put on board a hulk which lies there, till the ship which goes to the South Sea is ready to take them. He therefore took a boat, and went to the vessel to deliver up his prisoners. Some forms, which the jailer of Norwich had not been apprized of, having been omitted, the captain of the hulk at first refused to take them, and these miserable creatures were kept three hours in a open boat, before they were received into their new abode of wretchedness. And when they were admitted, the captain finding that one of them had an infant, peremptorily refused to take it on board, saying, that he had no orders to take children; neither the entreaties of Mr Simpson, nor the agonies of the poor wretch, could prevail upon the captain even to permit the babe to remain till instruction could be received from the minister. Simpson was therefore obliged to take the child, and the frantic mother was led to her cell, execrating the cruelty of the man under whose care she was now placed, and vowing to put an end to her life as soon as she could obtain the means. Shocked at the unparalleled brutality of the captain, and his humanity not less affected by the agonies of the poor woman, and the situation of the helpless babe, Mr Simpson resolved still, if possible, to get it restored to her. No way was left but an immediate personal application to Lord Sydney; and having once before been with his Lordship in a business of humanity, he was encouraged to hope he should succeed, could he but have an interview with him. He therefore immediately went back to Plymouth, and set off in the first coach to London, carrying the child all the way on his knee, and feeding it at the different inns he arrived at as well as he could.

When he came of London, he placed the child with a careful woman, and instantly posted to Lord Sydney's. Neither his Lordship nor his secretary were to be spoken to, at least this was told him when he addressed the person in waiting at the office; but humanity will not be restrained by forms. Acting under the influence of a superior power, it moves forward unchecked by the fear of offending any earthly one. Mr Simpson was denied admittance, but in vain, for he pressed forward into one of the offices, and told his story to one of the secretaries, who attended very properly to it, and promised to do all in his power to promote the object of his humane petition, but feared it would be impossible for him to see Lord Sydney for several days. He begged, however, of this gentleman to prepare an order for the restoration of the child, and determined to wait in the hall for the chance of seeing his Lordship pass, that he might prevail on him to sign it. Fortunately, not long after, he saw Lord Sydney descend the stairs. He instantly ran to him; his Lordship very naturally showed an unwillingness at first to attend to an application made to him in so strange and abrupt a manner, but Mr Simpson immediately related the reason of his intrusion, and described, as he felt, the exquisite misery he had lately been a witness to, expressing his fears, lest in the instant he was pleading for her, the unhappy woman, in the wildness of her despair, should have deprived herself of existence. Lord Sydney was greatly affected, and paid much attention to the particular circumstances of his narration, and instantly promised that the child should be restored, commending, at the same time, Mr Simpson's spirit and humanity. Encouraged by this, he made a further appeal to his Lordship's humanity in behalf of the father of the child, which proved equally successful; for his Lordship ordered, that he likewise should be sent to Plymouth to accompany the child and its mother, directing, at the same time, that they should be married before they went on board, and adding that he would himself pay the fees.

One of his Lordship's secretaries wrote immediately to Plymouth, that the woman might be informed of the success of Mr Simpson's application; and he, after visiting the child, and giving directions that it might be taken care of in his absence, set off for Norwich, where he arrived on Wednesday afternoon, and communicated the glad tidings to the unhappy father of the child. The poor man, who is a fine healthy young fellow, seemed very grateful to Lord Sydney and to Mr Simpson, [and] was made very happy by this change of circumstances; and it is hoped he may, notwithstanding his past situation, turn out a useful individual of the new community. He set off Friday night accompanied by Mr Simpson, who, after the fatigues, anxieties, and vexation of his first journey to Plymouth, having travelled three days and nights without sleep, no doubt will be amply recompensed by the satisfaction he must experience, in having thus been the means of rescuing two unhappy people from a situation of distress scarcely to be equalled.

It is proper to observe, that Captain Phillip, who is to go out with the convicts to Botany Bay, is a man of very different disposition to the person alluded to in this narrative, but he, unfortunately, had not power to interfere.

The conclusion of the above relation cannot be more properly given, than in the words of Mr Simpson himself, who wrote the following letter a few days ago to a gentleman in Bath:

Dear Sir,

It is with the utmost pleasure that I inform you of my safe arrival with my little charge at Plymouth; but it would take another pen than mine to describe the joy that the mother received her infant and her intended husband with. Suffice it to say, that their transport, that the tears which flowed from their eyes, with the innocent smiles of the babe, on sight of the mother, who had saved her milk for it, drew tears likewise from my eyes; and it was with the utmost regret that I parted with the child, after having travelled with it on my lap for upwards of 700 miles backwards and forwards. But the blessings I received at the different inns on the road, have amply paid me.

I am, with great respect, your humble servant,
John Simpson.[36]

The young man in question, Henry Cabell, had been convicted of burglary in February 1783 and sentenced to death, then reprieved to fourteen years' transportation to America. Susannah Holmes had been sentenced to death in March 1784 for the theft of clothing, linen and silver, then reprieved to fourteen years' transportation. They met in Norwich Castle, where both were held. Susannah was put on board the *Dunkirk* on 5 November, without her baby, who joined her with her husband-to-be on 15 November after John Simpson's heroic intervention. Initially the family sailed together for New South Wales in the *Friendship*, but Susannah and the baby shifted to the *Charlotte* at Cape Town. The parents married in Sydney on 10 February 1788.

Before they sailed, the publication of their plight and of their devotion to each other resulted in the public subscribing £20 to buy them goods, which was stolen on the *Alexander* during the voyage. In a gesture which would have been impossible in England, where felons were 'atteint' (i.e., dead from the point of view of legal rights), Phillip and Collins allowed Henry to sue the ship's master in the civil court, where he received £15 in damages. Over the next twenty years he and Susannah became prosperous, accumulating land, animals, shops and ships. Their lives were emblematic of the new society that would develop in New South Wales.

5.

The Ships

EVEN THOUGH THE EVIDENCE to gainsay the idea has been available for decades, it has become conventional wisdom that the ships of the First Fleet were clapped-out tubs.[1] It is therefore worthwhile to examine in detail the process by which the Navy Board selected them, for this provides further evidence of the care with which the Pitt administration prepared the expedition.

The Navy Board was the branch of government most concerned with the physical organization of the First Fleet. It was responsible for the Royal Navy's ships, for their upkeep and for the supplies held in the Navy's dockyards at home and abroad. It also was responsible for the appointment of 'warrant officers' (e.g., surgeons, pursers, masters, carpenters, gunners, sailmakers, etc.). The Navy Board was subservient to the Admiralty, which was responsible for the appointment and promotion of commissioned officers and for the deployment of Britain's powerful military marine. At times, relations between these boards could be quite tense, particularly when strong personalities headed them, as was the case in the mid-1780s, when Earl Howe was First Lord Commissioner of the Admiralty and Sir Charles Middleton the Comptroller of the Navy.

Middleton was a remarkable man. Born in 1726, he entered the Navy in 1741, was promoted to lieutenant in 1745 and captain in 1758. During the Seven Years' War he saw service in West Indian waters. He was appointed Comptroller in 1778, and during the next five years was responsible for the maintenance of the fleet during the conflict with the Americans, French, Spanish and Dutch, and assisted Lord Sandwich in the work of strengthening it and obtaining more stores. In the 1780s he oversaw the ambitious building programme that William Pitt insisted on, which by the end of the decade saw the Royal Navy more powerful than it had been in any previous time of peace.[2]

Middleton and the Prime Minister became good friends. Someone who was then a junior official later remembered: 'It was no uncommon thing for Mr Pitt to visit the Navy Office to discuss naval matters with the Comptroller, and to see the returns made from the yards of the progress in building and repairing the ships-of-the-line; he also desired to have a periodical statement from the Comptroller of the state of the fleet, wisely holding that officer responsible personally to him, without any regard to the Board.'[3] Against Howe's opposition, Pitt insisted on Middleton's promotion to rear-admiral in 1787; and, when Middleton was eighty, at a time when Napoleon was threatening to defeat Britain, Pitt appointed him First Lord Commissioner of the Admiralty.

Where the mounting of the First Fleet is concerned, Middleton was one of four administrative focal points. As the Home Office was responsible both for convicts and for colonies at this time (among many other things, of course), it was Evan Nepean's business to inform the Treasury of what measures were needed. One of the two Treasury Secretaries, George Rose or Thomas Steele, would then advise the Navy Board, which would set about hiring and fitting out ships and obtaining goods. Where military matters were involved, the Treasury Secretaries would also advise the Admiralty, usually via its Secretary, Sir Philip Stephens; however, given the nature of the Botany Bay business, these advices were less frequent than those to the Navy Board. The fourth focal point was Arthur Phillip, who knew that he was to be appointed governor of the colony at least by late September, and who thereafter also played a central role in the business, as he let both Middleton and Nepean know how he thought things should be done differently, and what more was needed. As we shall see, although lesser Navy Board officials were irritated by them, Middleton was tolerant of Phillip's demands, and the pair had a respectful relationship. Phillip and Nepean were friends, no doubt owing in part to Nepean's having been Phillip's spymaster when he operated in France.

When either the Treasury or Admiralty or Navy Board had queries or needed more information, the flow of correspondence was reversed. This was a somewhat cumbersome process, but it is because of it that we have such an extensive record of the mounting of the First Fleet. And the procedure itself does not seem to have caused any major delays. (That is, there were delays, but not because of this procedure.) Against the ignorant claims of some historians, it is difficult not to be impressed by these department heads' competence. They worked very long hours and attended to business diligently. Their industry is all the more remarkable when we remember that they wrote everything by hand.

*

The business of initiating and co-ordinating the multitude of arrangements necessary to prepare the ships for the voyage fell to two middle-ranking Navy Board officials: Joshua Thomas, the Board's secretary; and Captain George Teer, its agent for transports. As soon as he was appointed the agent for the First Fleet transports, Lieutenant John Shortland also participated in this detailed work. Shortland's appointment offers a minor illustration of the often-prickly relations between the Admiralty and Navy Board. Shortland had been agent for a transport convoy which had recently arrived from Nova Scotia; and, needing such a person for the First Fleet, the Navy Board offered him the post on 20 September. Belatedly, the Board realized that it should have sought Admiralty approval, which it did on 2 January 1787. The Admiralty replied tartly: 'Their Lordships have no objection to his being employed to superintend those transports, but ... they should have obtained their permission before they appointed him'.[4]

On 26 August, Thomas Steele notified the Navy Board of Sydney's advice about the Botany Bay colonization, and that the Treasury had endorsed it. Accordingly he asked the Navy Board to hire transport vessels for the 680 male and seventy female convicts; and to obtain 'such provisions, necessaries and implements for agriculture as may be requisite for their use after their arrival', including bedding. The provisions were to be for 1000 persons for two years after the voyage, with the women who might come from the Pacific Islands included in this number. The Navy Board was also to obtain 'a quantity of surgeon's instruments, medicines and necessaries for the sick'. These transport ships would be escorted by two Royal Navy vessels; and marines would guard the convicts at sea and on land.[5] Let us see how the business of hiring and equipping the ships then went forward.

Royal Navy ships

Sirius: On 6 September, the Admiralty instructed the Navy Board to prepare the *Berwick* and another vessel of about 200 tons burden for the task of escorting the transports to New South Wales.[6]

The *Berwick* was not, as has so often been said, an old East Indiaman.[7] Rather, it was an 'East Country' ship – that is, built for the Baltic trade. Accordingly, it had a spar deck, so that mast timber might be rolled on board. It is reasonable to speculate that it was chosen because of the service it was to perform at Norfolk Island.

Philip Gidley King, who sailed on it, reported that the *Berwick* had been built in 1780, and, after having burnt to the waterline, been purchased by the Navy Board as an armed storeship.[8] There must be considerable doubt about this, as the Deptford yard officers who inspected it before purchase in 1781 found it to be 'building' in Mr Watson's yard, and made no mention of any fire-damage. In any case, it had not been completed with the 'refuse of the yards', as Barnard Eldershaw claimed; neither was it in 1786 the 'worn-out' vessel that David Mackay represented it to have been. The repairs to it carried out in 1786–87 were to remedy defects that were only to be expected, given its service; and these repairs put it, as Henderson and Stanbury point out, in 'excellent condition'.[9]

The ship the officials saw was 89 feet 8 3/4 inches in length, 32 feet 9 inches in breath. Its depth in the hold was 13 feet, and its burden 511

83/94 tons. The officials recommended a number of alterations. These included enlarging the raft port on the lower deck so that it might accommodate '64- or 74-gun ships' masts', and ports and supports on its middle and upper decks for thirty 9-pounder cannons and four 18-pounder carronades. Altogether, the *Berwick* cost the Navy Board almost £6000.[10] It carried a substantial armament; and being of a 'full, round build' and 'all together a very capacious and convenient vessel',[11] was well-suited to carrying stores, which, again according to King, it did to North America in the last year of the war, and then to the West Indies.[12]

Perhaps not coincidentally, on 23 August the Admiralty Board instructed the Navy Board to prepare the *Berwick* for foreign service, and to report when it would be ready to receive a crew.[13] Upon receiving the formal advice that such a ship was needed for New South Wales, the Admiralty advised the Navy Board that it should be fitted out for this service 'with all possible despatch'. After inspecting it, the Deptford officers recommended a number of repairs and the replacement of some equipment, which they estimated would take forty men twenty-four days, for a total cost of £224.[14]

On 22 September, the Woolwich officers advised that the *Berwick* should be ready to receive men and stores on 16 October, which advice the Navy Board passed on to the Admiralty. But then, a week later, the Deptford officers provided a more extensive list of work to be done, which put back the date.[15]

On 9 and 11 October, the Deptford officers informed the Navy Board that yet more work needed to be done, which would occupy 116 men for ten days and cost £175, and that they wished to work 'two tides' so as to hasten the business.[16] The Board duly informed the Admiralty that this meant there would be a further two weeks' delay before the ship would be ready to receive men.[17]

On 12 October, the Admiralty instructed the Navy Board to register the ship as a 6th rate, by the name of the *Sirius*; that it was to have a complement of 160 men; that it was to be armed with four 6-pounder cannon, six 18-pounder carronades, and eight swivel guns; and that Arthur Phillip was to command it. The Admiralty requested this armament from the Duke of Richmond, the Master-General of the Ordnance, and advised Lord Sydney. King tells us that the ship was renamed after 'the bright star in the southern constellation of the Great Dog' – an unusually poetic gesture by the Admiralty.[18] On 25 October, the Navy Board advised the Admiralty that the ship would be ready in two days. It was commissioned on 1 November, with the Admiralty asking that it be fitted out 'for a voyage to remote parts', and to put twelve months' provisions on board. The same day, it told Phillip he was now in charge of the ship. Manning and provisioning then proceeded. A week later, the Admiralty ordered that both it and its tender receive 'such additional stores and provisions ... as [they] can conveniently stow'.[19]

The equipping of the *Sirius* did not conclude at this point, however.

On 31 October, Phillip asked for ten more 6-pounder cannons, and 'the iron work necessary for the carriages', as these extra guns might in future be 'of great use to us, on board or on shore'. The Admiralty agreed to this request, advising the Ordnance Board of it on 1 November.[20] This was a sign that Phillip was thinking beyond the immediate exigencies of a convict colony. Also at this time, the Admiralty ordered that both the *Sirius* and its tender be 'supplied with a camp forge and copper oven, and to have their coppers fitted with Mr Irving's apparatus for rendering salt water fresh, and to furnish them with Lieutenant Orsbridge's machine for rendering stinking water sweet'.[21]

The preparation of the *Sirius* continued through November and December. In mid-November, 20 tons of 'washed and screened shingle ballast' was put in its hold. Then, Phillip requested four more cables, of 15 1/2 inches diameter, to make a total of seven. At the same time, he asked the Board of Longitude for a chronometer, which was granted.[22]

Then there was the matter of ship's boats. On 12 September, the Navy Board ordered a yawl of 27 feet and a launch of 25 feet, with copper fastenings. By mid-November, the *Sirius*'s boats comprised a launch of 27-foot keel, and three cutters, of keels of 25, 22 and 18 feet. Phillip requested that he also be supplied with a 32-foot keeled, 16-oared boat in frame, for use in inshore exploration in New South Wales, which was agreed to. The *Supply* (see below) was also given a boat in frame.

As there was not room for them in the Royal Navy ships, they were loaded into the transports.[23]

Then there were foods and medicines to obtain for both ships. On 1 and 7 November, Phillip asked the Victualling Board for certain provisions, which were granted. On 8 November, it agreed to his request for 2 tons of essence of malt and 'as much sauerkraut as [he] may desire' (both considered to be anti-scorbutics, though in fact the malt contained no vitamin-C, and the pickled cabbage not very much); and one year's supply of 'wheat, sugar and mustard seed'. On 10 November it told him that the bread and other 'dry provisions' would be 'packed in tight casks'. On 14 November, he requested supplies of spirits; and then, another seven days on, four months' supply (7418 lbs) of molasses. Early in December, he asked for bread, wine and ox tongues; and then the *Sirius*'s 1st lieutenant asked for more bread, and beer.[24]

In the same manner, Phillip and the ship's surgeon requested additional medical supplies. George Worgan advised that 'Peruvian bark'[25] would be advantageous, but that 'from the high price of the drug navy surgeons cannot afford the vast quantity required to do justice to the men without wronging themselves'. When the Navy Board said that it did not provide this item, Phillip asked the Admiralty for permission to obtain it.[26]

On 30 December, John Hunter, now appointed second captain, asked for more iron ballast, which he received.[27] Then, Lieutenant Bradley requested more bread and beer. John Palmer, the purser, asked for 'two or three hogsheads' of tobacco for the voyage, but also that these be put into the *Prince of Wales*, as the *Sirius* was now so full. This was done.[28]

Supply: If the choice of the main ship was straightforward, that of its tender gave the Navy Board a great deal of trouble. The Deptford officers first inspected the French-built storeship *Eclipse*, only to find that it had been badly damaged when it had run aground in Ireland, and that 'by her appearance she is not a fit ship to accompany the *Berwick* storeship as a tender'. They next considered the *Rattlesnake*, an American-built sloop that had been offered for sale; but on surveying it they decided that from its age and build it was 'not a fit ship, either in substance or quality' to accompany the *Berwick*.[29]

Then, the Navy Board decided to purchase the *Grantham* packet boat, which its owner, Thomas Hubbert, had advertised for sale on 7 September:

> An extraordinary swift sailer, British-built, for the service of the Post Office; burden 230 tons, more or less; was lengthened about nine years ago, and copper-sheathed to light water mark about four years since; has copper fastenings to her bottom, and is now in extraordinary good condition, fit for immediate employ; has very great plenty of all sorts of stores, and may be sent to sea with the addition of provision only.[30]

It seemed a good buy, but as the Navy Board quickly found out, it was a very tart lemon. On inspection, the Deptford officers found that all its masts and yards were 'defective'; that its planks down to the water's edge were 'all in a decayed state'; that its frame was also decayed; that all its iron fastenings above water were corroded; that the planks underneath the copper sheathing were also decayed; and that the cables were also 'much worn and dry rotten', and, like the rigging, unfit for any 'purpose of government'. It would require 'a great repair' to make it seaworthy, which would employ many workmen for more than two months. And after having stripped it to establish all this, the Deptford officers reported that it would cost more to put it back together than it would then sell for.[31]

Accordingly, the Navy Board proposed using the *Supply*, a small Navy ship then at Portsmouth employed to carry naval stores from one yard to another. The Admiralty agreed to this, and the *Supply* became the *Sirius*'s companion.[32] Built in 1759, it was of 175 tons burden. Hunter said that 'it was a very firm strong little vessel, very flat floored, and roomy'; while King thought that it was 'much too small for so long a voyage'. Both said that it sailed badly, but its rate depended a good deal on weather conditions.[33]

When the *Supply* had arrived from Portsmouth, the Deptford officers surveyed it, and recommended repairs that would take forty men twenty days, and cost £156. At the same time, after consulting Phillip, they proposed that it carry four 18-pounder carronades on the main deck, four 4-pound canon on the quarterdeck, and twelve half-pounder swivel guns.[34]

The matter of the *Supply*'s armament then came in for extended consideration. The Admiralty suggested that it would be better to have four 6-pounder cannon on the main deck. On this suggestion being put to the Deptford officers, they decided that, yes, cannon would be better, but that 6-pounders would be too heavy. They therefore proposed four short 4-pounders.[35]

However, when he assumed command of the ship, Lieutenant Henry Ball advised that even 4-pounders would be too heavy, and recommended 3-pounders instead. This request went the usual path of Admiralty, Navy Board, Ordnance Board and back, and it was agreed to between 12 and 16 December.[36]

On 27 October, the Admiralty instructed the Navy Board that the *Supply* was to carry fifty-five officers and men, and that it was to be fitted out 'for a voyage to remote parts, … [and] victualled to twelve months'. The ship was listed on 28 October, with Lieutenant Henry Ball as its commander.[37]

There was still some work to be carried out on the ship. For example, carronade ports, additional chain plates, and copper sheathing needed to be fitted. Ball also wanted a new fire hearth. Then there were other things – new steering wheels, gratings, shot lockers, wedges for the masts. This work proceeded through November, though the Deptford officers advised that it would be ready to receive men on 11 November.[38]

Like Phillip for the *Sirius*, Ball had a series of requests for the *Supply*. On 11 November, he asked the Navy Board for supplies of ledgers and paper, which were granted. On 11, 13, 18, 22, 23 and 28 November, he asked the Victualling Board for provisions, which he received. On 2 December, in view of the ship's having been 'ordered upon a long and separate service', he asked the Navy Board for a quantity of portable soup, only to be told that this was not something it supplied. Then he asked for some wine, which was granted; but also for a warrant to buy coal, only to be told that the Victualling Board no longer provided this. On 6 December, he asked for 'surgeon's necessaries', upon which the Navy Board agreed to provide an eight-months' supply; and then a few days later, the Victualling Board agreed to provide fresh beef while the ship was in port.[39]

The transports

At the end of August and beginning of September, the Navy Board advertised 'for about 1,500 tons of shipping by the ton, to carry persons and provisions to Botany Bay on the coast of New South Wales', with tenders to close on 12 September.[40]

Turnbull, Macaulay and Gregory's offer, made to Nepean in August, was considered and they were asked to put it into a proper form.[41] Anthony Brough offered a number of 'Archangel-built ships, in the most prefect repair, which have been surveyed by the officers of the East India Company and declared very suitable for the China trade, three years old, and admirably calculated for long voyages'. The Navy Board told him that they would not use Russian ships 'for carrying convicts to New Holland'.[42]

The person who obtained the contract was William Richards Jr, of Walworth. Richards came up with a comprehensive plan, which involved the government's charting ships to carry people and goods out to Botany Bay, where they would be discharged from the government's service, and their going on to Canton, where the East India Company would hire them to bring back tea and other items. In this way, both the government and the Company would make substantial savings. In consultation with Middleton, Pitt and the deputy chairman of the East India Company, Richards developed this scheme over a number of weeks.[43]

On receiving the contract, and with George Rose having prepared the way, Richards offered five ships for the Company's approval: *Britannia, Britannia, Brothers, Scarborough, William and Mary*; and another three as storeships to the Navy Board: *Britannia, Columbus, George.*

The Company agreed to hire the five ships offered to it on 27 September, at £10 per ton, with the provisos that they should reach China by 15 January 1788, and not leave with crews of fewer than eight men and boys per 100 tons.[44]

The Navy Board was more demanding in its requirements and inspections, and in these we again see the care with which the administration approached the business of the First Fleet. The Deptford officers approved of the *Britannia* and *Friendship* as convict transports. They approved of the *George* as a storeship; but thought the *Columbus*, built of American timbers and with 'very indifferent' accommodations, not 'a proper ship'. They disapproved of the second *Britannia* as a storeship, for its copper sheathing had corroded some of its ironwork, and the sheathing itself was very thin. There were other faults, and they could not recommend it 'as fit for a voyage of so remote a nature'.[45] By mid-October, Richards had substituted the *Alexander* as a convict transport, and the *Borrowdale* and *Golden Grove* as storeships.[46]

Let me therefore give details only of those ships that made the voyage. Initially, there were five convict transports. The *Alexander* had been built at Hull, was three years old, and of 452 85/94 tons burden. The *Charlotte* had been built in the Thames, was two years old, and of 345 53/94 tons burden. The *Friendship* had been built at Scarborough, was two years old, and of 278 1/94 tons burden. The *Lady Penrhyn* had been built in the Thames, was less than a year old, and of 338 13/94 tons burden. The *Scarborough* was three and a half years old, and of 418 36/94 tons burden.[47]

In early December, as Teer and Phillip supervised the loading of equipment and provisions into these ships, and they and Middleton and Nepean discussed the dispositions of the people they would carry, it became clear that there simply wasn't enough space for people and things. Accordingly, the administration hired another ship, the *Prince of Wales*. This had been built in the Thames, was one year old, and of 333 67/94 tons burden.[48]

With the exception of the *Prince of Wales*, the owners of these ships completed the fitting-out they were responsible for in early November. The Navy Board then needed to make them capable of securing their human cargoes. It ordered them fitted with cabins and bulkheads 'for

[the] security of the convicts going to Botany Bay'. This work was completed by the end of the month. However, George Teer then suggested that it would be advisable to fit 'strong hatch bars in the between decks and over the gratings on the upper decks ... with strong locks as may be thought necessary', which was done.[49] But then, when a marine guard had arrived from Portsmouth, so that the first of the convicts might be put on board the *Alexander*, Lieutenant George Johnston complained that the ship's hatchway 'might with great ease be broke open, having only two cross bars, and them only secured with the common staple and padlock'. He recommended that more bars and bolts be added. He also pointed out that there were 'no loop holes to fire in upon them, supposing any riot or disobedience of orders should take place', and announced that 'under these circumstances I can't be answerable for the security of the convicts'. The Admiralty relayed the lieutenant's complaint to the Home Office, which told the Treasury, which directed the Navy Board to remedy the situation.[50]

Johnston also complained about the handcuffs the Navy Board had provided. The Board had ordered 350 double sets, 'such as are used in securing the convicts on board the hulks at Woolwich', from Mr Cross on 9 November; when they arrived, Teer distributed them among the ships 'agreeable to the number [of convicts] at first intended'. But Johnston found them 'by no means strong enough or calculated for the purpose intended', evidently because they were 'too long'. After some protest, the Board agreed to shorten them.[51]

The storeships

The *Borrowdale* had been built at Sunderland, was one and a half years old, and of 272 26/94 tons burden. The *Fishburn* had been built at Whitby, was six years old, and of 378 26/94 tons burden. The *Golden Grove* had been built at Whitby, was six years old, and of 331 30/94 tons burden.[52] None of these ships was hired by the East India Company. Teer reported on 30 October that the owners had completed their fitting out, and they were ready to receive provisions.[53]

*

There were also a number of arrangements of a different kind which needed to be made for the convict transports and storeships.

The Act 26 Geo. III, c. 60 required that privately owned, British-built ships should have formal permission to sail beyond Europe. The Admiralty sent licenses for the three storeships and four of the convict transports to the Customs Board in November 1786, and those for the others in December and January.[54]

These ships also needed to be licensed by the East India Company to proceed past the Cape of Good Hope. William Richards asked the Navy Board for advice concerning this on 15 December, which resulted in the Board sending a list of the ships to the Company.[55]

Third, in continued pursuit of William Richards's scheme to save the cost of ships returning empty, the government needed to conclude arrangements with the East India Company for those intended to load a cargo at Canton. On 18 October, the Navy Board reminded the Treasury that if the ships would 'reach China by 1 January 1788, they are to be discharged there, and we shall have made a most advantageous bargain for the public; but if unnecessarily detained in Botany Bay so as to be prevented from proceeding in time, we shall be obliged to keep them in pay until their return to Deptford'.[56]

Following standard procedure, George Rose then advised the Home Office and the Admiralty of the need to instruct Phillip accordingly. In mid-December, the East India Company informed its officers in Canton that it had chartered the *Alexander, Charlotte, Lady Penrhyn* and *Scarborough* to bring cargoes home, if they reached China by 15 January 1788. At the end of December, Richards seems to have substituted the *Prince of Wales* for the *Alexander*. In the event, though, only the *Charlotte, Lady Penrhyn* and *Scarborough* went on to China from New South Wales. When it became clear that the ships would not leave England until mid-1787, at the government's request the Company relaxed this deadline.[57]

*

It is clear, then, that the Navy Board did not select any clapped-out old ships that were available to carry the colonists out to Botany Bay.

Despite the faults that gradually revealed themselves, the *Sirius* and *Supply* were in the main sturdy ships, if indifferent sailers. The length of time the *Sirius* took to break up on the reef at Norfolk Island in March 1790 shows its basic strength.

The *Supply* was very much older than the other ships of the First Fleet, having been built in 1759. However, it was in good condition at the time it was chosen – for example, in November 1786 the Deptford officers inspected braces and pintles that had been fitted in April 1785, and found them 'in a perfect state'.[58] From New South Wales, it made a series of voyages – between Sydney and Norfolk Island ten times, and to Lord Howe Island once; to Batavia and back – before returning to England in April 1792. This was sterling service for a small ship, when the average life of a ship was about eight years.

None of the convict transports and storeships was more than six years old. Two were less than a year old; three were two years old; two were three years old; and two six years old. All were in good condition at the time of hiring. These were ships to take the convicts to their destination on the other side of the world, not to founder *en route*. The idea that these were decrepit ships is based on unexamined prejudice or inadequate research.

6.

Equipping the Colonists

The Navy Board followed standard procedure in letting contracts for food and goods for the Botany Bay colonists. However, there was at first a serious flaw in the way officials conceived of the voyage – one which might well have resulted in catastrophic failure. That this did not happen was because Phillip and his surgeons insisted on the need for change, and the Pitt administration agreed. I shall examine in detail what the problem was in Chapter 9. For the moment, let me describe how the Navy Board first went about equipping the colonists.

Food

The administration needed to provide food for two distinct phases of the venture: while the colonists were on board the ships, whether in one or other of the ports of southern England as they waited to sail or during the voyage; and once they were in the colony.

It was the contractor's responsibility to order the items and quantities needed in the first of these phases. The contract which the Navy Board concluded with William Richards on 12 September has seemingly not survived.[1] However, against the unexamined prejudices of some historians, the quality of the foods that Richards provided was high.[2]

As the government was to be the employer of the convicts in New South Wales, the Navy Board was directly responsible for providing them with food there. In his letter of 26 August, Steele asked the Board to order provisions for two years, even though the initial term of appointment of the officers and marines was three years.[3] This was because the administration was assuming that after the first year the colonists would be progressing towards self-sufficiency, so that, combined with local production, one year's provisions from England might be spread over the second and third years.

In return, the Navy Board asked for details of 'the quantity of each a ration is to consist of, distinguishing that for the convicts from [that for] the marines'. Steele sought Nepean's advice, who replied that 'the marines and convicts ... should after their landing be victualled in the same manner as the troops serving in the West India islands, excepting only the allowance of spirits; the women to have 2/3rds of the quantity of provisions supplied to a man'.[4]

As Steele then advised the Navy Board, the weekly ration for a troop in the West Indies was:

7 lbs bread, or in lieu thereof 7 lbs of flour

7 lbs of beef, or in lieu thereof 4 lbs of pork

3 pints of peas

6 ozs of butter (or 1 lb of flour or in lieu thereof 1/2 lb of rice).[5]

There was a good deal of formality to these exchanges, for the Navy Board knew perfectly well what this ration was, but administrative protocols needed to be observed: the Board might not act without explicit directions from the Treasury.

So instructed, the Board proceeded to calculate the weight of this allowance for two years for 1000 people, and the cargo space needed for it – that is, 860 rations for men (officials, marines, convicts), and 140 rations for women (convicts and Polynesians). Between them, the Navy Board and Victualling Board officials worked out that, as stated, the volume would be 1090 tons; but if 'flour is substituted for bread, pork for beef, and rice for flour, the amount will be only 786 3/4 [tons], with the addition of 516 1/2 tons should the bread be packed in casks [i.e., rather than in bags]'.[6]

The Navy Board then advertised for tenders, due on 27 September at 1 p.m.[7] Later correspondence shows that the contracts for the food went to the following firms:[8]

Dawson and Atkinson	butter
Reeve and Greene	flour
Jordaine and Shaw	beef, pork, rice
William Robertson	peas

At the turn of the year, when the administration had increased the number of women convicts to 150 and decided to allow about thirty marines' wives and children and thirty convicts' wives and children to go out, additional quantities of food were ordered.[9]

The quality of these provisions was also high. The flour, for example, was made from 'good sound corn, well-dried and calculated to keep [a] good eighteen months'. And, following the Navy Board's usual practice, Teer took representative casks as they were being loaded into the ships, to keep for twelve months so as then 'to ascertain the warranty' – i.e., to determine whether the contents had kept as they should have. On inspecting them twelve months later, Teer was satisfied, and the contents remained good enough for the contractors to purchase the casks back.[10]

Medicines, surgical instruments, surgeon's necessaries

In his letter to the Treasury announcing the decision, Sydney advised that 'a quantity of surgeon's instruments and medicines and necessaries for the sick will likewise be wanted, and as soon as an estimate can be formed it shall be transmitted to your Lordships'; and Thomas Steele repeated this advice to the Navy Board.[11]

On 24 October, George Rose asked Nepean for the details of the 'surgeon's instruments, medicines and necessaries for the sick for the use of the convicts destined to Botany Bay'. In advance of receiving this list, however, he requested the Navy Board to order a two years' supply. The Board accordingly asked the Apothecaries Company to provide 'a chest of medicines equal to the allowance of a 2nd-rate man-of-war with a complement of 750 men for two years'; and for 'a suitable set of instruments for that quantity of medicines'.[12] Given that the crews of the *Sirius* and *Supply* and the marines would be provided for separately in the way normal to their service, this was an adequate supply for the convicts, whose number at this point was 750.

Robert Adair, the surgeon-general to the Army and the King, and John White, the colony's chief surgeon, then drew up a very extensive list of medicines and surgical instruments and other equipment, including beds, which Nepean passed on to the Treasury on 14 November, whence it went to the Navy Board.[13]

It would require specialist knowledge to assess the competence of this list, which I simply do not have. However, my impression is that it was both much more extensive than might ordinarily have been expected, and was adapted to the needs of a land-based community – an impression presumably confirmed by the fact that in sending it, the Treasury advised the Navy Board that it was to supersede whatever may have been ordered as a consequence of Rose's earlier letter. The Board attended to this. In another sign that the administration saw how important good health was to the success of the venture, Steele also advised that White should oversee the distribution of the medicines and instruments into the various ships.[14]

The supplying of medical items continued into 1787. In January, for example, White asked for two stills, one ream of filtering paper, two pieces of bandage linen, and two sets of amputating and trepanning instruments, which were ordered.[15]

'Surgeon's necessaries' were small items that were then considered efficacious in aiding convalescence. They included almonds, barley, currants, garlic, mace, nutmeg, rice, sago, shalotts, sugar and tamarinds.[16] Later circumstances indicate that supplies of these items were not ordered for the convicts at this time. However wine, also considered a 'necessary', was thought of, with the surgeons recommending it, so that Nepean asked that Phillip be authorized to purchase 'about 30 pipes' of wine at Tenerife, which was done.[17]

Animals

While the records are sparse, some cattle and other animals were loaded on board the ships as they waited at Portsmouth to depart. The surgeon on the *Lady Penrhyn* recorded on 14 July 1787 that 'there were on board sheep, hogs, goats, puppies, kids, turkeys, geese, ducks, chickens, rabbits, pigeons, cats'. While some of these animals may have been loaded at Tenerife, at which the ships had called in early June, I think it likely that many of them were taken on board at Portsmouth.[18] However this may have been, the difficulties of preventing penned animals from being injured in pitching seas and of providing fodder for them on a very long voyage meant that it was sound policy to take the majority of the colony's animals on board at ports *en route*. The Treasury therefore gave Phillip permission to purchase 'live stock, seed etc. for the new settlement' at the Cape Verde Islands (thought of before Phillip had decided it would be better to call at Rio de Janeiro) and the Cape of Good Hope, but with the caution that he was to keep a proper account of his expenditure.[19]

When the ships were about to depart, Phillip announced that dogs were to be off-loaded. Banks's contemporareous advice to him and to the gardener who was to look after the breadfruit plants tells us that this was because of these animals' habit of burying their excrement, which might be most injurious to the plants being carried out in tubs. However, it is clear that not everyone obeyed this edict, including Phillip himself, who took some greyhounds with him for hunting game in the colony.[20]

Plants and seeds

Although the details are now lost, Phillip clearly consulted Sir Joseph Banks soon after he was appointed, for in his memorandum concerning the voyage and the colony, he remarked: 'such fruit trees and cuttings that will bear removing should be added to the seeds carried from England, as likewise roots that will bear keeping that length of time out of the ground'; and a few weeks later, he advised Nepean that the kitchen-garden seeds should be packed in 'very small parcels'. This was because they might then be distributed among the ships, so that if one ship went down, others would bring these precious items to their destination. This was done.[21]

Only some of the plants were obtained in England. Among those sent as nurslings or engrafted were peaches, nectarines, apricots, apples, pears, plums, cherries, pomegranates, oranges, lemons, limes, shaddocks, walnuts, almonds, figs, olives. There were strawberries, gooseberries, raspberries, filberts (hazelberries), vines, currants, mulberries. Among the common herbs were sage, mint, chives, tarragon, marjoram; and among the root garnishes horseradish, artichoke, garlic and shallot.[22]

Most of the seeds for the First Fleet, though by no means all, were taken from England. Under the direction of Sir Joseph Banks, these, vast in both variety and quantity, were obtained from James Dickson, the nurseryman with whom Banks habitually dealt. They were packed in camphor to stop them spoiling from heat and salt on the voyage, and roughly parallel assortments were loaded into different ships.

The list is very extensive. Among the cereals were spring wheat, winter wheat, barley, rye and oats. Of vegetables there were dwarf marrow peas, field peas, long orange carrot, early York cabbage, onions, leeks, kidney beans, asparagus, red and white beet, cauliflower, broccoli and parsnips. There were mustard, cress, nasturtium, spinach, parsley, fennel, thyme, basil, hyssop and balm. Among the pastures were lucerne, sainfoin, and red and white clover.

That is, a remarkable number of those grains, fruits, vegetables and herbs that Europeans had long cultivated, from the shores of the Mediterranean Sea north to England, Germany and Scandinavia, were sent on the First Fleet. We might see Banks's approach as something of a blunderbuss one; however, he was providing, as it were, a blanket insurance: if one variety of carrot or cabbage did not find the Botany Bay environment to its taste, another presumably would. If all – or even most – of the plants and vegetables that went out on the First Fleet were to flourish, then the New South Wales colonists would have a much greater range of food stuffs than was then available in any single English county.

It is worth pointing out that this was what in fact happened. In the first three years, when the colonists had to locate the areas of good soil and to learn about the environment, and when the long drought set them back in their efforts, the business of establishing horticulture and agriculture in New South Wales was certainly retarded. However, by about 1800, the colonists having had the benefit of additional shipments of animals, plants and seeds, the Cumberland Plain behind Sydney had become a prolific garden, spread over by fields of grain, fruit groves, vines, vegetable gardens and pastures. For example, one modern grower has estimated that there may have been as many as 160,000 peach trees by about 1802; so prolific were their yields that farmers fed their pigs upon them.[23] And behind Lieutenant-Governor Paterson's Sydney house was a 'vast garden', with a 'great number of useful vegetables ... which have been procured from every part of the world'.[24]

The colony's progress with grain cultivation and animal husbandry was equally impressive. By 1805, there were 12,700 acres under cereals; and on the native and introduced pastures grazed 517 horses, 4325 cattle, 20,617 sheep, 5123 goats and 23,050 pigs, as well as innumerable chickens, ducks and geese. François Péron, who arrived with the Baudin expedition in 1802 and visited Samuel Marsden's estate at Parramatta, wrote in awe: 'no longer ago than 1794, the whole of this spot was covered with immense and useless forests of Eucalyptus. This residence ... is ... isolated, in a manner, in the midst of woods; and it was over a very excellent road, in a very elegant chaise, that Mr Marsden drove me to it. What pains, what exertions must have been taken to open such communications! And these communications, these pastures, these fields, these harvests, these orchards, these flocks, are the work of eight years.'[25]

By the turn of the nineteenth century, that is, the New South Wales colonists had established that biota that had sustained Western Europeans for millennia (and added some exotics to it as well). And, benefiting from a better food supply, a benign climate, and free of the usual childhood illnesses, the first generation of native-born colonists grew up to six inches taller than their parents.[26]

Shelter

It was of course necessary for the colonists to have some shelter while they built their huts. For the ordinary marines and the convicts, the administration took tents out of the Ordnance store at Portsmouth.[27] In his letter of 26 August, Thomas Steele asked the Navy Board to obtain clothing and bedding for the colony's convicts, marines and officials. On 11 September, the Board called in Mr Simms, who agreed to deliver 750 beds for the convicts. These were ready about two weeks later.[28]

Providing for the officials and the marine officers proved more complicated. At the end of October, Phillip asked for some marquees for these two groups, and Nepean told Middleton privately in early December that twenty-two were required. The Treasury made this request official a week later, but the Navy Board advised that they could not be obtained in less than three weeks. Phillip then suggested that soldiers' tents be substituted, and volunteered to set an example to the others by using one himself, a move which would save something over £600. On 22 December Major Ross presented an extensive list of camp equipment needed for the marine officers, including forty-one tents and marquees, with Phillip annotating that these items were also 'wanted in addition for the governor, and eight officers of the staff'.[29]

The Admiralty then ordered Lieutenant Furzer, the marines' quartermaster, to Portsmouth, to see if items in store there left over from the American war might do. However, these had evidently become unserviceable, for on 4 January 1787 Middleton advised Nepean that the Navy Board was now ordering the tents, marquees, canteens and kettles. These were ready at the end of the month.[30]

There was also the matter of a temporary house for the governor, to serve while a permanent dwelling was being erected. On 8 November, the Navy Board ordered Mr Smith of Knightsbridge to make a prefabricated house of timber and canvas 45 feet long, 17 feet 6 inches wide, 8 feet high, with five windows on each side. While this dwelling did not provide as much comfort as Phillip hoped for – he wrote dismally from Sydney that it was 'neither wind nor water proof' – at least, it was better than nothing, as he waited for his permanent house to be completed.[31]

Clothing

The clothing ordered for the male convicts accorded with the list attached by Evan Nepean to Heads of a Plan, *viz.*, for one year:[32]

2 jackets
3 frocks
3 pairs trousers
4 woollen drawers
3 shirts
1 hat
4 pairs worsted stockings
3 pairs shoes

Nepean provided no such list of clothing for the female convicts, simply noting that 'the expense of clothing female convicts may be computed to amount to the same sum [as allowed for the men]. A proportion for two years to be provided'.[33] However, the Navy Board minute of 7 September 1786 and the list of items ordered in December for an additional thirty female convicts indicate that the yearly allowance for women was:[34]

4 white shifts
1 grey cotton jacket
1 white cotton jacket
2 check cotton jackets
2 linsey cotton jackets
2 canvas petticoats
[2 linsey woolsey petticoats][35]
1 serge petticoat
3 handkerchiefs
2 caps
1 hat
4 pairs yarn stockings
3 pairs shoes

The Navy Board ordered a two-years' supply of the men's and women's items on 7 September. The contracts were awarded to:

Mr Darby	woollen jackets and drawers
James Wadham	13 tons of 'slop' clothing[36]
W. and R. Borrowdale	1 ton of hats
John Yerbury	1/2 ton of stockings
Peter Pope	1/2 ton of stockings
William Goodman	2 1/2 tons of shoes[37]

When Nepean advised that there would be an extra thirty female convicts shipped from Newgate, the Navy Board ordered supplies of the same items for them.[38]

Tools and other implements

In his letter of 26 August 1786, Steele also asked the Navy Board to order 'tools and implements of agriculture' for the convicts and marines.[39] On 13 September, the Board asked the firm of Harrison, Gordon and Stanley to provide a long list of utensils, tools, implements and hardware.

Each of the male convicts and the marines was to have:

1 spade
1 shovel
1 grubbing hoe
1 West India hoe
1 garden hoe
1 felling axe
1 hatchet
1 knife
gimblets
wooden bowls, platters and spoons

Included in the list of communal tools, implements and hardware were: saws, adzes, broad axes, augers, chisels, planes, files, forges, bellows and anvils, grindstones, wheelbarrows, iron mills, ploughs, cooper's tools, nails, hinges, locks, bar iron, steel, glass, fishing lines, etc. But Sir Charles Middleton then had second thoughts about what was really needed, and drew up another list, telling Nepean that 'in the first list many things were wanting and other ill-sorted. I will take care that nothing superfluous is sent nor anything material omitted'.[40]

The items in the additional list are interesting, and give the lie to a number of hoary chestnuts, of which the most prominent is that no ploughs were sent. Plough and cart harnesses for six horses and six oxen were requested; a flax-dressing mill, together with 'the necessary articles for dressing flax'; mills for grinding cassava; canvas to make 250 beds for the colony's hospital; wheelbarrows; wheels on axles 'for the moving of timber, etc.'; bricks for chimneys and a kiln; 500 tin plates; coppers; stone mason's tools; scythes. The next day, the Board also asked for 'small shot of [different] sorts, 2 cwt from no. 1 downwards, with moulds for it'. On 31 October, at Phillip's request, the Board added an order for five dozen razors, and large and small combs. These items were ready for loading in mid-November.[41]

On 29 December, the Navy Board ordered 'a further quantity of 2 cwt of buck shot, 6 scythes and 5 dozen of razors'. Phillip considered these quantities 'very insufficient', and asked for an additional '20 scythes, 12 dozen of razors (at 12s a dozen) and 5 cwt of small shot, chiefly buck'. The Navy Board ordered another 6 cwt of small shot.[42]

Ordnance

Another of the matters that Phillip gave thought to soon after his appointment was the colony's defences.

In something I have never been able to get to the bottom of, at some point Phillip evidently trained as a soldier as well, for he had a specialized knowledge of artillery. This training is reflected in his remark in his memorandum about the colony that 'it will be necessary to throw up a slight work, as a defence against the natives … and against the convicts … For this my own little knowledge as a field engineer will be sufficient'; and a portrait done in London somewhere about this time shows him holding a plan of a pentangle redoubt.[43]

By the end of October, Phillip had asked for eight 12-pounder cannon to arm this fort, which the Duke of Richmond, the Master-General of the Ordnance, then reduced to four 12-pounders and four 6-pounders. Subsequently, this was changed again, to two iron 12-pounders 9 feet in length, two 12-pounders of 7 1/2 feet, and two 6-pounders of 8 feet, and two light brass 6-pounders of 4 1/2 feet.[44]

The Ordnance Board also gave him all the paraphernalia needed to keep these guns in good order, and to work them, including carriages, powder and shot, cartridges, handspikes, matches, sponges and rammer heads, fuses, hand grenades, blunderbusses, harness, lead aprons, ropes, laboratory knives, lanterns, tarpaulins, etc. As the muskets and cutlasses in the Portsmouth and Plymouth barracks stores were worn, the marines going to New South Wales were issued with 200 new ones, with the muskets to have steel rammers and bayonets, and with the attendant flints, locks, swivels and loops. As already indicated, quantities of ammunition were also provided.[45]

Bricks

On 26 October, the Navy Board ordered the Deptford officers to load 5000 bricks into the transports, to be used for building chimneys and kilns. This number was evidently later doubled, and brick moulds were also shipped. Under the supervision of the convict James Bloodworth, the kilns built at the brickfield about a mile to the southwest of the camp at Sydney, produced bricks that were used in the governor's permanent house.[46]

Implements for manufacturing cloth

From late Tudor times, southeastern Lancaster, in the English midlands, was a centre of cloth manufacture. With this development aided by easy river access to the major port of Liverpool, by the later eighteenth century proto-factories had been established in centres such as Preston, Blackburn, Bolton, Wigan and Stockport, with Manchester as the most important, and with a myriad individual spinners and weavers in the adjacent rural areas supplying them with yarn and cloth. The cloths ('fustian' or 'calico'[47]) were often a mixture of flax and cotton, with the flax coming from Ireland and the cotton from the Levant or the West Indies.

The market for linen and cotton cloths expanded in the eighteenth century, with demand for brightly coloured pieces in Africa, America and the West Indies, and with a growing domestic preference for women's dresses to be made of these materials.

And what, you may well ask, does this digression have to do with New South Wales? Well, as I explain in *Botany Bay: The Real Story*, one of the Pitt administration's reasons for establishing the colony was to obtain supplies of New Zealand flax (*Phormium tenax*), both to provide cloth with which to make clothes for the convicts and free settlers who might later arrive, and canvas and cordage for the warships stationed in Indian waters, but also for more general distribution – as Evan Nepean remarked in late October 1786, the colony's 'most considerable object' (i.e., apart from sending the convicts out of the kingdom) was 'the cultivation of the flax plant ... [which] has been found in that neighbourhood in the most luxuriant state, and small quantities have been brought to Europe and manufactured, and, from its superior quality, it will, it is hoped, soon become an article of commerce from that country'. The administration instructed Phillip that he was to attend to the cultivation and harvesting of this fibre plant,

> as it has been humbly represented unto us that advantages may be derived from the flax plant which is found in the islands not far distant from the intended settlement, not only as a means of acquiring clothing for the convicts and other person who may become settlers, but from its superior excellence for a variety of maritime purposes, and as it may ultimately become an article of export.

He was also to 'send home by every opportunity which may offer, samples of that article, in order that a judgement may be formed whether it may not be necessary to instruct you further upon this subject'.[48]

Therefore, it was necessary for the administration to provide Phillip with the means of doing so. In October, Nepean made contact with William Sharrow and John Singleton. William and George Sharrow (who may have been brothers) had first had a linen-manufacturing business in Ireland, which they then expanded into England, to Yorkshire and then to Birmingham, and with strong links to Manchester. Stating that, 'after much study and application, and at a great expense', they had 'invented a simple and easy process for dressing backings or hirds, being the common refuse of tow, dressed from flax, so as to answer the same end in several manufactures as cotton, particularly in the manufacture of checks, stripes and low-priced fustians; and also for candle wick and lamps, where real cotton is used', in February 1783 the Sharrows petitioned parliament for a financial reward, in return for which they offered to make their process generally available to linen and cotton manufacturers, which would 'be the means of a great saving in the imports of a foreign article of commerce'.[49]

Nepean's surviving correspondence with William Sharrow is not complete. Sharrow evidently wrote to him on 24 October, pointing out that the New Zealand flax might present problems of importation. Nepean replied on 27 October, thanking Sharrow, and asking for details of how he thought the fibre might be managed, 'so as to serve as an instruction to the people who may be employed in its cultivation, and tend to remove those objections to its importation which you suggest'. Sharrow answered three days later, that, 'on arrival of the convicts', the cultivation of it would 'employ men, women and children'. He asked for a sample of it, so that he might 'do everything in my power to communicate the improvement of the flax plant, [so as] to make it eligible for importation, which certainly is a great national object, as the manufacturers of this country will reap a considerable advantage from it (far more so than is yet seen)'. A week later, he asked if it would be too late for him to present his 'report and instructions ... the middle of next month' (i.e., December), as he would then be in London.[50] These documents have not been found. My assumption is that they were given to Phillip without being copied, for him to pass them on to those whom he sent to Norfolk Island.

Simultaneously, and at Phillip's urging, Nepean sought advice from John Singleton, a Wigan check manufacturer, about the cultivation of cotton in New South Wales. Saying that he had talked to 'a West India merchant who tells me he is sure cotton will thrive in [the] South Seas', Singleton offered to send seeds of different varieties, adding that 'it is very possible the profit in [the] end may be considerable to this country'.[51] As the following quote shows, Singleton provided seeds. Phillip subsequently took on more seeds, and plants, at Rio de Janeiro. King sowed cotton immediately on landing at Norfolk Island; but this planting evidently did not succeed, for Phillip later reported that 'of the cotton seed brought from England very little vegetated'.[52]

Given the intermingling of flax and cotton in cloth manufacturing then, these conversations must have been linked. Indeed, it is possible that the Sharrows and Singleton made a joint approach to the administration; but whether or not this was so, officials duly provided for the refinement of fibres and the manufacture of cloth in the colony, when they shipped 'twenty-four spinning whorls, forty-eight spinning brasses, nine hackles for flax, nine hackle pins, three flax dresser's brushes, 127 dozen combs, [and] one machine for dressing flax, with iron work and brushes'; and a 'loom for weaving canvas, complete'.[53]

There were many other small items that the administration needed to provide, many of them necessary for the various officers to be able to fulfil their duties – e.g., in January 1787 Andrew Miller, the commissary, spent £20.11.0 on stationery 'for the business of his department'.[54] Often, these items were so routine that they were provided without record. And on 4 December, at Phillip's request, the Navy Board ordered sets of weights and measures – weights from 1/4 cwt down to 1 lb; and 1/2 bushel and smaller measures according to the Winchester standard.[55]

Trade goods

The administration also thought that, in line with Matra's suggestion, the colony might obtain animals at places closer to New South Wales than Europe or the Cape of Good Hope – for instance, from Savu in the Molucca Islands and from the Pacific Islands.

Accordingly, at the end of October, Phillip asked Nepean what items had been ordered as 'presents' for the natives; and suggested some additions. Nepean then asked the Treasury to obtain £50-worth of ducats and 'two or three cask of beer' to bribe the Dutch at Savu; and 200 muskets and cutlasses to induce the local inhabitants to pass over their 'black cattle, goats and hogs'. He asked also for £150-worth of 'small hatchets, some of them made in the Tahiti fashion, glass beads, chiefly white, pocket looking glasses [i.e., mirrors], nails and gimlets, and a few *real* red feathers' to trade with the Society islanders. The Treasury ordered these from Brook Watson's firm, Rashleigh and Company. They were ready four weeks later. (One newspaper reported also that 'an immense number of toys are to be sent ... for the natives'; but this may only be a garbled version of the above.)[56]

Equipping the marines

As we have seen, both the marines and convicts going out to New South Wales were victualled in the manner of troops sent to the West Indies, with the qualification that the convicts were not allowed spirits. However, because they were part of the regular peacetime naval establishment, the marines were otherwise equipped separately from the convicts, and by the Admiralty and Navy Board rather than by the Home Office.

Clothing and Goods: In November, Phillip Stephens told the marine storekeeper at Portsmouth that it was intended that the troops should be supplied with clothing in the colony; and on 5 December, he ordered a long list of 'necessaries', including shirts, stockings, shoes, ribbons, knapsacks, kitchen utensils, shears, needles and threads, combs and razors. The majority of these items were ready by the end of the month.[57]

Wine and Spirits: At the beginning of November, the Navy Board queried the Treasury's earlier advice that the marines were not to be provided with spirits at Botany Bay, to be told that this was indeed so.[58] In keeping with this intention, the administration also did not make any provision for spirits or wine (except, as mentioned, what would be required for the sick). Curiously, a merchant firm offered to supply the marines with Tenerife wine 'at 20 shillings per gallon delivered on board at the island of Santa Cruz, in stout pipes with a proper quantity of hoops'. Treasury referred this offer to the Navy Board, which replied 'that by the orders we have received for providing the rations of provisions for them, there is not any mention of wine or spirits'.[59]

Officials had a foreboding about the trouble these exemptions would cause for months before it became a tumult. Phillip put it to the Navy Board that the marines should be supplied with spirits in New South Wales, to be told that he must approach the Treasury. He then asked Nepean to do so, saying that he feared 'much discontent in the garrison if there is no allowance of wine or spirits (to which they have ever been accustomed)'; and that he could take on wine at either Tenerife or the Cape of Good Hope.[60] At this time, however, he received no satisfaction on this point.

Equipping the colony for science

Lieutenant William Dawes was included in the marine officers going to New South Wales because of his scientific expertise. He came to London for consultations at the end of October 1786. On 14 November, Neville Maskelyne, the Astronomer Royal, told Board members that Dawes was interested in making 'useful nautical and astronomical observations in his passage [to Botany Bay], and during his stay there', and had asked the Board to lend him instruments and manuals; and that he 'was capable of making proper use of them'.[61]

Dawes had earlier presented the Royal Society with a long list of instruments he wished to have, but this was now reduced according to what the Board of Longitude had available. These included an astronomical quadrant; a sextant; an acromatic telescope with a micrometer; various clocks and watches; barometers and thermometers; tables of logarithms; and nautical almanacs. However, believing that the governor would be in a position to take better care of them than Dawes, the Board stipulated that the 'said instruments and books should be ... delivered into the charge of Captain Phillip'. The Board also added a Kendall chronometer for Phillip, 'he giving a receipt for the same and promising to return it at the expiration of his voyage'.[62]

Long afterwards, Dawes received £100 from the Board 'as an allowance for my observations made in New South Wales'.[63]

Providing for the soul

As well as to their physical needs, authorities thought to attend to the spiritual welfare of the convicts. Following a request from the Archbishop of Canterbury, the Society for the Propagation of the Gospel provided the Reverend Richard Johnson with large numbers of bibles, prayer books, catechisms and improving tracts, including *Religion Made Easy, Great Importance of a Religious Life, Christian Soldier, Offices for the Penitent, Admonitions* – and more to the point, perhaps, *Plain Exhortations to Prisoners, Dissuasive from Stealing, Caution of Profane Swearers* and *Exhortations to Chastity*.[64]

We may wonder how many of the convicts were suitably appreciative of these presents.

Providing for commerce

In the list of seeds sent in the *Sirius*, Banks included a category for 'commerce' – i.e., for trade with passing ships or for export: hemp, flax, rhubarb, tobacco, potato seed and oats.[65]

At first glance, this is a curious mixture, but it has a not-immediately-obvious significance. As just discussed, one of the reasons for establishing the colony was to manufacture the New Zealand flax; and if *Phormium tenax* flourished in the islands of the southwest Pacific Ocean, so too might the European fibre plants. Rhubarb was then widely used in medicine as a laxative. Tobacco was a common return cargo for ships visiting the southern American colonies. Light and able to be compressed, it was a convenient item to carry. It was also a staple of a sailor's life. Oatmeal was an integral part of the ration on Royal Navy ships, being served on three days out of seven. Brought from America after Columbus's voyages, the potato was being widely cultivated in Europe by the end of the eighteenth century, when it had become a common food for the poor (most famously in Ireland). It was also a common substitute in the naval ration for bread, with the established proportions being 2 lbs of potato for 1 lb bread.[66]

These examples show how such items were relevant to ships doing business in the great ocean. In 1793-4, James Colnett undertook a voyage into the Pacific Ocean, which was to have been an official one but which, after the outbreak of war with France, went forward privately, although Colnett continued to see himself as fulfilling Admiralty intentions. Its purpose was to search for places where Southern whalers might refresh, and Colnett planted 'garden seeds, of every kind, for the benefit and comfort of those who might come after us'. Similarly, early in the nineteenth century, reflecting their contact with Euopeans and their acumen, Maori at the Bay of Islands had extensive fields of wheat and beds of turnips, potatoes and sweet potatoes, which they traded to visiting ships.[67]

The items that Banks annotated 'For Commerce', then, were all such as ships would require – not only those ships which would carry convicts out in the future, but also those which would pursue trade independently – a development in line with Phillip's expectation that in time 'ships of all nations' would come to the colony.

7.

Loading the Ships and Embarking the People

THERE WAS A MYRIAD arrangements to be made, and items to be shipped. What I offer here is an indicative description only, not a comprehensive analysis. Also, the chronology of steps was in reality more convoluted than I make it seem here. For example, while a certain number of officers went on board the ships as soon as they were fitted out, so as to begin preparing them for the voyage, others who were either appointed subsequently or who needed to make extensive preparations for their particular roles in the colony embarked much later. Among this latter group were the governor, the chief surgeon and some of his deputies, the surveyor, the commandant of marines, the quartermaster and the astronomer.

Fitting out and loading the ships
On 25 October 1786, the Admiralty advised the Navy Board that Arthur Phillip would command the *Sirius*, which should carry a crew of 160 (including twenty-two marines), and 'be fitted out for a voyage to remote parts, ... victualled to twelve months of all species of provisions at whole allowance and stored to a proper proportion for foreign service'.[1] The same day the Deptford officers advised the Navy Board that the *Sirius* would be ready to receive its crew on 27 October. A skeleton crew began rigging it on 28 October. This work continued for some weeks, as the number of crew increased. On 9 November, the ship shifted down to

Loading the Ships and Embarking the People

Long Reach to take on its cannon and other ordnance stores. During this time, officers and crew were accommodated on the *Flora*, so as 'to keep them clear of the artificers'. John Hunter assumed day-to-day command of the ship on 5 December.[2]

On 27 October, the Admiralty similarly advised the Navy Board that Lieutenant Henry Ball would command the *Supply*, which was to have a crew of fifty-five (including twelve marines), and be fitted out and provisioned for a voyage to remote parts in the same manner as the *Sirius*.[3] On 1 November, the Deptford officers proposed further works on it; and on 6 November, they advised that it would be ready to receive its crew on 11 November.[4] It took on provisions in the second half of November, and its guns in December.

Since they were needed to work them, the crews of the transport ships also went on board at an early stage.

*

Captain George Teer was the Navy Board official responsible for overseeing the fitting out and the loading of the transport ships, after their owners had done some basic work on them. On 30 October, he told the Board that the storeships – *Borrowdale*, *Fishburn* and *Golden Grove* – were ready to receive stores, which was done through November.[5] Soon after, the first of the convict transports, the *Lady Penrhyn*, was ready to receive stores. On 4 November, for example, it took on board five barrels of tar and two of pitch, two casks of rosin, eight dozen brooms, two gallons of oil, one horse hide, eight casks of oakum 'and other small stores for [the] ship's use'.[6]

On 20 November, the Navy Board advised the Treasury that the *Alexander*, *Charlotte*, *Friendship* and *Scarborough* were also ready to receive stores. They were then loaded, with the *Alexander*, for example, taking on 'government stores' on 23 November, 'four cases of hats' on 27 November, and 'sundry' articles and stores on 30 November and 1 and 2 December.[7]

The stowing of eighteenth-century sailing ships was a complicated business, what with the need to carry ballast, cables, sails, water, fuel (timber or coal), food and goods, and still to leave room for people. Various items (e.g., butter, beef, wine, spirits, water) were packed in different-sized casks, which created further difficulties. And the loading of the First Fleet ships was even more complicated than was normal, given that they were to carry criminals, and implements, animals, a two-years' supply of provisions for the colony, and the knocked-down boats for the *Sirius* and *Supply*. The business required a great deal of expertise, which might only be born of experience. This George Teer certainly had; but Arthur Phillip thought he had it too, so there was soon tension between the two. On some points, Phillip was right – for example, the gunpowder on board the *Alexander* certainly could not be put where the convicts might get their hands on it.[8] But Phillip's 'advice', suggesting as it did faults in Teer's management, clearly riled the Navy Board official.

After Phillip wrote to the Navy Board on 4 December with several criticisms about how items were being stowed, Teer exploded with frustration:

> I beg leave to acquaint you that Captain Phillip has from time to time so increased the orders for stores, and implements for Botany Bay, and increased the number of marines from 74 up to 160 – I believe I may venture to assure you, they will occupy amongst all the ships upwards of three hundred tons space – each day and week continuing to add more, that I was obliged to put a stop to his wishes still to add more.

The Board replied that if there were space after all the stores ordered by the Treasury had been stowed, he was to meet Phillip's requests.[9]

Phillip wrote again on 7 December, with additional comments about how the beds were arranged, the need for fresh air in the holds, and the amount of water being carried. Teer replied at length, which must have been an unwelcome distraction from his work. He had recommended scuttles rather than hatchways, he said, since these would better deliver fresh air into the holds where the convicts would be held. Since some of the ships were to carry few convicts, he did not see the need for barricades on them. The beds were placed 'in the best manner they possibly can be'. He conceded there was a need for night-time toilet 'tubs'; but Phillip had made a mistake about the size of the water casks (70 gallons in a Navy ship, but 126 gallons in a merchant one), so that in fact the transports would carry sufficient water. He concluded: 'the convicts' ships are *completely fitted*, their provisions and accommodations are better than any set of transports I have ever had any directions in, as they have more water and provisions on board than any of those that went to India with Commodore Johnstone's fleet'.[10]

Already acute, this problem of lack of space was exacerbated by the Home Office's decision to increase the number of women convicts to 150 and to permit a certain number of convicts' wives and children to go out, decisions which meant, not only were there more people to ship, but also the clothes, food and water for them.[11] After considering the various possibilities, Middleton came up with an arrangement to distribute the female convicts among three ships, two of them also carrying men. This was contrary to the earlier decision of the Treasury, that the women should be accommodated together on one ship, 'so as to keep them separate from the men'.[12] When Nepean very diffidently proposed an alternative arrangement, Middleton himself grew testy, telling the Under-Secretary that 'it is absolutely impracticable to arrange the transports in any other manner than we have done without unloading and new fitting all the ships, and which would require at least three weeks from this time'. He also pointed out that 'the women cannot be more crowded than they are, having only 1 1/2 tons allowed to each, and which is as little as possible for so long a voyage'. He concluded by saying that he would 'be very happy in following any mode that can be pointed out for putting an end to this disagreeable and troublesome business'.[13]

Despite these problems, the loading of the five convict transports was largely completed by 6 December, when the Navy Board informed the Admiralty and Treasury that they would be ready to leave Deptford (i.e., to receive people) after they had been fitted with beds for the marines who were to go on them.[14] But once people were on board, it became clear that more items were needed. Four chests of arms for the marines were put into the *Charlotte* in mid-December, for example, and ordnance from the Tower into various of the ships. In mid-January, arms and accoutrement chests were ordered for the *Friendship*, and 200 sets of new muskets and cutlasses were loaded onto the *Sirius* for carriage to Portsmouth.[15]

Then, in early January, the marines on board the transports found that they were not provided with all the things they needed – that is, while the detachments going on normal sea service into the *Sirius* and *Supply* would be equipped in the usual manner, the contractor and masters were not obliged to supply certain items for the marines on the transports. Telling him that he would be recompensed, the Navy Board asked Richards to provide candles on 8 January.[16] Six days later, Captain Tench complained that 'camp utensils' were also lacking, and that, when asked about them, the master of his ship had said that 'as he had no allowance of necessary money from the Navy Board, he did not consider himself bound in any state to furnish us with these indispensable requisites'. Ross took up the complaint with the Admiralty, which referred it to the Navy Board, which asked Richards to supply those items that were allowed on the King's ships.[17]

There was a set of colours needed for the marines to parade with, and drums, drumsticks and fifes. Then, two years' supply of light clothing needed to be loaded for those who were to serve in New South Wales, and one year's supply for those on the *Sirius* and *Supply*. It was also thought proper to order 150 new 'check' shirts for the troops.[18]

On 21 January, John Shortland complained that the kitchen coppers on the *Alexander* were much too small, which necessitated two preparations of food. Expressing 'surprize' at this, the Navy Board directed Richards to replace them.[19]

*

Well before this, however – by 7 December in fact – it had become apparent that another ship was needed. In what was clearly a concerted move, Phillip suggested this to Nepean on 12 December, saying 'I do not see that it is possible to put all the marines and the number of women allowed to go with their husbands on board the transports intended to carry the convicts; and by the quantity of provisions and stores put on board the storeships, none can be received in those ships'. Nepean so advised the Treasury, which told the Navy Board to 'hasten the equipment of the *Prince of Wales* transport' – that is, before the Treasury had formally agreed to the request, and before William Richards had offered this ship to the Board (27 December 1786) and the Deptford officers had inspected it (29 December 1786).[20]

The *Prince of Wales* was fitted and loaded in January 1787. On board it were put (among other items) the 18 tons of camp equipment Major Ross considered indispensable for the marines; the tobacco for the sailors and marines on the *Sirius*; additional clothing and provisions for the extra women and children; and also provisions to be taken round to Portsmouth to replace those which were first intended for the voyage but which were now being consumed as the ships waited.[21]

*

In loading the ships, there were also a number of routine legal requirements to be met. These included Customs and Excise approvals for the technical exportation of some of the goods. On 6 November, Messrs Harrison, Gordon and Stanley asked the Navy Board to obtain exemptions from the Customs Board to permit those they had supplied 'to be shipped free of duties and fees'. The Board referred this request to the Treasury, for George Rose to ask for 'a list of the several articles and the name of the ship or ships on board of which they are intended to be sent, in order that the same may accompany the warrant for permitting the exportation of the same duty free'. Subsequently, the Board approached Customs for 'free cockets and bills [of health] for the transports ... hired to carry convicts to Botany Bay'.[22]

Then, William Richards requested the Navy Board to obtain exemption from excise charges for the rum he was loading for the marines going to Botany Bay (i.e., for the voyage, not for after landing).

The Navy Board approached the Treasury, which approached the Excise Board, which gave approval. Subsequently, the Navy Board and Treasury also requested exemptions for the rum loaded into the *Prince of Wales*.[23]

There was one such request that the Commissioners of Customs and Excise refused to grant, however. Phillip was intending to take a considerable amount of goods out with him, including two pipes and 104 dozen bottles of port; two puncheons of rum; twelve barrels of porter (a dark, bitter beer); twenty hundredweight of sugar; thirty-four dozen glasses; and forty decanters. Considering that he ran the risk of 'losing half those articles' if they were sent in a transport, he asked that the *Sirius* be included in the list of ships which qualified for the 'drawback' – i.e., the reimbursement of any duties which had previously been paid on the goods being shipped out. Nepean approached the Treasury on his behalf, which asked Customs, to be told that this was legally impossible, since the goods were to be carried on a Royal Navy ship and not a merchantman.[24]

Marines and convicts

Putting the various groups of colonists on board the ships of the First Fleet also proved an intricate and protracted business, with four steps – three legal and one practical – needing to be taken in order to embark the convicts.

The first of the legal steps was an order for transportation. As discussed in *Botany Bay: The Real Story*, the comprehensive Transportation Act of August 1784 (24 Geo. III, c. 56) had provided for the King-in-Council's fixing the place to which felons sentenced to transportation would be sent. The places identified for those so sentenced into the mid-1780s had been America or Africa, or the more general 'part or parts beyond the seas'. Therefore, New South Wales had now to be specified as the place for each of those intended to be sent there. On 1 December, asking that this be done, Sydney sent the Lord President of the Privy Council lists of those so destined. In a series of Orders-in-Council and warrants the Privy Council identified their new destination as 'the eastern coast of New South Wales extending from the latitude of 10°37' to the latitude of 43°39' south, or some one or other of the islands lying between those latitudes to the Eastward of the said coast of New South Wales within the southern Pacific Ocean'.[25]

The Orders are as follow. On 6 December, one containing the names of 321 persons sentenced to transportation 'beyond the seas'; and one containing the names of fifty persons sentenced to transportation to America or Africa. On 22 December, one containing the names of four women sentenced to transportation to America, and of fifteen sentenced to Africa; and another containing the names of eighty-one women sentenced to 'beyond the seas'. On 12 February 1787, one containing the names of thirty-three persons sentenced to 'beyond the seas'; and another containing the names of four persons sentenced to America or Africa. On 20 April, one containing the names of twenty-seven persons sentenced to 'beyond the seas'; and one containing the names of one person sentenced to America, and two to Africa.[26] When these Orders did not quite fill up the intended complement of 750 convicts, the Privy Council and the Home Office began issuing Orders identifying New South Wales as the place for individuals or small groups recently sentenced to death, but reprieved on condition of transportation.[27]

The second step was the drawing up of warrants authorizing the keepers of convicts to deliver them over for transportation. Those for Duncan Campbell, for example, were issued on 3 and 20 January and 24 February 1787; and that for Henry Bradley at Plymouth on 5 March.[28] Others for convicts held in county jails followed – e.g., for the Kingston-upon-Thames jailor on 10 March, and for the High Sheriff of Leicester on 11 April.

The third step was that those taking 'jail delivery' of the convicts needed to sign contracts and post bonds for receiving them and delivering them to their destination. The concluding of these certificates was a tedious business, as it had to be done with representatives of the courts which had sentenced the prisoners. Nepean pointed out this need to Middleton on 9 December, saying that 'the owners as well as the masters and mates [of the ships] must enter into the bonds which the acts of parliament require, for the safe custody of the convicts whilst on board the transports. If that has not been done new difficulties will arise, for the courts will not vest them with the custody of the convicts without it.' Middleton replied that he could see 'a real difficulty unless the King's authority can supersede the usual practice of the courts in dispensing with [the requirement]', because, unlike as with earlier transportation to North America, those concluding the bonds would have no vested interest in delivering the convicts safely.[29]

Nepean circulated the forms to be completed for the convicts to go on board the *Alexander* to the clerks of the various assize circuits on 13 December, and announced that William Richards and Duncan Sinclair, its master, would be at the Home Office in the morning of Friday, 15 December, in order to sign them. When some of the clerks queried the need to conclude contracts, Sydney sought the Law Officers' opinion, which was that 'in order to comply with the requisites of the acts relative to the transportation of offenders, that the persons agreeing to transport the offenders should contract for the due performance of such transportation with two justices of [the] peace appointed by the court before whom the prisoners were respectively tried, or by a subsequent court held with the like authority'.[30]

These contracts were then drawn up for each of the convicts transported. Curiously, although there were once more than 750 of these, it seems only one is now extant, that made on 27 January 1787 by the magistrates of the town of Kingston-upon-Thames to deliver Mary Mitchell to Richards and William Sever for embarkation on the *Lady Penrhyn* and transportation 'to the eastern coast of New South Wales or some one or other of the islands adjacent in pursuance of His Majesty's Order-in-Council lately made in that behalf by virtue of the statute'.[31]

*

The practical step was to place the marine guards on board the transports before they received their convicts – or at least, on those that were to receive male convicts, for the women were put on board the *Lady Penrhyn* ahead of a marine detachment.

Only two of the six transports, the *Alexander* and the *Lady Penrhyn*, loaded their convicts in London. As those dangerous rogues who had earlier been selected for transportation to Africa went in the *Alexander*, it was particularly important that there be a strong guard for them. Under the command of Lieutenant George Johnston, thirty-seven marines marched overland from Portsmouth, reaching London on 6 December. They went on board the ship on 14 December, but Johnston soon reported that the security arrangements for the convicts were inadequate, so that these had to be increased.[32] On 6 January 1787, 184 convicts went from the hulks into the *Alexander* – 101 from the *Ceres*, fifty-one from the *Justitia* and thirty-two from the *Censor*. On 15 January (five days ahead of the relevant warrant being issued), another twenty-five convicts went into this ship, bringing its number very close to the planned 210.[33]

The women from Newgate and Southwark jail were also put on board the *Lady Penrhyn* through January – fifty-six on 6 January, 'victualled ... the same day agreeable to Mr Richards's plan'; six women and three children on 9 January; sixteen women and one child on 26 January; and twenty-two women on 31 January.[34]

The Admiralty began directing parties of marines to board the other ships in mid-January. The *Sirius* and *Supply* received their complement on reaching Portsmouth on 24 February.[35] Lieutenant William Collins went on board the *Lady Penrhyn* on 17 March, and his servant three days later. Captain James Campbell and his nephew joined them on 3 May.[36]

On 20 and 24 February, the Home Office sent Campbell lists containing the names of some 191 convicts, of whom 184 were to be sent on board the *Scarborough*, and others on the *Alexander*.[37] It was now necessary to send these overland. Nepean arranged for six wagons to carry them, for a cavalry guard to escort them, for the marine guard to go on board the *Scarborough* (which it did on 27 February), and for Portsmouth authorities to provide lighters, etc., to take them from shore to ship.[38]

This caravan left London on 27 February, and reached Portsmouth on 2 March. One young naval officer later remembered:

> All the ship windows and doors of Portsmouth [were] closed on this occasion, and the streets were lined with troops, while the wagons ... passed to Point Beach, where the boats were ready to receive them; as soon as they were embarked, they gave three tremendous cheers.[39]

However, the weather had turned so bad that it was impossible to ferry the convicts out at the Mother Bank. Instead, they were temporarily put on board the *Gorgon*, and fed out of the Navy's stores, until 4 March, when the weather moderated enough for them to be embarked on their proper ships.[40]

On 5 March, the Home Office directed Henry Bradley, the keeper of the *Dunkirk* hulk at Plymouth, that he was to put eighty male and twenty-two female convicts on board the *Friendship*, and ninety-nine men and twenty-two women on board the *Charlotte*; and another twenty-six male convicts, who were to be transferred to the *Scarborough* on arrival at Portsmouth. John White, the colony's chief surgeon, travelled west to oversee the business. The marine guards went on board these ships on 9 and 10 March, but gales made it impossible to load the prisoners until 11 March. The men were shackled, but not the women.[41]

A number of disparate groups went on board the *Prince of Wales* at Portsmouth. There were single marines; the married ones who had received permission to take their wives and children with them; the wives and children of the convicts; and some late additions to the number of female convicts. On 7 March, twenty-nine marines and four wives were embarked; two female convicts from Chester a week later; and four female convicts and one child on 28 March. A warrant for jail delivery having been issued on 27 April, at the beginning of May, a second convoy of two wagons took two men, thirty-seven women and one child to Portsmouth, most of whom were put on board the *Prince of Wales*.[42] There were also transfers to and from other ships. All in all, when it sailed it carried some (it is impossible to give precise figures) thirty marines, twenty-eight marines' wives, twenty-five female convicts, twenty-five convicts' wives, and some children.

*

Loading the Ships and Embarking the People

As the ships waited at Portsmouth to sail, there were various additions and alterations to the numbers of people on them. Some of the crewmen of the *Sirius* and *Supply* and some of the marines died or were invalided ashore, and were replaced by others. Lieutenant Long and Lieutenant Furzer were ordered on board the *Sirius* on 21 February; Major Ross and Captain Collins (together with one sergeant, three drummers and six privates) on 2 March; and Andrew Miller, the colony's commissary of stores, on 30 April.[43] Phillip was the last official to embark on the flagship, arriving from London on 7 May.

The situation was similar with the convicts. In March and April, in order to complete complements, or as some of those on board were released or died, more convicts were sent to the ships. Two women were transferred from the *Friendship* to the *Lady Penrhyn* after arriving from Plymouth. Three women and two children went on board the *Friendship* on 17 April.[44]

On 26 April and 6 and 8 May, the convict transports seem (because lists vary slightly) to have been carrying:[45]

	Men		Women		Children	
	26 April	6/8 May	26 April	6/8 May	26 April	6/8 May
Alexander	197	195				
Scarborough	205	205				
Charlotte	86	86	20	20	2	2
Friendship	76	76	21	21	5	4
Lady Penrhyn[46]	1	1	101	101	5	5
Prince of Wales		2	10*	47*	1	2
Totals	565	561	152*	189*	13	13

* These figures include convicts' wives.

At the beginning of June, when the First Fleet reached Tenerife, these totals were: 558 male convicts, 192 female convicts and wives, thirteen convicts' children; together with twenty-eight marines' wives and seventeen children. The ages of the children ranged from infants up to fifteen years.[48]

Together with the officials and marines, these were the people who would found the New South Wales colony. Theirs was a strange destiny. As children in their villages and towns, and as feckless or desperate adults who transgressed their society's rules, they could have had no inkling of the voyage they were going on, or of what awaited them at its end.

PART THREE:
PREPARING TO SAIL

8.

At Portsmouth

IN THE EVENT, THE FIRST FLEET sailed some six months after administration officials thought it would.

On 5 September 1786, the Navy Board advised the Treasury that 'the shipping for carrying the convicts may be got ready in about six weeks'. In mid-October, the Home Office advised various county officials that the ships would sail at the end of the month, or the beginning of November.[1] Various newspapers then announced that they would depart in mid-November, then late December, then mid-January.

In January 1787, as the ships gathered at Portsmouth, Evan Nepean began a memorandum concerning their route to Botany Bay with: 'In case of no unforeseen accident, it is expected that the instructions will be ready, the convicts be embarked, and the convoy prepared in all respects for their departure by the first or second week in March'.[2] At the end of February, the *General Evening Post* reported that the Fleet would sail 'in two or three days'. On 7 March, General Collins, commandant of the Portsmouth Barracks, ordered that the equipping of the marine companies be completed as soon as possible, so that they might be ready to embark 'at an hour's notice'.[3]

But still weeks went by. On 17 April, Newton Fowell wrote to his father that he did not expect to sail 'this month'. On Wednesday 18 April, Nepean told Middleton that, as Phillip's commissions were to be approved by the Privy Council on Friday, he hoped the governor would leave London for Portsmouth on Saturday. In the event, however, the Privy Council did not approve the commission and instructions until 25 April, and the Admiralty did not issue the last of the legal instruments until 5 May. Phillip reached Portsmouth on 7 May, and the ships sailed six days later.[4]

There were a number of causes of this delay. First, it took William Richards and the Navy Board longer than they expected to select the transport ships, what with a number of those first proposed proving unsatisfactory, and owners evidently withdrawing others. Then, following the administration's decision to double the number of female convicts and to allow some convicts' wives and children to go out, another ship had to be added, fitted out and loaded. This decision also meant that the additional women had to be brought from jails about England to London and Plymouth. Both these things took time. Then there were the outbreaks of 'jail fever' and dysentery on the *Alexander*, which made it necessary to clear and disinfect that ship when it reached Portsmouth.

A greater factor, however, was the administration's realization in November 1786 that the colony needed to be governed under civil law. This required the pursuit of complicated administrative processes and the issuing of lengthy legal instruments, neither of which could be done overnight. For example, the administration could not introduce the bill providing for a criminal court in New South Wales before parliament resumed at the end of January 1787. And of course, Botany Bay was not the only extensive business government departments had to deal with between August 1786 and May 1787.

Nonetheless, there was a significant elapse of time between decision and departure. Fundamentally, there are two ways to view this 'delay'. The first is that taken by the traditionalist historians: that it shows the Pitt administration's incompetence. Manning Clark wrote that 'an indescribable hopelessness and confusion dominated the [Portsmouth] scene'. A.G.L. Shaw concluded that the government was 'rather inefficient and did not seriously consider the needs of a new settlement, penal or otherwise'. Robert Hughes wrote that 'the late winter and spring of

1787 went by in a stream of blunders and delays'. James Thomas said that 'the First Fleet's hallmark proved to be endless delay'.[5]

It is striking that these historians did not offer any example of an equivalent expedition that was more efficiently mounted, so as to establish a valid comparison. How long did it take to prepare for expeditions of 1500 soldiers to the East Indies, for example – two months, three months, four months? But then, such expeditions required no innovations in administrative and legal arrangements. Were there any real analogies for what the administration was attempting with the First Fleet? If so, how long did it take to send them off? The traditionalist historians have never asked these questions. They concluded that the mounting of the First Fleet was a shambles, and assumed that this judgment does not require any proof.

The second way to view the 'delay' between the decision to establish a convict colony at Botany Bay and the sailing of the First Fleet is that the sheer intricacy and extent of the preparations needed only became apparent as the business proceeded; that, as they realized what was needed, officials worked diligently to ensure that the venture would succeed; and that this took more time than they initially expected.

Rendezvous at Portsmouth

The Home Office, Treasury and Admiralty began assembling the First Fleet from 7 December, once the Navy Board had all but completed the fitting out of the ships and the loading of goods into them. Progressively, they were ordered to rendezvous at Portsmouth.[6] The *Scarborough, Fishburn, Golden Grove* and *Borrowdale* left the Thames on 15 December. The *Scarborough* reached Spithead on 21 December, followed by the *Fishburn* two days later. The *Golden Grove* came in on 24 December, and the *Borrowdale* arrived on 28 December. The *Sirius* met the *Alexander* and *Lady Penrhyn* at Gravesend on 31 January, and the three went on to the Nore, where they were joined by the *Supply*. The *Lady Penrhyn* then went ahead, reaching Portsmouth on 10 February. Gales forced the others to anchor in the Downs, on the southeast coast of Kent, from 4 to 19 February, when they proceeded into the English Channel, joining the *Scarborough*, *Lady Penrhyn*, *Prince of Wales*, *Borrowdale*, *Fishburn* and *Golden Grove* at the Mother Bank on 21 and 22 February. The *Friendship* and *Charlotte* left for Plymouth on 15 and 16 December, with the *Friendship* arriving on 21 December 1786, and the *Charlotte* on 7 January 1787. The *Charlotte* and *Friendship* came into Portsmouth from Plymouth on 15 and 16 March.[7]

In mid-January 1787, at the request of the Home Office and the Treasury, the Admiralty and Navy Board began ordering the masters of the transports to put themselves under Phillip's orders. Once the ships were all assembled at the Mother Bank, the Admiralty formally ordered Phillip to take charge of them 'and give them such orders for their further proceedings as you may judge necessary'. As Phillip remained in London until early May completing administrative arrangements, in practice this meant that John Hunter had immediate charge of the ships in February, March and April.[8]

*

Inevitably, there were many adjustments to the ships and goods during this time. A number of the ships needed further repairs and adjustments to their fittings. Because the *Sirius* was dragging its anchors in strong winds, Phillip asked for larger anchors to be fitted, and for another cable, both of which were granted. It emerged that the ship also needed further work, for water was getting into the sail room, a bulkhead needed to be moved, the hawse holes were damaging the cables, two eye bolts were missing from the main topmast, and the gun room ports were faulty. Then, rotten planks were found on the gun deck. The Navy Board ordered that these defects be fixed. The work took a week, and the Admiralty asked the Board to explain how the ship had been let out of the Deptford yard 'without being thoroughly inspected'. At the end of March 1787, Phillip asked for a set of magnetic bars (used to minimize the deflection of the compass needle caused by the ship's iron fittings), which he received.[9]

The situation was similar with the *Supply*. As it was about to leave the Thames, two ships collided with it, which necessitated replacing its bowsprit and repairing other damage, which was done by 11 January. By the time it reached Portsmouth, however, it had become clear that the new bowsprit needed to be refitted.[10]

Phillip asked for additional crewmen for the *Sirius*. There were also deficiencies of stores to be made up and extra items to be ordered.[11] Ball also asked for boatswain's and carpenter's stores, which he received. Then, he suggested that the ship's ballast be lessened by five tons, which was done.[12] Phillip asked for 200 lbs of portable soup in addition to the 50 lbs already supplied, 'as it is probable that the ship's company will be on salt provisions for some months after they arrive on the coast of New South Wales', which he received.[13]

There were problems to remedy on the transports, too. John Shortland asked for some flags and old canvas, which he received. He asked for 'junk' – shredded cable used to caulk the deck planks, a task which was often the responsibility of a ship's crew rather than of dockyard artificers. He received several hundredweight, and also paint for his cutter and a new windsail (used to introduce fresh air into the hold) for the *Alexander*.[14]

Adjustments to the transport ships' accommodations continued. For greater security, all the others were altered as the *Alexander* had been, with Phillip pointing out the need to do so before the convicts to be sent there overland were embarked. Towards the end of January, the marine officers on the *Charlotte*, who were then at Plymouth waiting to load its convicts, complained that the arrangement of the troops' and convicts' sleeping quarters was 'such that very serious consequences may be apprehended in case of an insurrection'. The Navy Board asked the commissioner at Plymouth to change things as he saw fit. The *Friendship*'s master and commanding marine officer then asked that its accommodation be similarly altered, which was done.[15] The grating on the *Prince of Wales* was closed, so as to prevent 'any communication in conversation' between the marines and the female convicts. The Navy Board also ordered thirty more sets of handcuffs and 'a dozen heavy irons for such of the convicts as are refractory'.[16]

Then, Major Ross suggested that the way the marines were berthed in the *Alexander* might have contributed to the spread of illness: they were 'excluded from all air but what passes through the hatchway leading from the seamen's berth, which must in some degree render it putrid before it reaches the others'. The ship's accommodation was consequently altered, though it is unclear whether Hunter's suggestion of a round house on the upper deck was followed.[17]

John White asked for, and received, sick kettles for the ships. Two cots, for the senior marine officers, were put into the *Scarborough* and *Prince of Wales*. Those on the *Friendship* and *Charlotte* then asked for the same favour. Soon all the marine officers and surgeons on the transports asked for cots to take ashore with them on reaching New South Wales, which they got. Phillip asked for extra hammocks, which he did not get, because there were not enough in store. Hunter wanted twelve leather hides for the *Sirius*, which he got.[18]

Then there was the need to keep replenishing provisions and stores used up as the ships waited to depart. As mentioned, Phillip and Ball each asked for more stores at the end of February, which necessitated the Navy Board authorizing them to be issued at Portsmouth (though in fact, Captain Marshall had already ordered this by the time he received this official notice). As the cost of these additional supplies could not be met out of the regular funding of the Portsmouth and Plymouth yards, the Board asked the officers there to keep separate accounts of the cost of items provided to the First Fleet ships. At intervals, the Board also directed William Richards to keep up the provisions on the transports to eight months' supply, the expected duration of the voyage.[19]

More clothing was also needed for the marines and the convicts. At the end of February, the Admiralty ordered the Portsmouth storekeeper to put supplies of 'light clothing' on board the *Alexander, Scarborough* and *Prince of Wales*, which was done. The Plymouth storekeeper likewise put light clothing on board the *Charlotte* and *Friendship*, and also 200 'check' shirts. The marines also needed extra ammunition. The problem was that in peacetime the barracks commandants ordered only enough supplies from the Ordnance to meet routine needs. When Ross pointed out that his companies might require greater amounts than normal to put down a convict insurrection, whether at Portsmouth or during the voyage, the Admiralty Secretary instructed Generals Smith and Collins accordingly. The Navy Board also put chests on board each of the convict transports 'for securing the ammunition for the marine guard'. In the event, the Botany Bay marines seem not to have received sufficient extra supplies; nor, evidently, were they provided with additional amounts of cartridge paper and sets of armourer's tools.[20]

There was also the question of how the wives of the marines and convicts who had been given permission to go on the voyage, and their children, were to be fed. No allowance for people in these categories had been made in the original contracts with William Richards, and now they were deprived. Ross wrote of one case on the *Alexander* where a marine, his wife and their two children were trying to live on 1 1/2 rations. Prompted by the Home Office, Treasury and Admiralty, the Navy Board fixed the rations at 1/2 for a marine's wife and 1/4 for a child, which had the curious consequence of a convict's wife (3/4) and child (1/2) being better fed than a marine's. Before this, however, Richards had been providing food for these women and children, in the expectation that the matter would be dealt with.[21]

Then there was the need to send Phillip the beer and ducats he was to use to obtain stock from the Molucca Islands.[22] And there was the need to pay Jonathan Altree, the young surgeon who had been ministering on a temporary basis to the women on the *Lady Penrhyn*. Phillip pleaded his case, and the Navy Board granted him £30.[23]

In short, there was a myriad day-to-day arrangements that needed to be made. Mostly, these were conveyed by notes passed between Hunter, Shortland, the masters of the transports, and the naval and marine officers. There must have been hundreds, if not thousands, of these notes, but they were ephemeral, and only a handful now remain. Two examples give their flavour. On 23 April, Ralph Clark told Richard Johnson that a newborn convict baby on the *Friendship* was dying and needed to be baptized. The next day, Clark asked Shortland to send a boat to take one of the officers to see Hunter on the *Sirius*.[24]

Disgruntlements

At Portsmouth a number of problems arose from the vagaries of human nature, and the pressure of incompatible people being confined together for extended times.

In mid-March, the master and the surgeon of the *Supply* complained to the Navy Board that Lieutenant Ball had altered their mess accommodation for the worse. The Admiralty directed him to restore the space to what it had been when the ship left Deptford. Hunter investigated the complaint, to find that Ball had not made any alteration to the ship. The Admiralty directed Hunter to 'reprimand the master and surgeon for making so groundless a charge'.[25]

No sooner had Ball dealt with this complaint than the master made another against him, more serious because it bore on the interest of the whole crew. On 18 March, Christopher Holmes showed Ball a letter which he said he intended to send to the Admiralty, complaining that he was stinting the crew of their proper rations. Nine days later, having heard nothing further, Ball demanded a formal enquiry. The Admiralty asked Samuel Marshall, the senior officer at Portsmouth, to put together a group of captains to investigate. These found that the crew 'never had made a complaint, or ever thought of so doing', and advised the Admiralty that 'we all are fully satisfied with the propriety of Lieutenant Ball's conduct'. The Admiralty directed the Navy Board to dismiss Holmes, and to appoint another in his place.[26]

John White, the surgeon, thought it unfair that, while the Admiralty had denied him a servant, the Reverend Richard Johnson was taking one out with him. White argued: 'without a servant my situation must be truly uncomfortable, ... not only on the passage but after landing. I have applied to Captain Phillip, who has no objection, and admits the propriety (if not necessity) of it.' He was given a servant.[27]

Newton Fowell, midshipman on the *Sirius*, took a keen interest in his prospects of promotion, and fretted about when it might happen.[28]

Because their lives were otherwise in turmoil, or because the reality of service in far-distant New South Wales was drawing closer, some young marine officers found that they preferred not to go. Lieutenant

James Morrison was first absent from the Portsmouth barracks without leave in February 1787. When he returned apologetically in March, his commandant interceded successfully with the Admiralty on his behalf. He was reprimanded and his pay restored, and he went on board the *Scarborough*. But then, two weeks later, he disappeared again, and was replaced by Lieutenant Maxwell.[29]

Lieutenant Ralph Clark might well have done the same. As the time to departure shortened, he grew increasingly anxious about the coming long separation from his wife. Repeatedly, and against the advice of his friends, he implored the authorities for permission to take her and their son with him, even offering to pay the cost himself. It was to no avail. Phillip clarified the situation with the Home Office, and told him firmly, No. He asked a second time, to get the same answer. He asked Lord Howe, again to be told, No. Then, he asked for ten days' leave to see his family at Plymouth. Phillip told him he should have applied via Ross, but that in any case the answer would have been No, as they were soon to sail.[30]

Clark's discontent continued. He was appalled by the coarse and violent behaviour of some of the convict women during the voyage. In June, when four whom he had put in irons for fighting were released, he commented: 'there was never three great[er] whores living than they are, the four of them that went through the bulkhead while we lay at the Mother Bank. I am convinced they will not be long out of them, they are a disgrace to their whole sex, bitches that they are. I wish all the women were out of the ship.' When the women were put into another ship at Cape Town to make way for sheep, he thought that these would prove more congenial companions. During the voyage to the colony and once he was there, he dreamed repeatedly of sexual congress with his 'beloved' Betsey Alicia.[31] Mind you, these sentiments did not prevent him from taking a convict woman as his mistress.

There was also tension between the marines and sailors in the *Alexander*. When Ross asked for the marines' accommodation to be changed in a way that would have disadvantaged the crew, the sailors promptly said they would not go.[32]

At Portsmouth, all the ordinary marines grew most disgruntled when they learned that they would not be given spirits in New South Wales. There were two reasons for their unhappiness. The first was that they felt betrayed. In his initial advice to the Admiralty, Sydney had stated that they would be 'properly victualled by a commissary immediately after their landing', and the Admiralty Secretary had repeated this when he wrote to the recruiting officers at the barracks at Portsmouth and Plymouth. So too did Major Ross.[33] To the ordinary troops, being 'properly victualled by a commissary' meant that they would be supplied with spirits, or at least with wine, as per established practice. The second reason for their unhappiness was that they realized that while they would not have 'this principal necessary of life' in the colony, their brothers-in-arms on the *Sirius* and *Supply* would, since those marines would continue in sea service.

From early April, the marines on the transports petitioned their officers to change the situation. The *Alexander*'s detachment felt themselves 'much injured'. They were committed to using 'their utmost endeavours in defending the just rights of their King and country'; however, in view of the hardship being imposed on them, they – all of them volunteers – would prefer not to go. Those on the *Prince of Wales* pleaded, 'as the allowance of liquor is a great support to nature it will be an utter disappointment to the whole detachment as we all embarked with the idea that we should have been victualled as on board any of His Majesty's ships'. Those on the *Scarborough* held that a 'moderate distribution' of spirituous liquor or wine was 'indispensably requisite for the preservation of our lives, which change of climate and the extreme fatigue we shall be necessarily exposed to may probably endanger'. 'In the most respectful and dutiful manner', those on board the *Charlotte* pointed out the hardships 'which being thus deprived of our grog will subject us to from our being placed on an island where nothing of the kind can by any other means be procured, and the necessity of it to soldiers whose duty will be active and unremitting; … besides which we believe it is extended to all garrisons abroad'. Ross and Phillip took up the matter again with the Admiralty and the Home Office.[34]

Before this, however, Middleton and Sydney had discussed the situation, and decided to give way. Just before the ships sailed, the London officials told Phillip and Ross that Phillip had approval to purchase *en route* 'such a quantity of spirits and wine for [the marines'] use as he can for £200'. The letters made clear, however, that this indulgence would not be continued after the initial three years.[35] In this ruling, I think, lie the origins of the colony's notorious rum trade of the 1790s.

Finally, there were the convicts. It is difficult now to know what these thought of the business. Many of them were illiterate, and for all they knew about New South Wales they might as well have been going to China or the moon. However, some of them did write to friends on shore. At the end of April, Ross ordered the marine officers to inspect their letters. Tench described this duty as 'not one of the least tiresome and disagreeable'. However, he was also often surprised at the contents. These 'varied according to the dispositions of the writers', he said; 'but their constant language was, an apprehension of the impracticability of returning home, the dread of a sickly passage, and the fearful prospect of a distant and barbarous country'. Tench saw pretence too, however, for he considered that the gloomy sentiments were often 'an artifice to awaken compassion, and call forth relief; the correspondence invariably ending in a petition for money and tobacco'.[36]

*

While these were largely mundane matters, and most of them were slight, the attending to them meant the First Fleet sailed better prepared that it otherwise would have been. However, there were other things of crucial importance to the success of the voyage that were addressed at Portsmouth, which I shall now describe.

9.

Preparing Bodies for the Voyage

HAPPILY, THE VAST MAJORITY of the First Fleet convicts survived the long and arduous voyage. However, it was not inevitable that they should have done so.

We should consider that there were three major phases in the process of ensuring the good health necessary to their doing so: first the Navy Board's laying an adequate basis, by ordering good-quality supplies for the voyage; second, detailed preparations in the months and weeks before departure; and third, the management of the voyage itself. In the event, it was the second of these phases that was the most important, for it was at Portsmouth, as a consequence of the surgeons' agitations and Phillip's insistence, that the colonists' health was raised to a different level. These Portsmouth preparations had a number of facets, some specific, others more general.

Clothing the women
The fact that a full supply of women's clothing was not loaded has become a notorious sign of the supposed general negligence that afflicted the First Fleet. In addition to Manning Clark's lurid, unhistorical description of the women lolling semi-naked on the decks of the transports (discussed in the Introduction), there is Shaw's catalogue of woes: 'there were ... not enough clothing, no anti-scorbutics, insufficient surgical supplies ... Perhaps no more can be deduced from this than that

the government was rather inefficient and did not seriously consider the needs of a new settlement, penal or otherwise'. Mackay, Hughes and Hill each highlighted how Phillip complained. Mackay: 'In the course of the preparations, Phillip had cause to complain about the inadequacy of the medical supplies, agricultural implements, ordnance stores, victualling (particularly the meat, bread and flour), the convicts' clothing, the anti-scorbutics and the wine'. Hughes: 'The pale, ragged, lousy prisoners, thin as wading birds from their jail diet, were herded on board and spent the next several months below; orders forbade them to exercise on deck until the flotilla was out of sight of land. The condition of the women provoked Phillip to a furious outburst: "The situation in which the magistrates sent the women on board … stamps them with infamy – tho' almost naked, and so very filthy …"'. Hill: 'When the Fleet eventually sailed from Portsmouth … it left without enough clothing for the women'.[1]

What we have in these writers' accounts is a history only of the illness, not of its cure. None of them recognized that Phillip was complaining (as he put it) about 'evils [that] may be redressed', nor acknowledged that (with one partial exception), this was in fact done. Let us see what the real story was.

In the first place, this shortage in the supply of women's clothing arose because of the acute need to clothe the female convicts sent from Newgate and Southwark jails in the depth of winter. It was to these that Phillip referred when he indignantly said, 'the situation in which the magistrates sent the women on board the *Lady Penrhyn* stamps them [i.e., the magistrates] with infamy – though almost naked, and so very filthy, that nothing but clothing them could have prevented them from perishing, and which could not be done in time to prevent a fever, that is still on board that ship'.[2] In order to succour these women immediately, the ships' agent and surgeon drew on the slop clothing supplied for life in the colony.

In the second place, the shortage arose because the number of women was doubled. The Navy Board did order extra supplies of clothing in December, which were put into the *Prince of Wales* for transshipment to Portsmouth.[3] Before these arrived, however, on 20 January the Navy Board directed Shortland to send

> a list of the convict women on board the *Lady Penrhyn* without loss of time and to demand of the storekeeper at Portsmouth the beds and slops that are to be left there by Gustavus Vasa, to replace what may be ordered to be issued here, reporting to us if there is any deficiency that it may be provided for and sent in the *Prince of Wales*, observing that he is not to make any difficulty in supply[ing] the women with men's clothing if there is not a sufficiency for the women.[4]

This expedient was evidently a temporary one, for on 14 March Shortland asked the Navy Board that the deficiencies be 'made up', and the Board ordered that this be done. But then, the problem was exacerbated by the arrival of the *Charlotte* and *Friendship* from Plymouth with more women – as Phillip told Nepean on 18 March,

> the giving clothes to those convicts who have been embarked at Plymouth is so very necessary that I have ordered it to be done, and presume the Navy Board will replace the clothing, but as there are more convicts to be sent on board the different ships, unless orders are given for their being washed and clothed on their leaving the prison or the hulks, all that we may do will be to no purpose.

These new arrivals were clothed too, but by once more drawing on the supplies that had been ordered for issue in the colony – as Nepean subsequently told Middleton,

> I find from Captain Phillip that some of the convicts are almost destitute of clothing, and that it will be necessary to supply them with such articles as are needful immediately. Captain Hunter and Lieutenant Shortland have been desired to inquire into their wants and to supply them, and Lord Sydney will be glad if the quantity which they may issue out of the general stock be replaced.[5]

Shortland continued to issue these women with clothing from the 'general stock' into April, but this stock was also evidently insufficient. The Board authorized further purchases on 20 April, which either did not happen or were again insufficient.[6] When Shortland and Phillip pointed this out to the officials in London, the Treasury authorized the Navy Board to purchase additional quantities on 10 May. The next day, the Board sent a directive for this to be done at Portsmouth, but the authority did not reach Phillip before he sailed. Simultaneously, the Board asked six London contractors to send supplies to Portsmouth 'with the greatest despatch possible', only to have to cancel these requests three days later on receiving news that the ships had sailed.[7] It may be that we are justified in finding some inefficiency here, but given the many arrangements necessary to send the ships off, it is hardly surprising that there should have been some mistakes. In any case, what is the more significant is that the shortage arose not from a callous disregard of, but from a humane concern for, the women's welfare; and that it was progressively, if not completely, redressed.

Containing illness

'Jail fever' or 'jail distemper' was an ever-present reality where the convicts were concerned. This was a blanket term for either typhus or typhoid fever, which were undifferentiated at the time. Its prevalence arose from the exceptionally poor conditions of the prisons; and it was frequently brought into the hulks by infected persons arriving from metropolitan and country jails.

Consider the following collection of observations on the conditions of English jails made by the reformer John Howard in the 1770s and 1780s. During his extended tours, Howard found that, often, prisoners were kept in small, dark, dank and very unhygienic conditions, without beds, or even straw; without water or toilet facilities; without infirmaries; and usually without adequate food. In 1773, eleven prisoners in the Oxford jail died of smallpox, and the illness continued for the next two years, with five dying of it in mid-1775. Howard commented: 'No infirmary: no bath: no straw: the prisoners lie in their clothes on mats.

The men's dungeon swarms with vermin'. The keeper of the Petworth Bridewell told him in 1774 that 'all his prisoners upon discharge, were much weakened by the close confinement, and small allowance [of food]'; and in January 1776 three men died there of privation. In the spring of 1779 at Cambridge he found seventeen women confined in a room about 6 metres square, which had no fireplace or sewer. 'This made it extremely offensive, and occasioned a fever or sickness among them ... Two or three died within a few days'. At Maidstone Bridewell, he saw 'two prisoners with the smallpox, lying on loose straw, and their only covering was common mats'. At St George's Fields, Southwark, he found 'several sick on the floors: the county allows no bedding nor straw ... A woman sick on the floor. The rooms were dirty: in two or three of them were fowls'. In January 1783 at the Clerkenwell Bridewell in London, he saw in the male infirmary five sick and one dying, 'with little or no covering. In another room one was dead. In the women's sick ward twelve were lying in the clothes on the barrack-bedstead and floor, without any bedding.' When he visited the New Jail in Southwark in October 1783, he found many prisoners 'sick on the dirty floors; one of the turnkeys had lately died of a fever'. Howard explained, 'I had seen on board the hulks a few days before, several sickly objects, who told me they had lately come from this and other jails; which, by the looks of those convicts, I was persuaded must be in a bad state'.[8] It was from the Southwark jail that some women went to the *Lady Penrhyn*.

There was illness on two of the First Fleet transports during embarkation. The surgeons seem to have controlled the fever on the *Lady Penrhyn* quickly but that and the 'fluxes' (dysentry or cholera) that swept through the marines and convicts on board the *Alexander* were a good deal more virulent. These appeared in January and February, while the ship was still in the Downs. After reaching Portsmouth, it was evacuated, cleaned with vinegar, and 'smoked' (dried out). By the end of April, when the infections were at last contained, eleven convicts and an unknown number of marines and sailors had died. (The uncertainty arises because many sick marines were taken on shore and replaced by new recruits.) But at least the ships sailed free of infection.[9]

The scourge of scurvy

Until the end of the eighteenth century, scurvy was the bane of those undertaking long voyages. Resulting from a deficiency of vitamin C, in its extreme state scurvy caused dizziness, swelling of limbs and gums, loose teeth, foetid breath, haemorrhages (ulcers and old wounds re-opening) and loss of energy; death followed the emergence of these symptoms within days, or even hours. Modern clinical studies have established that, without any replenishment, the body loses its store of vitamin C in sixty-eight to ninety days; and that labour in wet and cold conditions, lack of hygiene, and high intakes of salt and alcohol increase the rate of loss.

It is now also known that a very small daily intake of 15–28 milligrams of vitamin C is sufficient to maintain health – hence the seemingly miraculous recovery of scurvy patients once put ashore and given a diet of fresh food, including fruits and vegetables. Take the case of the crew of the *Sirius* as it sailed to Cape Town at the end of 1788:

> Going round the Horn this passage, the ship's company was taken with the scurvy till we had but thirteen in the watch with the carpenter's crew. I was carried below three times in one night, but I done my duty the next day. Some died in sight of the Cape of Good Hope, or Table Bay … The doctor went to town and brought a quantity of fruit on board to be served out to both sick and well, for even those that were doing their duty, when biting an apple, pear, or peach, the blood would run out of our mouth from our gums with the scurvy. The next day we run up to Table Bay and moored ship. By Captain Hunter's orders and at the insistance of the doctor, we were supplied with the best of provisions the Cape could afford. Mutton and vegetables was the most suitable for the scurvy, and the captain allowed us to send for as much wine as we thought fit to make use of, the ship's company recovering daily, till we were all well and hearty.[10]

For hundreds of years, scurvy wreaked a fearsome havoc at sea. Naval squadrons leaving England in the first months of the year were particularly prone to epidemics, as the crews had not had the benefit of early spring vegetables (such as brussels sprouts) and summer fruits. So, too, were those whose crews were not in good health in the first place. In 1740 Lord Anson sailed from England with eight ships and 1955 men, many of them old or ill, to attack the Spanish settlements on the west coasts of the Americas. By the time the squadron entered the Pacific, there had been hundreds of deaths from malaria, dysentery and scurvy. In all, 1415 of the original complements died, 997 of them of scurvy.[11] In 1780, after a six weeks' cruise, there were 2400 cases of scurvy among the crews of the Channel squadron.

The true cause of scurvy remained unknown until the turn of the twentieth century, when vitamins were identified and their dietary roles established. Before this, some far-fetched theories of its causes were entertained, including that of foul air in the holds of ships. However, experienced naval commanders knew that scurvy appeared during prolonged voyages when people fed on salt provisions; that it was important that people should keep themselves clean and their clothing and bedding dry; that they should have fresh air and exercise regularly; that they should be provided with anti-scorbutics; and that they should revert to a diet of fresh foods wherever possible.

Some astute people understood more. In 1593, for example, Sir John Hawkins praised the efficacy of oranges and lemons in curing the disease: 'This is a wonderful secret of the power and wisdom of God, that hath hidden so great and unknown virtue in this fruit, to be a certain remedy for this infirmity.'[12] Indeed, in 1747, in a clinical experiment, the naval surgeon James Lind proved conclusively the value of these citrus fruits; but the official view lost sight of this knowledge for fifty years, partly as a consequence of James Cook's unfortunate preference for sauerkraut and wort of malt. Despite this lack of official recognition, there is evidence that belief in the virtue of citrus fruits continued amongst those experienced in long voyages. When he showed signs of scurvy on the *Endeavour* voyage, for example, Joseph Banks drank some of the lemon juice he had brought with him.[13]

Like most naval officers, Arthur Phillip had had first-hand experience of scurvy. As a boy, he had sailed on the squadron which Admiral Byng had taken out from Portsmouth on 6 April 1756, some of whose sailors were afflicted by the time it reached Gibraltar in early May. Later, he had commanded a ship in the squadron of twelve which Sir Richard King took out from Madras on 2 October 1783. When they reached the Cape of Good Hope on 9 December, they had 1800 cases of scurvy, and many more sailors had died on the passage. And if the story of Phillip's having taken 400 Portuguese convicts to Brazil is true, he had additional close experience of the disease.

So Phillip knew only too well the danger that scurvy would pose during the First Fleet's voyage. When he drew up his memorandum concerning the colony at the beginning of October 1786, he noted that 'sickness must be the consequence in so long a voyage' and that 'scurvy must make a great ravage amongst people naturally indolent and not cleanly'. As he had become aware of how the Navy Board officials were treating the voyage as one to America rather than to 'the extremity of the globe', his apprehension increased. He feared, he told Sydney in mid-March, 'that it may be said hereafter the officer who took charge of the expedition should have known that it was more than probable he [would lose] half the garrison and convicts, crowded and victualled in such a manner for so long a voyage'.[14]

Given what we now know about the etiology of scurvy, the underlying health of the colonists as the ships gathered at Portsmouth becomes a pertinent question. Since they were fed the usual naval rations and had medical care, the crews of the *Sirius* and *Supply* would probably have been in reasonable health but, given the season, their bodily stores of vitamins would likely have been at lower levels than modern science recommends. The situation of the marines would have been similar, though perhaps not quite so good. That of the convicts who came from the Thames hulks may have been, if anything, somewhat superior to that of the marines, for these had been required to wash, they had had medical attention, and they had been adequately clothed and fed. The situation of those convicts from the country jails who gathered at Plymouth and in London, and that of those who went directly to Portsmouth, was manifestly the worst of all, for these had been poorly clothed, were ill-fed, and had had little or no medical care. It was no doubt these whom Collins had in mind when he recorded that many convicts 'were embarked in a very sickly state' (where 'embarked' means when they were put aboard the ships, not when they sailed).[15]

As the ships were assembling at Portsmouth, Phillip and his officers campaigned to improve the health of all. William Balmain, the *Alexander*'s surgeon, was convinced that serving fresh food was an essential measure if the illness on that ship was to be contained, as he told Shortland on 17 February:

> As some of the marines are much impaired in health from fever and a number of the convicts severely afflicted with fluxes, I think it my duty to acquaint you that I am of opinion if an allowance of fresh provision (from which broth and other nutritious aliment might be extracted) could be procured in the room of salt it would greatly assist in restoring the sick to health and strength, and if during our stay in England fresh food could be conveniently got for the whole it might in a great measure prevent the growth of disease. A small quantity of wine would also be a powerful restorative to the sick.

Shortland passed this request to the Navy Board, which sought the Treasury's opinion, which replied (no doubt after consulting the Home Office) that it should be acceded to. Accordingly, the Board told Richards that he was to provide fresh meat. It told Shortland that he was to see 'that no more is provided for than the surgeons think actually necessary'; and that in any case he was to limit expenditure on fresh provisions to 1s per person per day.[16]

The difficult point here was that the Navy Board had long since concluded with Richards a contract for feeding the convicts and marines that did not include fresh provisions. Any alteration to it would constitute an additional charge, not against the contractor but against the government, so that the Treasury's approval was needed. At the end of the month, Phillip increased the pressure for this, when he asked Sydney 'that orders may be given for the supplying both marines and convicts with fresh meat and vegetables while they remain at Spithead, and that a small quantity of wine may be allowed for the sick'. Warning that the surgeons attending the marines and convicts were 'decidedly of opinion that unless they are supplied with fresh meat, vegetables and other refreshments a great mortality amongst them may be expected', Nepean passed on this request to Middleton on the same day, who replied: 'In consequence of a letter lately received from the Treasury, the contractor proceeded to Portsmouth on Saturday to furnish the sick with fresh provisions and vegetables, and which may be extended to the convicts and marines in general if an order is sent from the Treasury for that purpose.'[17]

There clearly was some delay in the Home Office's arranging this, for on 6 March the Navy Board told Shortland that 'we have no directions to allow fresh provisions etc. to any but the sick convicts and marines'.[18] Phillip pressed the point again on 18 March, stating that 'fresh meat for all the convicts and wine for the sick I was informed had been ordered in consequence of the representation I made as soon as the ships got round to Portsmouth, *but the sick only* have fresh meat'. Now he had his way. On 21 March the Navy Board told Richards 'to cause all the marines and convicts to be victualled with fresh provisions on the same terms already fixed on for the sick during their continuance at Portsmouth, and with wine for the sick according to the discretion of the surgeons, and to provide 1 ton weight of essence of malt'. Thereafter, Tench says, fresh foods were given 'indiscriminately' to the marines and convicts, well and sick.[19]

Preparing for illness on the voyage

For Phillip, a larger issue underlay that of feeding the people with fresh foods while they were at Portsmouth, important as this undoubtedly was.

There is no question but that in the beginning the Navy Board officials and the contractor did not conceptualize the voyage adequately. As Middleton told Nepean at the end of February 1787,

> the Navy Board, in contracting for the victualling of the convicts
> on their passage, have observed the same rule that has been always

followed with soldiers on board of transports – that is, 2/3rds of what is allowed to the troops serving in the West Indies, spirits excepted.[20]

Although it is yet to be found, ancillary correspondence makes clear that the contract which the Board concluded with William Richards on 12 September was indeed drawn up according to this model.

Middleton defended this decision on the ground that since they would not have the opportunity of much exercise during the passage, the convicts did not need more food. From Middleton's perspective, this may have been a justifiable view. As well, however, the model allowed rice to be substituted for the flour usual in the Royal Navy ration, and did not provide for either anti-scorbutics or 'necessaries' for the sick. A naval officer experienced in very long voyages, one aware of the health record on Anson's 1740–44 circumnavigation, of Lind's subsequent clinical trial and of Cook's regimen, might only see the model's limitation – as Phillip told Sydney:

> I have repeatedly pointed out the consequences that must be expected from the men being crowded on board such small ships, and from victualling the marines according to the contract, which allows no flour, as is customary in the Navy. This must be fatal to many, and the more so as no anti-scorbutics are allowed on board the transports for either marine or convict. In fact, my Lord, the garrison and convicts are sent to the extremity of the globe as they would be sent to America – a six-weeks' passage.[21]

It is important to note here that Phillip's complaint was not that not enough food was being provided, but rather that certain items needed for a very long voyage were not – i.e., that the voyage needed to be conceptualized as one of eight months, during which scurvy would inevitably appear, rather than one of six weeks, when it perhaps would not.

Since he was convinced that 'if salt meat is issued, without any proportion of flour – the scurvy must prove fatal to the greatest part' of the marines and convicts, Phillip pursued the matter for a number of months, asking for the rations to be altered, and also that he be able to provide fresh provisions for all when in port *en route*. Initially, the Admiralty told him that it could give him no directions on these points, and the Navy Board told him that it could not agree to alterations to the contract, as to do so would increase the cost of the voyage.[22]

Phillip turned to the Home Office, asking Sydney 'whether it may not be advisable to make some alteration in the provisions, by allowing the marines *a proportion of flour* in lieu of a certain proportion of salt meat; and some addition to the provisions served to the convicts: at present a convict has only, for forty-two days, 16 lbs of bread'. He added: 'The contractor's having a power of substituting a 1/2 lb of rice in lieu of 1 lb of flour will be very severely felt by the convicts'. When Nepean referred these requests on, Middleton gave a little ground, telling Nepean that 'if flour is preferred to rice, Captain Phillip may direct a preference on the passage, and repay it out of the storeships on their arrival'. However, at the same time he cautioned that 'the substitute of rice for flour is agreeable to the army contract, and so paid by the Treasury'.[23]

Phillip wanted still greater latitude. Pointing out that 'the contracts for the garrison and convicts were made before I ever saw the Navy Board on this business', he asked again for those things the army-type contract lacked – flour, anti-scorbutics and fresh foods *en route*. The Board explained wearily to him on 25 April that

> not having received any orders from the Treasury to direct the contractor to purchase fresh meat etc. for the marines and convicts at such places as the ships may stop at, or wine and spirits for the marines and officers of the garrison so long as they shall be victualled by him, we have not given him any directions thereon;

that

> it was consented to that the contractor might make such alteration in the provisions as Captain Phillip desired, provided the expense

> should not be increased to the public, but we have no authority to make any alteration that would require additional tonnage without orders from the Treasury;

and that

> his apprehensions of the consequence that may attend the not allowing the usual quantity of flour and not allowing more bread instead of salt provisions for the convicts will be more properly represented to the Treasury, as the ration provided is in consequence of their orders and therefore we conclude has been properly considered.[24]

Even as the Navy Board restated this position, however, it was being subverted, for on this same day (25 April) the Privy Council issued Phillip's instructions, which included an authority to purchase provisions *en route*; and Nepean wrote to William Richards concerning this need. Before he sailed, Phillip took on board quantities of 'good, though coarse' bread for the convicts.[25]

Purser's and surgeon's necessaries

Other deficiencies were remedied while the ships were at Portsmouth. In the late eighteenth century, two classes of 'necessaries' were carried on Royal Navy ships – 'purser's necessaries', including the (supposed) anti-scorbutics, sauerkraut and wort of malt; and 'surgeon's necessaries', small foodstuffs for the sick, which, as explained in Chapter 6, included almonds, barley, currants, garlic, mace and nutmeg, rice, sago, shallots, sugar and tamarinds. Oatmeal, for making gruel, was sometimes included under the one heading, sometimes under the other.[26]

The nature of the Navy Board's contract with William Richards meant that these items had also not been supplied for the marines and convicts for the voyage. On 7 February, John White told Phillip of this. Pointing out that these people were 'equally subject to the diseases incident to men embarked on board the King's ships', he asked that these items be provided 'in the usual manner of the Navy'. Phillip told Nepean and Stephens, with the latter telling the Navy Board on 10 February. The Board instructed its commissioners at Portsmouth and Plymouth to 'cause such a quantity to be put on board – as shall be a proper proportion for the number of marines and convicts on board each ship during the passage'. It turned out that there were insufficient stocks on hand at these ports, so on 28 February the Board asked George Cawthorne to supply 'necessaries for the number of marines and convicts embarked on board each transport in the same proportion as for the King's ships for six months'. On 12 March, following a request from White, now at Plymouth, the Navy Board ordered necessaries for the *Charlotte* and *Friendship* to be sent from London to Portsmouth, the ships' next destination.[27]

Phillip continued to pursue this business. Pointing out that it was his 'duty to repeat complaints *that may be redressed*', on 18 March he asked for wine for the sick, among other things. The Navy Board ordered two pipes the next day, along with 1 ton of essence of malt for distribution among the transport ships.[28]

At the beginning of April, as the time till departure shortened, White asked for the supplies of necessaries to be completed to eight months, the expected duration of the voyage. The Navy Board minuted that 'the deficiency may be sent on board a few days before they sail', and asked Cawthorne to make up quantities 'to the period that the other species of provisions are'. A week later, Phillip asked for more portable soup and sauerkraut. Another week on, Nepean asked for casks of oatmeal to be put on board to make gruel for the sick, which were to be considered 'as surgeon's necessaries'. The Navy Board ordered two casks for each ship. Then, on 23 April, White asked for another pipe of wine, which was supplied. The additional supplies of necessaries reached Portsmouth on 10 May, and were loaded onto the ships.[29]

The surgeon of the *Lady Penrhyn* recorded receiving 1 lb almonds, 6 lbs currants, 40 lbs (moist) sugar, 6 lbs sage, 100 lbs 'fine' rice, a 'large quantity' of French barley and smaller quantities of mace and cinnamon, 'some portable soup, tea, lump sugar', two kegs of 'fine essence of malt', and 10 gallons of 'red port wine'. We may assume that these quantities are indicative of what all the transport ships received.[30]

A hospital ship

Arthur Phillip also knew that if there were epidemics during the course of the voyage, he would need to isolate the sick – as David Collins observed, 'prior to our departure it was generally conjectured, that before we should have been a month at sea one of the transports would have been converted into a hospital ship'.[31] Accordingly, Phillip asked for permission to use a ship for this purpose, which the Navy Board gave. When the illness spread in the *Alexander* at Portsmouth, he thought to convert the *Friendship*, but the need abated, and never arose again.[32]

*

In April 1787, in its usual dismissive fashion, the *Bath Chronicle* observed, 'from the mortality that has already taken place on board the transports, it is supposed that not more than one in five [of the convicts] will survive the voyage'.[33] It's a pity that today's practice of newspapers printing 'Corrections' or 'Retractions' did not exist then. For, against this dire prediction, the voyage of the First Fleet was a striking success. From the time of the ships' leaving England to that of their arrival at Botany Bay, only twenty male and three female convicts and five of their children died. Among the marines and their families there were only three deaths (one man, one woman, one child). This health record speaks for itself; but if we remember Collins's caveat that many of the convicts 'were embarked in a very sickly state', it speaks with even more purpose, and eloquently refutes the charge that the First Fleet colonists were ill-prepared for the voyage to New South Wales.[34]

While the story of the First Fleet's extraordinary health record is told mostly in these mortality figures, it is also told in another way, one that turns on a profound difference between our perceptions of good health and those held by late eighteenth-century people.

In September 1785, when Lieutenant Henry Pemberton extolled the virtues of the southern coast of Africa near the Krome River as a site for a convict settlement, he pointed out how the Dutch settlers in the vicinity 'are remarkably healthy and live to a great age'; and to the women, 'whose prodigious stature and florid complexion announced the most perfect state of health'. In October 1792, from Norfolk Island, Charles Grimes wrote home that 'I have been very ill on the voyage here, and [for] some time prior to my leaving the Cape, but I am now much better and fatter than when I left England'. In September 1802, when Mary Hutchinson married Dorothy Wordsworth's brother William, Dorothy wrote that her sister-in-law 'looked so fat and well that we were made very happy by the sight of her'.[35] To these people, plumpness indicated good health.

So it was on the First Fleet. When the ships reached Rio de Janeiro, Phillip remarked that the convicts were 'much healthier than when we left England'. What he meant was that they were *fatter*. From Cape Town, David Collins wrote home that 'my brother William as well as myself have enjoyed our healths perfectly since we sailed. William is grown so tall and stout withal you would hardly know him'.[36]

Now, it is hardly surprising that the people on the First Fleet should have gained weight during the voyage. It has been estimated that the male convict's preserved ration 'had a daily energy value of between 4000 and 5500 k cals, far in excess of the 3,350 k cals required by the average 65-kilogram man employed on heavy labour'; and when in port, they were given what are to us very large quantities of food – at Rio de Janeiro, for example, 20 ounces (c. 560 grams) of meat daily.[37] They were certainly not burning these calories on the ships, for they were not labouring and had only very limited opportunities to exercise. However, they would not have grown plumper without the basis of good health they were given at Portsmouth.

*

It is true that, at first, the Navy Board's following of established ways was an obstacle to achieving this success; but the more significant point is that in the end, rather than rigidly adhering to these ways, those planning the voyage circumvented or abandoned them. Roger Knight makes the good point that, since the business was undertaken in peacetime, the officials were able to attend to it in a detailed, thorough manner.[38]

Indeed, in the preparations at Portsmouth for the First Fleet's voyage, what we see is a group of officials progressively recognizing that they needed to do things differently from how they were accustomed to if the venture were to succeed. They did – and it did.

As described at the beginning of Chapter 8, traditionalist historians have seen the ships' long sojourn at Portsmouth as yet another sign of the Pitt administration's incompetence. It is certainly true that officials did not manage to send the First Fleet off nearly as quickly as they initially expected. But the delay had a particular benefit, for it enabled Phillip and his surgeons and, indeed, the contractor William Richards too, to prepare the people as well as they knew how to for such a long voyage. Their insistence on clothing the people adequately and on cleanliness; on containing illness; on having ample supplies of anti-scorbutics and necessaries; and on providing fresh foods while they waited to sail meant that the twelve weeks from late February to 12 May were crucial to the success of the voyage, for the colonists left with their illnesses cured and their bodily stores of vitamins replenished.

Rather than continuing to gaze at the mirage of the Pitt administration's callous disregard of the convicts' welfare, we should attend to the real story.

PART FOUR:
THE VOYAGE

10.

Leaving the World

ONCE – DECADES AGO NOW – I boarded a long-haul flight in Melbourne bound for England, in order to continue my research into the British colonization of New South Wales. This particular flight path took us to Bombay, then over southern Iran, Turkey and Europe to London.

As it happened, I had previously walked among the Hittite ruins in Central Anatolia and visited the Persian cities of southern Iran – Isfahan with its great madan and stunning Blue Mosque; Shiraz with its rose gardens; and Persepolis, its austere ruins splendid in the arid air. At Isfahan, I had stayed at a converted caravanserai, where drivers and their camels would rest before beginning the long trek through present Iran, Irak and Turkey to Constantinople. In the old days, this trek would take six months, leaving the beasts – as T.S. Eliot put it memorably – 'galled, sore-footed, refractory', and the men 'wanting their liquor and women'. In my aircraft, we covered the distance in six hours. Of course we did not have to endure the annoyances of land travel through sand and snow and over rocky mountains; but then, neither did we have the experience of olden-time passage across the great earth.

In the early twenty-first century, when we have become accomplished international travellers as a consequence of fast jet aircraft, it is all too easy for us to forget the realities of travel in earlier ages. Then, long sea voyages were no less arduous than land treks – perhaps more so, if for different reasons. Before the mid-nineteenth century, when steel hulls powered by steam engines began to render passages independent of the tyrannies of oceanic winds and currents, and to make voyages much less hazardous to health (because safer and faster), sea travellers often had a very hard time of it. The tedium of voyages was legendary, the mortality from scurvy terrible.

In the early decades of the fifteenth century, Prince Henry of Portugal ('the Navigator') sent ships from Portugal to reconnoitre the islands in the Atlantic Ocean and the western coasts of Africa. In 1488, Bartolomeu Dias reached the Cape of Good Hope, thus showing there was a sea route to India; and in 1498 Vasco da Gama rounded it to reach India. In 1500, sailing further west than these predecessors, Cabral discovered Brazil on his way to the East.

These voyages established the basic routes that Europeans pursued for three centuries in their quest for the eastern spices, cloths and porcelains that they so much desired, and that they had previously been able to obtain only from the Arab traders who had brought them overland by camel train, or by boat up the Red Sea. The routes were determined by the prevailing winds and currents of the Atlantic and Indian oceans. From western Europe, ships would proceed down the Atlantic more or less parallel to the African coast to Madeira, the Canary, Azores and Cape Verde islands; but then they needed to sail south and west towards Brazil, which led to the growth of Rio de Janeiro as an important port of supply.

From Brazil, they made a broad sweep though the southern Atlantic Ocean until, with the winds and currents of the 'Roaring Forties' at their back, they turned east for the Indian Ocean. Once round southern Africa they turned north or northeast for India or the East Indies. Early, the Portuguese established ports of refreshment and supply in Moçambique; later, the Dutch did so at the Cape of Good Hope, and the French at Mauritius. All but one of the major European maritime trading nations established bases in India or the East Indies; and some did also in China and Japan. Spain was the exception. The papal division of the non-European world between Portugal and Spain by the Treaty of Tordesillas in 1493 meant that Spanish navigators were required to approach Asia by rounding South America and crossing the Pacific Ocean, so that Spain's bases were in Argentina, Chile, Peru, on the west coasts of Central America and in the Philippines.

By the 1780s, centuries of voyaging had made these basic routes to and from the East familiar to Europeans, and they naturally provided some analogy for that to New South Wales – hence the appearance of the East India Company's shipping official Charles Coggan before the House of Commons Committee enquiring into transportation in 1785.[1] But this analogy could not be a complete one. Once past the Cape of Good Hope, East India Company ships and Royal Navy warships and transports proceeding to India had well-established routes whose hazards (winds and currents, shoals) were known, and on or adjacent to which were places where ships in need might stop – Madagascar, the Coromo Islands, Mauritius, Ceylon, the coasts of India, the many islands of the East Indies. This was not the case of the First Fleet ships intended for Botany Bay. Once they would leave the Cape of Good Hope, they would head into a largely unknown ocean which offered no places of refreshment until Van Diemen's Land.

In fact, in 1786 there were only three precedents for the voyage of the First Fleet. These were that by Abel Tasman in 1642, when he had sailed west from Batavia to Mauritius, then south and east to Van Diemen's Land, before crossing to New Zealand and returning to Batavia by going north of New Guinea; James Cook's second voyage, when he went from the Cape of Good Hope through the southern Indian Ocean to the south island of New Zealand; and Cook's third voyage, when, after leaving Cape Town, he took the *Resolution* across to New Zealand, and his companion Charles Clarke in the *Discovery* called at Van Diemen's Land on the way to New Zealand. Moreover, a voyage through unknown seas by a discovery ship specially equipped for the purpose, and carrying an appropriate crew, was one thing; that by a group of transports carrying convicts was another.

There are many accounts of the voyage of the First Fleet. I do not intend to deal with it in all its aspects here. Rather, I shall concentrate on the commanders' continuing efforts to make it a success, and to obtain additional items that the colony would need.

Planning the voyage

In planning the voyage of the First Fleet, Arthur Phillip drew not only on accumulated European experience but also on his own deriving from his voyages to Brazil and India.[2]

He saw the ships stopping at Tenerife in the Azores, at the Cape Verde Islands and perhaps at Rio de Janeiro, in order to replenish water, and to obtain fresh foods and certain other items, such as wine. At Cape Town, the ships would take on a large amount of additional supplies, particularly animals. From Cape Town, he would go on ahead, for:

> By arriving at the settlement two or three months before the transports, many and very great advantages would be gained. Huts would be ready to receive those convicts who were sick, and they would find vegetables, or which it may naturally be supposed they will stand in great need, as scurvy must make a great ravage amongst people naturally indolent, and not cleanly. Huts would be ready for the women, the stores would be properly lodged, and defended from the convicts in such a manner as to prevent their making any attempt on them. The cattle and stock would be likewise properly secured; and the ground marked out for the convicts.

He and the lieutenant-governor should go in separate ships; and the goods and animals should also be distributed among the various ships, so that at least part of them would arrive. As he would reach Botany Bay first, he should take with him some of 'the articles of husbandry, stores, corn, seeds, and of the articles for traffic [i.e., trade]'. And he would need to provide the people with fresh foods when in port *en route*, so as to keep them healthy.[3]

So was the basic outline of the voyage fixed. About the beginning of 1787, when officials thought departure was eight to ten weeks off, Evan Nepean wrote:

> The convoy will probably arrive at Tenerife in three weeks, which will bring it to the last week in March or first in April.

The passage from thence to the Cape of Good Hope direct may be about seven weeks at most. But it is imagined that it may be of advantage to touch at Rio de Janeiro, where there is a certainty of obtaining supplies, and which is not to be depended upon at the Cape. The passage will of course be lengthened, and will most likely delay their arrival at the Cape till the latter end of July or the beginning of August.

The passage from the Cape of Good Hope to Botany Bay will most likely be effected in two months, which will bring it up to the latter end of October or beginning of November, the spring of that country.

It will be a winter passage from the Cape to Botany Bay, but if the favourable season was to be preferred, it would occasion a considerable delay and the convoy would arrive at a time when the settlers ought to be employed in gathering their crop.[4]

Nepean's estimate of an eight-months' duration proved accurate, even if, in the event, the Fleet didn't sail until mid-May.

Fuelled by such descriptions as George Worgan's of the failure of the initial plantings of vegetables –

The spots of ground that we have cultivated for gardens, have brought forth most of the seeds that we put in soon after our arrival here … but whether from any unfriendly, deleterious quality of the soil or the season, nothing seems to flourish vigorously long, but they shoot up suddenly after being put into the ground, look green and luxuriant for a little time, blossom early, fructify slowly and weakly, and ripen before they come to their proper size

– it has been one of the most hoary of old chestnuts in the historiography of the Botany Bay colonization that the British were so inept they didn't even know that the seasons were reversed in the Antipodes. Nepean's estimate that the ships would likely arrive at 'the latter end of October or beginning of November, the spring of that country' should immolate this baseless idea forever. The colonists planted vegetables at Sydney in February 1788 because they needed them to cure the sick of scurvy, not because they didn't know that it was autumn in the southern hemisphere. The failure that occurred was only to be expected – as Worgan himself observed, 'this circumstance must be considered, they were sown [at] the very worst season'.[5]

In its various instructions to Phillip, the administration provided for the voyage to proceed as he and Nepean outlined. In those issued on 25 April 1787, he was given permission 'to call with the ships and vessels under your convoy at the island of Tenerife, at the Rio de Janeiro, and also at the Cape of Good Hope, for supplies of water, and other refreshments for the voyage'. He might buy wine at Tenerife; and at any or all of these places, seed grain and 'any number of black cattle, sheep, goats, or hogs which you can procure', and 'any fresh provisions which it may be requisite to procure' for the marines and convicts.[6]

At the beginning of May, Nepean arranged with Middleton that, should the fresh provisions *en route* cost more that the dry ones contracted for, then Richards would be paid the difference.[7] And the Home Office arranged with the Admiralty that, after leaving the Cape of Good Hope, Phillip might, 'if he thinks fit, [proceed] to the said coast of New South Wales in the *Supply* tender, leaving the convoy to be escorted by the *Sirius* to the rendezvous which he may fix upon'.[8]

This is precisely how the voyage went forward. After leaving Portsmouth, Phillip went down the Atlantic Ocean to Tenerife; then crossed southwestwards to Rio de Janeiro, then southeastwards to Cape Town. After Cape Town, he went aboard the *Supply*, and, together with the *Alexander, Friendship* and *Scarborough*, set out ahead of the rest of the convoy for New South Wales. To Phillip's enemies in the First Fleet (for already by this time there were some), this was another example of his wilful incapacity – as the surgeon of the *Lady Penrhyn* wrote: 'Had he conceived the idea, and put it in practice at leaving Rio de Janeiro, it might have succeeded in some measure, but as it was now produced it was a mere abortion of the brain, a whim which struck him at the time'.[9] But all this comment really shows is that, like some of the later historians of the venture, Smyth didn't know what he was talking about. As we have just seen, Phillip's going ahead was envisaged from the first, and was part of the administration's careful planning.

The voyage

All business in London having been effectively concluded, Arthur Phillip reached Portsmouth on 7 May, bringing with him the chronometer and sextant from the Board of Longitude. He gave the chronometer to William Bayly, the astronomer who had sailed with Cook and who was now headmaster of the Portsmouth Naval Academy, to determine its accuracy precisely. This is another sign of the care with which the administration equipped the expedition. The use of the chronometer in navigation was a recent development. On his first voyage, Cook had calculated longitude using direct observation and lunar tables; on the second and third voyages, he used chronometers, which allowed him and his astronomers to determine the difference in time between Greenwich and whatever was their present position. In 1785, the India Board recommended that the East India Company issue chronometers to the officers it was to send to survey the ocean between India and Africa. Now, one was given to Phillip for the First Fleet, and another to Bligh for the breadfruit voyage.[10] These are signs, less immediately obvious than some others, but telling nevertheless, that the administration wanted these expeditions to succeed.

On 10 May, Phillip signalled the ships gathered at the Mother Bank to prepare to put to sea. He paid the crews of the *Sirius* and *Supply* two months' advance on 12 May, and the *Hyaena* arrived, to help guard against any mutiny by the convicts while the transports were within reach of England.

Several new difficulties appeared. Quantities of clothes ordered for the women convicts did not arrive, and the marines did not take on enough musket balls and armourer's tools. And, protesting that their ships' masters had not advanced them wages to purchase goods for the voyage, the crews of the transports declined to put to sea. The lack of the clothing and musket balls did not bother Phillip greatly, for he knew that he might either obtain them at a port *en route*, or that they might follow in the *Bounty* or another ship.[11] But the difficulty with the sailors was another matter, and he spent the day rectifying it.

On 13 May, at daybreak, with the wind from the southeast, the *Sirius* weighed anchor 'and made sail to the westward within the Isle of Wight, in company His Majesty's ship *Hyaena*, armed tender *Supply* with six transports and three storeships under convoy'.[12] At 9 a.m. they passed through the Needles into the English Channel. Forty-eight years old, and a traveller of goodly states and kingdoms and wide oceans, Arthur Phillip was on his way out of the world. So too were the 1200 colonists in his charge.

The voyage began auspiciously. Whereas on the last occasion Phillip had sailed from Europe, winter storms had shattered the squadron in the Bay of Biscay and he had had to proceed alone, now he sailed in 'fine' weather with a 'good breeze' at east southeast.[13] Five hundred kilometres out from Portsmouth, he farewelled the *Hyaena* and headed his ships southwest into the Atlantic.

Sailing down the route that thousands of voyages had made second nature to European navigators, the First Fleet reached for the Canaries. The weather continued good. Preparing for the tasks of colonization, Phillip gathered details of the convicts' 'different trades and occupations'; and with him and his surgeons paying particular attention to diet and hygiene, the general level of health far exceeded expectation. Especially was this true of the convicts. After three weeks, not only were they 'not so sickly as when we sailed', but all the ships were 'remarkably healthy'.[14] And already, in their behaviour, they showed the benefit of a change of circumstance. There was a brief worry with some rogues on the *Scarborough*, but the officers quickly put paid to their intended mutiny. Indeed, Phillip found so little cause for concern that he gave permission for the males to be unfettered, and for all to be allowed above deck at intervals. He reported from Tenerife, 'in general, the convicts have behaved well ... they are quiet and contented'.[15]

The Fleet reached the Canaries in the first days of June. The position of these islands across southerly winds and currents meant that they were ideally situated to be a place of refreshment for ships sailing to the West Indies, South America, Africa and India. After settling them in the fifteenth century, the Spanish colonists had quickly provided for this demand, raising animals and poultry, vegetables and fruit. In time, they also produced goods for the European mainland – first sugar, then wines. By the 1780s, Santa Cruz, the chief town on Tenerife, had become the group's central port, and had a population of more than 6000. To it came a great variety of European goods – beef, pork, butter, fish, candles, wheat, maize, rice, timber, cloths. From it went wines, silk and orchilla.

Having sighted the famous Peak of Tenerife the previous day, the ships reached Santa Cruz on 3 June, and the governor received Phillip helpfully. In the next week, Phillip obtained fresh food, considering this 'absolutely necessary' for the colonists' present and future wellbeing. The marines and their wives received 1 lb of fresh beef per day, together with rice, wine, and what vegetables and fruit were available. The convicts had 3/4 lb of beef and 3/4 lb of bread daily, and vegetables. Phillip also took the opportunity to replenish the ships' supplies of water.[16]

During these days, the officers inspected Santa Cruz and its surrounding districts. They found the town to be 'very irregular and ill-built', but nonetheless to have some 'spacious' and 'convenient' houses; and they were shocked at the 'restless importunity' of the beggars and the brazen behaviour of the prostitutes. Beyond the port and Laguna, the island's capital, they found 'fertile' valleys and 'a romantic pleasant country'.[17] Nevertheless, the First Fleet people did not see the Canaries at their best. Vegetables were scarce, and few fruits were in season. Still, in the solidity of the town's buildings, the fertility of its environs, the production of wines, dye, cotton and silk, and the establishment of a regular government over the mixed population, they saw enough to gain a sense of how a small-scale European colonization might succeed. Tenerife was the first in a series of such experiences during the voyage to prepare them for the business they were about.

Phillip took the ships to sea again on 10 June. A week later, when at the Cape Verde Islands, he decided the voyage was going well enough for him not to need to stop, so he pressed on for Brazil. Despite some tropical heat and storms, the weather continued favourable, and the people's health good. The waters swarmed with fish, with which the colonists supplemented their diet.

When they reached Brazil early in August, they had lost only fifteen convicts and one marine's child; and most of these had been on embarkation 'such objects as could not have been supposed would have lived, had they remained in England'.[18]

The arrival at Rio de Janeiro was something of a homecoming for Phillip, who brought his convoy through the heads with flags flying and cannon sounding. His friend the Marquis of Lavradio was no longer viceroy; but the new ruler, Luis de Vasconcelos e Souza, greeted him as an equal, returning his salute, providing him with accommodation on shore, and ordering the palace guard to receive him formally whenever he landed. Phillip found the soldiers' attention a hindrance to the efficient conduct of his business, and sometimes sought to avoid it by landing where they were not expecting him – which led to the comical sight of desperate soldiers running to meet him and hastily drawing themselves up on parade. Inconvenient as this attention was, Phillip had for the most part to accept it, for he needed the help that went with it. The viceroy made the country's resources freely available; and, in a rare gesture, he permitted the British officers to move without military escort about the city and its environs. This was in sharp contrast to the obstacles that Lavradio had placed in Cook's way in 1769, and it reflected Vasconcelos's awareness of his nation's debt to Phillip.

As I have explained, the basis of the First Fleet colonists' good health was laid during the months at Portsmouth. It was brought to another peak during the stay at Rio de Janeiro. The day after the ships came to anchor, canoes swarmed round them, with the Negro crews selling oranges at two dozen and then four dozen for 6d. And when the officers toured ashore, they found themselves besieged with offers of fresh fruits. Ralph Clark recorded how on one trip into the country, 'we stepped into a grove of oranges when the gentleman asked us if we would walk in and offered us knives and go and eat oranges in the grove. He sent his servant with us to pull them off of the trees for us where we eat as many as we could and stuffed our pockets full and he would take nothing for them.' Smyth recorded of another walk, 'an old gentleman ... seeing us pass his garden, by signs invited us in and treated us in the most friendly manner, insisting upon our eating of every fruit his garden afforded, viz.: oranges of many sorts, sweet and sour lemons, pineapples, bananas, guavas. He also loaded us home with presents of each.'[19] Many of these fruits are very rich in vitamin C: a medium-sized orange contains from 25 to 50 milligrams, a tangerine 31, a persimmon 40, a guava an astonishing 200.

It was not only officers whose health benefited from Rio de Janeiro's bounty. Smyth recorded how on 8 August the *Lady Penrhyn*'s captain 'went early on shore and brought off great plenty of vegetables, fruits, etc. The canoes alongside brought prodigious quantities of oranges of two sorts, one very small, of a dark red colour; very sweet and rich flavoured; and the other remarkable large. The officer of the guard boat brought a bucketful as a present, of the largest I ever saw, which measured a foot in circumference, with the stalks and leaves adhering to them.'[20]

And so too did the convicts benefit. As before, Phillip's concern was the health of all in his charge. Immediately on arrival, he obtained 'great plenty' of vegetables, fruits, and fresh beef; and he saw that all persons continued to have supplies throughout their stay. These foods were cheap, and Phillip ordered very generous allowances – more than 1 1/4 lbs of beef per adult per day; 1 lb of rice; yams, plantains, radishes, cabbages, lettuce and endive; and large quantities of oranges, limes, guavas and bananas. (John Easty recorded serving the marines and convicts on the *Scarborough* ten oranges each on 12 August.) He landed the sick at the Ilha das Cobras; and the fresh air and fresh foods 'soon removed every symptom of the scurvy prevalent among them'. By the time the ships sailed from Rio de Janeiro, the convicts were 'much healthier than when we left England'.[21]

As he attended to immediate needs, Phillip also looked ahead, purchasing items that they would need either during the rest of the voyage or in New South Wales: 115 pipes of rum and 15 of wine; 100 sacks of the bread substitute cassava; 10,000 musket balls.[22] He gathered plants and seeds, too – some rare varieties to send back to Sir Joseph Banks, and others he expected would flourish in New South Wales – fruits, vines, coffee, cocoa, indigo, cotton and some cochineal. David Collins enlarged this list to include coffee (both seed and plant), cocoa (in the nut), cotton (seed), banana (plant), oranges (various sorts, seed and plant), lemon (seed and plant), guava (seed), tamarind, prickly pear plant (with the cochineal on it) and Eugenia or *pomme rose*.[23]

While Phillip forwent the pleasures of the city, the officers, to whom it was unfamiliar, walked about it. Some, like John White and William Dawes, discussed professional matters with their Portuguese counterparts. Others were simply tourists, and wandered to admire the imposing civic square, the towering aqueduct and the churches. Many joined the throngs at the colourful festivals, enjoyed the displays of fireworks, and sought out 'tender' attachments. As those who have travelled since to this romantic city have found, while it offered great contrasts of wealth and poverty, it also offered an abundant sense of life.

To the officers, it was a welcome interlude between tedious wastes of ocean; and it showed them how European colonization might succeed on a grand scale. They might have enjoyed it less, however, had they understood as Phillip did the difficulties that lay ahead.

*

The company refreshed, the ships reprovisioned and bearing more of what the party would need in New South Wales, Phillip sailed from Rio de Janeiro for the Cape of Good Hope on 4 September. The good fortune continued. Despite the weather being rougher than before, there were no serious incidents; and while some were sick with scurvy and dysentery by the time they sighted the Cape on 13 October, in general the expedition remained unusually healthy.

At Cape Town, Phillip followed a similar procedure to that at Rio de Janeiro. He saluted the fort as the ships entered Table Bay and, after the port master had ascertained that the ships carried no contagious illnesses, he paid his compliments to the governor and requested permission to purchase food and livestock. At first, the Dutch authorities restricted the amounts of bread and flour, citing the failure of crops two years before. The Dutch merchants' charging double or treble their usual prices was another annoyance, but as he could not manage without their supplies, there was little Phillip could do about this. He must have found the situation all too familiar; and the difficulties entirely justified his and Nepean's decision that he should first call at Rio de Janeiro, and not sail ahead of the Fleet until they had left Cape Town.

Despite the initial difficulties he encountered, Phillip persisted with his requests, and his persistence paid dividends. After repeated applications and explanations, he received permission to buy most of what he wanted, and the people once more benefited from daily fresh food, with the convicts, 'men, women, and children [having] the same allowance as the troops, except wine' – '1 1/2 lbs of soft bread, and an equal amount of beef or mutton daily' together with 'a liberal allowance of vegetables'. In this circumstance he found it unnecessary to land the few sick, who were 'perfectly re-established in three or four days'.[24] On the face of things, there was little reason for the party not to be confident. The voyage was going well, far better than might reasonably have been expected.

Phillip and some of the officers lodged ashore. As always, he was more concerned with business than pleasure; John White, for example, was moved to speak of his 'sagacity and industrious zeal for the service';[25] but his juniors again looked interestedly about a place that was strange to most of them.

They noticed the township's regularity and neatness, and its avenues of oak. Predictably, they were most struck by the Dutch East India Company's garden, by its fertility, its cool passages and its menagerie, which put a number in mind of St James's Park; and Governor Graaf added to their pleasure by entertaining them at his residence. As it had done in Brazil, the experience suggested they might expect a happy outcome to their own venture. 'The Cape is situated in a fine climate,' one wrote, 'and yields most of the necessaries of life, and some of its luxuries. We have good hopes of Botany Bay, it being in nearly the same latitude.'[26]

But a distinct sobering of outlook also attended their arrival at the Cape; officers' writings from this time reveal a loss of optimism, and the growth of a sense of menace. The Cape colony itself occasioned the first manifestations of this sense. Though prosperous enough, Cape Town was no Rio de Janeiro; however much they enjoyed it, the officers found that the Dutch settlement 'certainly suffer[ed]' in comparison. Here there were no 'picturesque and beautiful' environs 'abounding with the most luxuriant flowers and aromatic shrubs', but rather the forbidding Table Mountain, on whose bleak rocks renegade slaves took refuge.[27] Here there were no taverns for the officers to lodge at, provisions were dear, and the governor was reluctant to allow the British access to them. The regularity with which the township was laid out, and the regulation of its inhabitants' lives bespoke the Calvinism of the Dutch. Here were no exuberant festivals. Here ladies did not let passionate glances slip past enticing veils, throw nosegays from balconies, gather at the gates of convents to encourage assignations, or mingle with the festival crowds to achieve them. Rather, they sat demurely in the middle of austere churches, with the men about the walls so as to surround them. Wearing black, couples married only on Sundays. Slaves moved about the streets in fear, not in celebration.

To some extent, the change in their mood resulted directly from what the British officers saw at the Cape; but there were other causes, one quite practical. Knowing that they were destined for a region 'that does not furnish any of the necessaries of life', Phillip acted to take on as many of these as he possibly could. He shifted persons from one ship to another, crowding them together to make room for the stalls which he filled with animals: 'bulls, cows, horses, mares, colts, sheep, hogs, goats, fowls and other living creatures by pairs'. Hunter said that the government stock consisted of: one stallion, three mares, three colts, two bulls, six cows, forty-four sheep, four goats and twenty-eight pigs; and then there were fowls of all kinds. Phillip spent some £2000 on livestock. Some of the officers also bought stock for the small farms they intended to establish in the colony, but found themselves constrained by the high cost of feed.[28]

Taking advice from the botanist Francis Masson, who was collecting at the Cape of Good Hope for Banks for the second time, and from Colonel Gordon, the commander of the Dutch troops, Phillip likewise gathered 'a vast number of plants, seeds and other garden articles, such as orange, lime, lemon, quince apple, pear tree – in a word, every vegetable production that the Cape afforded'. These also included fig trees, sugarcane, vines, strawberries, oak and myrtle.[29] And the company at large now felt the urgency of the need. 'This is the last port we touch at in our way to the new settlement,' a junior officer wrote, '[and it] has been a time of constant bustle – indeed it is right to take every advantage of it, for the leaving behind of any of the many articles that are requisite, and necessary, would be now irreparable.'[30]

There was a deeper, less tangible cause. Instinctively, the officers knew that when they left the Cape of Good Hope for the southern Indian Ocean they would leave the known world. As Cook had written from the Cape to his old master and friend John Walker in November 1772, 'having nothing new to communicate I should hardly have troubled you with a letter was it not customary for men to take leave of their friends before they go out of the world, for I can hardly think myself in it so long as I am deprived from having any connections with the civilized part of it, and this will soon be my case for two years at least'. Now, those on the First Fleet faced this reality. 'The land behind us was the abode of a civilized people,' David Collins observed as they prepared to sail, 'that before us was the residence of savages. When, if ever, we might again enjoy the commerce of the world, was doubtful and uncertain'.[31]

In this atmosphere, the voyagers clutched at the intangibles of their world. Some of them had received letters just before they sailed, and as the ships moved away from the Cape, they encountered the *Kent* whaler: 'On our first discovering her, as she seemed desirous of joining or speaking to the Fleet, we were in hopes of her being from England, probably to us, or at least that we might get letters by her; but our suspense on these points, a suspense only to be conceived by persons on long voyages, was soon put an end to by hearing she had been so many months out.' The disappointment gave finality to the move from the Cape. 'We weighed anchor,' Tench wrote, 'and soon left far behind every scene of civilization and humanized manners.'[32]

With each ship like 'another Noah's ark', crowded with cattle, sheep, pigs, horses and poultry, and loaded deep with food and extra water for these beasts and the plants, with his own cabin 'like a small green house', Phillip sailed again on 11 November.[33] He did so without Masson, whom some had expected to join the expedition.[34]

Phillip now decided finally to go on ahead. Shifting into the *Supply*, and taking trusted junior officers and some convict artificers with him, he set off with three of the faster sailers. This advance party lost sight of the body of the convoy on 27 November, and proceeded eastward through a 'great number' of black and blue petrels and albatrosses and a 'prodigious quantity of whales', as well as frequent squalls and high seas. On 24 December, for example, the squalls were 'very violent', with 'great quantities of rain, sleet and large hail stones'. Phillip described how the wind was 'seldom more than twenty-four hours in one quarter, veering regularly from the northward to the westward where it seldom stood more than a few hours, ... [and was] seldom to the eastward and then for a few hours only'. Interspersed were days of 'very pleasant and serene weather'. The *Supply* sighted the South Cape of Van Diemen's Land on 3 January, and entered Botany Bay in the afternoon of 18 January 1788, to be followed by the three transports the next day.[35]

Meanwhile, Phillip's departure had increased the psychic dislocation amongst the main party. Hunter, now responsible for seven ships and about 1000 persons, became excessively cautious. Put out by Phillip's not consulting him about his decision to sail ahead, Major Ross grew bitter. The convicts fell back into old patterns of behaviour, and became fractious. In December, the passage grew distinctly worse. The ships wallowed constantly in the great swell, and encountered fogs and gales. So as to preserve the water for the animals and plants, Hunter put the colonists on 3 1/2 pints a day. Illness increased, and there were frequent injuries from the ships' equipment shifting in the gales and seas. As they entered the longitudes of New Holland, the officers pored over the charts deriving from Cook's voyages, so as to know when theirs would end. At Christmas, nostalgia for country and friends half a world away engulfed them.

In this final stage of the voyage, accidents, disease and cold damaged the plants and caused great mortality among the animals, whose food grew short. The master of the *Fishburn* reported that he had lost many sheep and 'three dozen fowls out of four dozen'; that of the *Golden Grove* that he had also lost 'the greatest part of his fowls'; that of the *Prince of Wales* reported that he too had lost 'almost the whole of his fowls'. On the night of 31 December, when the sea was 'mountains high', the chicken coups on the *Lady Penrhyn* 'gave way and came with such violence against the side as to drive the goat house all in pieces and lamed the goat and kid'. Nine days later, there was only one day's supply of hay left on this last ship, and in 'a greater swell than at any other period ... the tubs in the cabin with the banana plants, grape vines etc. broke from their fastenings and were thrown out of the tubs and much hurt'.[36]

Then came those portents the voyagers were longing for. Some of the plants from Rio de Janeiro began to bloom, and on 6 January 1788 they sighted the southern coast of Van Diemen's Land. Cook's charts allowed them to identify their position, and the captains distributed wine. They swung away from land again, but more briefly now they knew, to have a clear run up to their destination. On 19 January, they came upon the coast of New South Wales just south of Botany Bay. The wind was 'fair', the sky 'serene, though a little hazy', the temperature 'delightfully pleasant', the coastline as Cook and Banks had described it. The next day, they entered Botany Bay, to find the ships which had gone ahead.[37]

As the ships of the second division arrived so quickly after him, Phillip was not able to prepare beforehand as he had intended. However, this was the only blemish in an achievement remarkable on a number of counts. To have eleven indifferently-sailing ships follow a route that only Tasman and Cook had previously taken, through 'a long track of ocean ... totally unknown' to their masters,[38] and arrive within two days of each other, was a remarkable feat of navigation, which says much for Phillip's and Hunter's technical competence. To pass such a long voyage without any serious incidents on the ships, too, reflects the alert care with which the commanders supervised the venture. While there were several plots laid on the *Scarborough* and *Alexander,* these were quickly discovered, and the murmers of rebellion easily silenced. When we consider what happened among the shipwrecked people of the *Batavia* 160 years earlier we may see how easily it might have been otherwise.

Collins caught the magnitude of the achievement best:

> Thus, under the blessing of God, was happily completed, in eight months and one week, a voyage which, before it was undertaken, the mind hardly dared venture to contemplate, and on which it was impossible to reflect without some apprehensions as to its termination. ... In the above space of time we had sailed 5021 leagues; had touched at the American and African Continents; and had at last rested within a few days sail of the antipodes of our native country, without meeting any accident in a fleet of eleven sail, nine of which were merchantmen that had never before sailed in that distant and imperfectly explored ocean: and when it is considered, that there was on board a large body of convicts, many of whom were embarked in a very sickly state, we might be deemed peculiarly fortunate, that of the whole number of all descriptions of persons coming to form the new settlement, only thirty-two had died since their leaving England, among whom were to be included one or two deaths by accidents; although previous to our departure it was generally conjectured, that before we should have been a month at sea one of the transports would have been converted into a hospital ship.[39]

This was an extraordinary accomplishment; and it was made possible by the care with which the voyage was planned, the skill of the people who conducted it, and the foods that the colonists were given.

*

Arthur Phillip quickly decided that Botany Bay was not a suitable site for a large settlement and, after investigating the splendid Port Jackson, established the colony about Sydney Cove.

Having unloaded most of the stores and stock, and landed the convicts, on 7 February 1788 Phillip formally established the colony. At ten in the morning he had assembled all the colonists at the marines' parade ground on the west side of the cove. When the convicts had been gathered together and ordered to sit, the marines entered, led by their band and with their colours flying, to form an encircling guard. Phillip stood bare-headed in the centre, in company with his principal officers. David Collins, the deputy judge-advocate, read Phillip's commission and the Letters-Patent establishing the colony's courts. At intervals, the marines fired volleys of muskets and the band played bars of 'God Save the King'.

Empowered as the giver of law and dispenser of mercy, Phillip addressed the convicts – in a 'short speech, extremely well adapted to the people he had to govern', according to one officer who heard it; in a 'mild and humane manner', said another; in an 'excellently adapted speech, accompanied with many judicious exhortations', said a third. From the records of these observers, we can reconstruct a good deal of what Phillip said at this, the colony's formal beginning. He praised those who had behaved well during the voyage, and pointed out how he had been lenient towards those who had not. He was convinced, he said, that there were many fundamentally good persons amongst them, who had succumbed to vice in moments of misfortune, or drunkenness, or under the influence of bad companions. But he also feared that 'there were some men and women among them, so thoroughly abandoned in their wickedness, as to have lost every good principle'. He urged all 'to forget the habits of vice and indolence in which too many of them had hitherto lived; and exhorted them to be honest amongst themselves, obedient to their overseers, and attentive to the several works in which they were about to be employed'. He pointed out that only 200 of the 600 men had done the work in the past days, while the others had 'skulked' in the woods. Henceforth, those who would not work would not eat, for the '*good* men ... should not be slaves for the *bad*'. He forbade the theft and slaughter of the colony's livestock, and assured his audience that all transgressions would be punished with the utmost severity, no matter how 'it might distress his feelings'. He said the sentries would fire on any men trying to enter the women's tents at night, and he urged the convicts to form regular relationships by marrying. He told the convicts that it was 'entirely in their power to atone to their country for the wrongs done at home, that nothing but a new repetition of their former demerits could draw down upon them the severity of those laws of which he was invested with the dispensation'. He would ever be ready, he said, 'to show approbation and encouragement to those who proved themselves worthy of them by good conduct and attention to orders; while on the other hand, such as were determined to act in opposition to propriety, and observe a contrary conduct, would inevitably meet with the punishment which they deserved'. He extolled the humanity of the law which they had transgressed and, citing the absence of temptation in their new situation, pointed out how this offered the opportunity, not only 'to expiate their offences', but also 'to become good, and even opulent men, as many of the first settlers in the western world had been convicts like themselves.' 'Nor,' said he, 'could shame be imputed to such as reformed and became useful members of society.' He concluded by wishing them 'reformation, happiness, and prosperity, in this new country' – and by giving them the day free from labour.[40]

These officers, marines and convicts were European Australia's first colonists, and the new world was all before them.

PART FIVE: THE COST

11.

No Cheaper Mode?

A RECURRING CLAIM IN THE historiography of the Botany Bay decision is that the Pitt administration was seeking an inexpensive solution to a pressing problem. 'The Government of Pitt chose New South Wales as a prison, commodious, conveniently distant, and, it was hoped, cheap', wrote Hancock in 1930. Fifty years later, Mackay said: 'From the moment the decision was announced (and attacks on it began) the planners of the First Fleet, and its commander, were enjoined to economy. Everything was done to reduce the cost of the enterprise. The stores were cheap and shoddy. The equipment level was low.' In arguing that the existence of any other motive for the venture was 'only speculation', Shaw cited Pitt's remarks to the House of Commons in February 1791: '"No cheaper mode of disposing of the convicts could be found"', declared Pitt, 'and that has to be explained by those who urge that other reasons were more important'.[1] *No cheaper mode of disposing of the convicts could be found*? But did the politicians really think that New South Wales would be a cheap solution to the convict problem? On the assumption that this is what Pitt and his advisers believed, the historians have found them sadly wanting. Let us see what the story really is.

In the mid-1780s the administration was paying Campbell approximately £28 per annum to keep a convict on a hulk,[2] and in 1778 the House of Commons Committee had accepted that the value of his labour constituted a return of about one-third of this cost. If the ministers thought that transporting convicts halfway around the globe would cost less than £18 per person, then clearly common sense had deserted them. On the other hand, the ministers were obviously incompetent if, knowing how costly it was likely to prove, they decided to transport convicts to Botany Bay because they simply could not think of another way to dispose of them. As Molony wrote:

> In England some critics thought that the settlement in New South Wales was absurd, impractical and grossly expensive. Half a million pounds had been spent up until the end of 1792, but Pitt was convinced that no cheaper method could be devised of disposing of the Kingdom's worst criminals who, at home, would help to corrupt others.[3]

The business of estimating in detail the cost of carrying convicts to New South Wales began in 1785, with the Beauchamp Committee. Members heard from Charles Coggan, the East India Company's chief shipping official, that it cost £25.2.9 to send a soldier from England to India, when the Company had to meet the expense of the outward section of the voyage only. The Committee also interviewed Duncan Campbell, whom they asked, 'If you were to carry convicts a voyage of probably six months to a place where no kind of trade is carried on, how much per man would you contract for?' Campbell answered that if the ship were of 700 or 800 tons with a crew of seventy to eighty men, and the round voyage of fifteen months duration, then the cost might be £30 per person for 300 convicts, or £40 per person for 200.[4]

In January 1786 Nepean took the question up again. Starting from the idea that the expedition would comprise a 40-gun warship, a tender and two transports, he asked Campbell to estimate the cost of sending out 260 or 270 male convicts per transport, together with surgeons and a guard of thirty marines, and maintaining them for one year in New South Wales. It is worth looking at these estimates in detail.

Nepean: What would be demanded for the conveyance of 260 or 270 male convicts to New South Wales, together with any provisions and stores that the ship can conveniently stow? (The contractors to furnish the convicts with provisions during their passage.)

Campbell: The vessel being hired and fitted for the sole purpose of carrying out the convicts: I apprehend the cost, and charges of wages and provisions during the voyage, less what she may be supposed to sell for on her return, will be the expense of sending out 270 convicts. See the calculation of the expense, which amounts to £50. 8.2 per man.

Nepean: The ship must also be of sufficient size to take about thirty marines as guards. What would be the charge of their victualling to New South Wales, and of the surgeon* and a mate or two*, in addition to the above?

[*Campbell's annotation*: These are provided for in the calculation for the ship's company.]

Campbell: The ship being of a size sufficient for this purpose, the only charge for these will be victualling, which I suppose may be done for 1s per diem each. Government to find water casks.

Nepean: What is supposed to be the annual expense of a year's clothing for a convict?

Campbell: £2.2.0 in a warm climate.

Nepean: Each convict must have a bed and hammock: what is the price of each?

Campbell: Perhaps a better mode than a hammock may be adopted and the expense included in the allowance of 10d per diem mentioned in the calculation.

Nepean: What is it supposed an allowance of beef or pork for one year would amount to for the support of 600 convicts on shore, with a proportion of flour and any other species of provisions that may be requisite for their use in addition thereto, to be sent from this country? NB: In this we suppose that the quantities, whatever they may be, may be sent out in the 40-gun ship, the tender and the two convict ships, so that no freight can be charged.

Campbell: Allowing 4 lbs for six men per day and five days in the week would require 520 barrels [of] beef and pork. Bread and flour, allowing 1 lb of either per day to each man, will require 109,500 lb bread, and also of flour 109,500 lbs. To hold the first will require 240 sugar barrels; and to hold the last will require 291 barrels or sack casks. Allowing 3 pints per mess of six men of peas and barley or oatmeal for their soup on meat and bargoo days, will require as per calculation 10,355 bushels or 217 barrels for every six men. A cheese two days in the week will require 10 tons of cheese. The provisions for the country expenditure for twelve months will amount to £3567.

Nepean: What sort of tools and utensils for building and implements for agriculture are proper for the use of the convicts; and what would the assortment amount to for 600 convicts and the marine guards consisting of three companies?

Campbell: Stores and implements £958

Added to the £3567 allowed for provisions, Campbell noted, this made for a sum of £4525. Concerning his estimate of £50.8.2 for transportation, Campbell pointed out: 'But if this calculation is right government must pay considerably more, because no man can be expected to undertake such a contract but with considerable prospect of gain.' However, he qualified this caution with: 'Should the ship be permitted to take in a load at China for Britain, in that case the contractor might be able to obtain a handsome profit by the voyage, and of course to relax in their terms.'[5]

Sometime about the beginning of August 1786, after T.B. Thompson's unfavourable report concerning Das Voltas Bay had led the administration to concentrate on Botany Bay, officials again pursued the question. An estimate, probably drawn up by the Navy Board, states:[6]

By Mr Campbell's estimate:
The charge of taking the convicts to New South Wales will amount to £50.8.2 per man. But it is to be observed that in forming

this estimate, he includes, 1st, their provision and clothing for eight months; 2nd, the provision for thirty marines during that time at 1s per day; 3rd, the ship to be navigated by seventy men, and their provision charged at £1.15.0 per month, although by the answers from the Admiralty Office it appears that the public expense of victualling seamen and marines amounts but to 10 67/100 d each per day.

This charge may therefore be considerably reduced by government's undertaking to victual the ship's crew, marines and convicts, and by the reducing the ship's crew from seventy to fifty men, for the latter number is equal to the mere purpose of navigating her, and thirty marines joined to the crew will be a sufficient guard.

Upon this foundation the *whole estimate* will stand nearly as follows:

	£
A 40-gun ship, every charge included, per annum	4392
A tender of 200 ton if freighted	1400
The annual pay of two companies of marines	2451
Victualling the same	...
Clothing 600 convicts per annum	1260
Victualling 600 convicts per year, no liquor included*	3567
Annual charge not including the victualling of the marines	13,070
Tools etc., necessary for 600 convicts if bought	1000
Victualling the crew of the convict ships, 100 men for eight months	1117
Freight of 600 convicts at £40 each	24,000
	26,117
Total	39,187

* As the convicts when on shore will be victualled but for one year at most, the annual expense after the first year will be reduced [by] £3567.

Neither Campbell's estimate nor this one contained any provision for a civil establishment. This was added by Nepean in the next calculation in the series, in which he also increased the number of marines to three companies and the amount to be allowed for tools, and included provision for purchasing stock and seeds:[7]

	£
[Annual charge of warship and tender]	5792
Annual pay of three companies of marines (say 180)	3676
Victualling of ditto	2874
Annual clothing [for] 600 convicts	1260
Victualling 600, no liquor allowed	3567
Annual pay of the superintendent	500
	17,669

It is presumed that after the first year one half of the victualling of the marines and convicts may be saved, so that instead of £17,669 per annum it will be reduced to £14,449.10.0; and that the service of the tender after the second year or even the 40-gun ship will not be necessary, so that the expense of the establishment at the end of three years will probably not exceed £7000 per year.

Freight of 600 convicts, including all the expenses of the crew of the two ships which convey them, including their victualling for eight months and the pay and victuals of the crew etc., calculated upon a supposition that the ships may be absent fifteen months, [at] £45 each	27,000
Tools to be purchased	1000
Stock to be purchased and seeds	1300
	46,969

Before his next revision, Nepean estimated the cost of an enlarged staff establishment:[8]

Yearly salary

The naval commander to be appointed governor or superintendent-general	500
The commanding officer of the marines, to be appointed lieutenant-governor or deputy-superintendent	250
The commissary of stores and provisions, for himself and assistants (to be appointed or named by the contractors for the provisions)	200
Pay of a surgeon	182.10.0
Ditto of two mates	182.10.0
Chaplain	182.10.0
	1497.10.00

He then incorporated this figure into an extended estimate:[9]

Annual expense of a ship equal in size to one of 40-gun according to the Navy Board's calculation, supposing no unusual accidents to happen	1500
Annual pay of her officers and men, supposing her crew to consist of eighty	1600
Annual expense of victualling her crew, including the water casks, necessary money, etc.	1292
Annual expense of a tender of 200 tons, including her crew, provisions, etc.	1400
Annual pay of three companies of marines, supposed to consist of 180	3676
Annual expense of victualling them	2874
Annual expense of clothing 600 convicts	1260
Ditto of victualling them, no liquor allowed	3567
Annual pay of superintendent and staff establishment	1500
Total	18,669

It is presumed that after the first year, one half of the expense of victualling the convicts and marines may be saved, so that instead of an annual charge of £18,669 it will be reduced to £15,449.10.0. That after the second year the service of the tender will be unnecessary, and after the third, or possibly the second, the 40-gun ship may return home. So that the annual expense of the whole establishment will probably not exceed £7000 per annum:

Freight of 600 convicts, including all the expenses of the two ships and the victualling of the convicts during their passage, which it is presumed may be about eight months, calculated at £45 per man	27,000
Tools to be purchased and implements for agriculture, etc.	1000
Stock and seeds for the settlement	1300
	29,300

That is, Nepean came to the conclusion that it would cost £48.10.0 to transport a convict to New South Wales, and to equip him for his tasks; and that the cost of maintaining 600 convicts there, a marine guard of 180 men, and a civil establishment would drop from £18,669 to about £7000 per annum over three years, as the colony grew towards self-sufficiency – or roughly £23 per annum per convict. It was on this basis that in August 1786 the Pitt administration found it financially feasible to establish a convict colony at Botany Bay.

*

However, as soon as the administration moved to implement this decision, there began that 'blow out' so familiar in modern government budgets and contracts. One reason for this was that the intricacy of the business of establishing a colony of convicts in a place so far away, where local resources were slender and points of succour remote, only emerged as it was pursued. As it did, the administration increased the quantity of some items and added others. Another reason was that new aspects were added to the scheme – for example, bringing Polynesian women to the settlement, and sending one of the transports to New Zealand for the flax plant, and to the Friendly Islands [Tonga] to obtain breadfruit plants for the West Indies. By December, when, at Pitt's request, Nepean asked Sir Charles Middleton for an estimate of the 'expenses which it is supposed will be incurred under the direction of the Navy Board for the providing of provisions, clothing, implements, etc. for the convicts, and sending them out to Botany Bay, including the expenses incurred for the detachment of marines', Middleton replied with the following figures:[10]

Freight of convicts, no. 750	6734
Freight of provisions	7840
Expenses of extra etc.	460
Provisions [for] convicts for two years	15,758
Victualling convicts and marines in their passage	6169
Slops and beds for convicts	3042
Medicines for garrison	1500
Implements, necessaries, etc.	3000
Agent	220
	44,723

He added: 'NB: If this embarkation is detained so as to prevent the convict ships from reaching China by January 1788, £10,000 more must be added to the freight'.

At this point, Middleton implicitly saw that the remaining period of embarkation and the voyage would constitute twelve months, so that his estimates covered a three-year period. The above figures did not include all the costs, however. To be added were those for:[11]

The Navy ships, the *Sirius* and *Supply*	31,663
The annual pay and clothing of the marine establishment for three years	14,089
The cost of the civil establishment	8632
Ordnance	2435
	56,819

Therefore, on a still very incomplete reckoning, by mid-December 1786 the members of the Pitt administration knew that it was going to cost in the vicinity of £100,000 over a three-year period to establish a colony of 750 convicts in New South Wales, or some £45 per convict per annum – and more if the transports did not obtain a return cargo.

In April 1787, four weeks before the First Fleet sailed, Middleton drew up a more nearly complete account:[12]

Freight of convicts	19,464
Freight of provisions	7840
Provisions for the convicts for two years	15,578
Victualling convicts and marines on the passage	8000
Slops and beds for convicts and medicines for garrison	4600
Implements and necessaries	3000
Agent and extra expenses	700
Expense of *Sirius* and *Supply* tender, including stores, wages, provisions and wear and tear for three years	34,375
Marine establishment, including officers and victualling for two years	12,220
	105,777

Missing from this account are those costs that did not fall within Middleton's purview:

Civil establishment for three years	8632
Ordnance	2435
	11,067

So that, by mid-April 1787, the administration's estimate of the cost of the colony over a three-year period had risen to some £116,000, or to £52 per convict per year.

*

When the final accounts came in, the cost was still higher. According to the returns that Nepean and Middleton prepared for the Treasury in February 1790,[13] over the three-year period from January 1787 to the end of 1789, the costs of the New South Wales venture had variously been:

Preparations in England

Clothing Bedding etc. purchased by the Navy Board for the supply of 680 male and 70[14] female convicts who composed the first embarkation, supposed to be sufficient for their use during the passage to New South Wales and for two years after their arrival	5156
Tools and implements of husbandry, for erecting public edifices, including nails, glass etc.	3056
Medicines, surgeon's instruments, necessaries of different sorts, etc., for the hospitals	1202
Seed grain	286
Handcuffs and irons for securing the convicts	42
Marquees for the governor, the civil and marine officers	389
Old canvas supplied from Portsmouth dockyard for tents, etc. for the convicts, until huts could be erected	69
Portable house for the governor[15]	130
Stationery for the commissary of stores and provisions	20
Provisions for two years for the settlement [1000 rations per year]	16,205
Mr Richards, for provisions supplied the marine guard and convicts from the time of their embarkation to the time of their sailing from Spithead, including a quantity of wine, essence of malt and other necessaries of that nature purchased by him	4705
Fees paid upon Governor Phillip's commission and for that of establishing courts of justice	627
Expenses incurred in conveying convicts from the Old Bailey to Portsmouth to embark on board the transports	84

The Reverend Mr Johnson to enable him to provide necessaries for the voyage	50
Travelling expenses of Captain Norman and other persons charged with despatches from Governor Phillip and other trifling expenses	79
Fees on the above payments	57
Subtotal	32,157

On the Voyage

Mr Richards, for freight of transport ships[16]	40,993
Ditto for provisions etc. supplied the above-mentioned marines and convicts from the time of their sailing to the time of their disembarkation in New South Wales including 2 1/8 per cent discount on Navy bills	7612
Lieutenant Shortland, agent for transports, his pay and disbursements during the passage	881
Commissioner Miller's bills for wine, fresh provisions, etc., purchased at Tenerife	76
Governor Phillip's bills from Rio de Janeiro for supplies	135
Commissioner Miller's bills for fresh provisions, etc., at Rio de Janeiro	2303
Ditto for fresh provisions, cattle and seed and grain purchased at the Cape of Good Hope	1966
Subtotal	53,966

In New South Wales

[Mr Richards] for surplus salt beef provided by him for the supply of the above marines and convicts landed as per agreement in New South Wales, for which he obtained bills upon the Treasury	436
Pay of the artificers belonging to the *Sirius* and *Supply* employed on the public works at Port Jackson, for which bills have been drawn upon the Treasury	172

Flour, grain and surgeon's necessaries purchased by Captain
    Hunter of the *Sirius* at the Cape of Good Hope, to which place
    he was sent by Governor Phillip after the establishment had
    been made at Port Jackson   128
Subtotal   736

To this list we need to add:

Cost of the *Sirius* and *Supply* for three years
    (as per estimate)[17]   39,209
Civil establishment for three years   8632
Marine establishment for three years   14,088
Ordnance   2435
Compensation made to Mr William Richards, Jr, for [the]
    value of the *Friendship*[18] transport, which was scuttled
    and sunk on her passage home   1972
Value of casks, etc. supplied by him to the settlement, and
    for some other articles lost in the *Friendship* transport   350
     66,686
Total   153,545

That is, the cost as the administration knew it in February 1790 of the colony in its first three and a quarter years was £153,544, or £63 per convict per year, so that sending the convicts to New South Wales had cost about 2.25 times what it would have cost to keep them on hulks in the Thames. This ignores the simple benefit of the hulk convicts' labour. If we take this into account but on the other hand assume that, in this early period, there was little equivalent benefit to be had from the labour of the convicts sent to New South Wales, the differential increases still further. The initial cost of maintaining a convict in New South Wales, then, was approximately 2.25 to 3.5 times as great as that of keeping him on a hulk.

These ratios increase sharply when the cost of the *Guardian*'s voyage is taken into some account. Partly because one-quarter of the items ordered for it went on the *Lady Juliana*, and partly because some of the supplies it carried did reach the colony eventually, it is impossible to calculate this cost precisely. However, the sources give us the following partial list:[19]

Expenses attending the equipment of His Majesty's ship *Guardian* employed in carrying out provisions and stores etc.	7710
Expense of victualling twenty-five convicts (artificers) and eight superintendents	209
Pay of her commander and crew, provisions, ordnance, wear and tear	6756
Clothing sent out in the *Lady Juliana* and *Guardian*	3962
Hospital stores ditto	4767
Implements for husbandry etc.	2656
Sundry stores	810
Provisions sent out in the above ships	12,034
Bill drawn by Lt Riou of the *Guardian* for wine purchased at Tenerife	220
	39,124

This calculation does not include Riou's claim that the *Guardian* carried £70,000 worth of food and stores, nor the cost of the wrecked ship. If, however, for the sake of a rough comparison, we say that the *Guardian*'s voyage took the cost of the New South Wales colony between October 1786 and the end of 1789 past £200,000, then the raw cost per convict per year was £82, or between 2.5 and 4.5 times the cost of keeping them at home.

*

Major Robert Ross's contemporary claim that it would have been cheaper to have fed 'the convicts on turtle and venison at the London Tavern', then, was a valid, if caustic, one; or, in Blainey's less emotive assessment, 'the settling of eastern Australia was a startlingly costly solution to the crowded British prisons'.[20] Indeed it was – and the Pitt administration knew this at the time. Why then did the ministers decide to do so?

Because they were incompetent – or because they saw that it would serve a number of purposes?

If in February 1791 Pitt claimed that 'no cheaper mode of disposing of the convicts ... could be found' than to dump them at Botany Bay, then he was either lying or tacitly admitted to massive incompetence – but was this really what he said? Shaw has misrepresented Pitt's speech, the contemporary report of which is:

> Mr *Pitt* said, he had no objection to the motion; on the contrary, he was glad it had been made, because, if reports prevailed that the settlement at Botany Bay was disastrous, and contrary to the purpose intended, it was most desirable that the public should be relieved from the prejudices which such opinions necessarily created, by having the real situation of the colony explained, and stated upon grounds of authority. Government, he said, were convinced that the reverse was the fact, and that there was no reason whatever for any such apprehensions as had been hinted at.
>
> With regard to what the learned gentleman [Sir *Charles Bunbury*] had said, relative to the suspension of the sailing of the vessels now going with convicts abroad, he should betray his trust, as a minister of the Crown, if he were to advise a moment's delay, in despatching those vessels to the place of their destination. What good purpose did the learned gentleman suppose could be answered by it, granting, for the sake of argument, that Botany Bay had proved improper for such a colony? Were the convicts now embarked to be detained till some new place of settlement was explored, and all the first expense again encountered? Or, if it was thought better to distribute them in penitentiary houses, were they to wait until proper houses were erected? In what way were they to be disposed of in the interim?
>
> If Botany Bay was not capable of receiving them, he would freely acknowledge, that ministers were highly reprehensible for sending out so many as were now on the point of going there; but government had no reason to suppose it to be the case. In point of expense, no cheaper mode of disposing of the convicts, he was satisfied, could

be found. The chief expense of the establishment of the colony was already passed and paid. Why, then, were they, unless strong reasons indeed operated to enforce the measure, to begin *de novo*, and make a new colony? And where it could be made to more advantage he was really a stranger.[21]

Rather than to the whole Botany Bay venture, as Shaw supposes, I think these comments refer to the convicts on the Third Fleet ships. That is, what Pitt effectively said was: 'Now that the government has met the initial costs of establishing the colony in New South Wales, no cheaper mode of disposing of convicts sentenced to transportation is to be found.' The wording of the motion put by Bunbury, to which Pitt was responding, confirms this reading: 'That there be laid before this House, an account of the number of convicts which had been shipped from England for New South Wales, *and of the number intended to be sent in the ships now under orders for that service*' (my emphasis).

And if, in February 1791, Pitt was making a specific point about costs, it is inconceivable that he did not also have specific returns on investment in mind when he said that he did not know where else a colony might be founded to more advantage. The report of his speech (which evidently is not a complete one) does not indicate what he then considered these to be. However, we do not have far to look to find them. In February and March 1791 the administration was negotiating with the East India Company to obtain three major trading innovations in the East. As I describe in *Botany Bay: The Real Story*,[22] Pitt, Dundas and Hawkesbury wanted the Southern whalers and the Nootka Sound fur traders to be able to operate without licences; to be able to operate anywhere in the Pacific Ocean east of the latitude of Canton (113°E) – that is, to be able to trade not only among the Pacific Islands and to Korea and Japan, but also to the Philippines, among the Molucca Islands, and along the coasts of New Guinea and New Holland; and, 'when they come into the seas of the East Indies', they wanted them to be considered as 'country' (i.e., local) traders, and to be free to operate accordingly.[23]

No, Pitt evidently did not at this time enlarge publicly on how Britain would benefit from the new colony's being built about splendid Port Jackson, which lay adjacent to one of the only three feasible routes into the Pacific Ocean. But the next year, writing to Phillip in New South Wales, the Prime Minister's confidant Henry Dundas, who had now become Home Secretary, pointed to the advantages 'which must always be derived from a port so capacious and secure as Port Jackson'[24] – advantages which helped to justify the colony's huge cost.

Conclusion

A GREAT DEAL OF VERY poor history has been written about the First Fleet. Clark's comment about the near-naked women convicts 'lolling' on the decks at Portsmouth, and Wilson's about the venal incompetence of the civil servants are on a par, really, for lurid error. Such comments – wilful because unexamined – arise from entrenched assumptions. These writers *know* what the members of the Pitt administration and the departmental officials thought of the convicts and how they dealt with the First Fleet; and they don't need to examine the sources carefully to know what they know. Coming to the questions with their opinions already well-developed, they attend only to those fragments of the very extensive historical record that seem to confirm their prejudices.

The evidence I have presented makes it abundantly clear how wrong such claims are. More invidious – because at first glance less obviously faulty – are the many statements which agree with one hundred years and more of historiography, but which do not take account of the countervailing evidence. I have pointed to some of these statements in the Introduction and the body of this work. Let me now give you two more examples. Mackay claims that 'the despatch of the First Fleet to Botany Bay was a reckless act on the part of a desperate ministry. The intended site for the settlement was insufficiently known; the expedition itself was poorly organized and badly equipped'.[1] But he offers no extended analysis of the third and fourth of these points, which, as this full-length study shows, the historical record simply doesn't support. Neither does he establish any comparisons with similar ventures, which might give some weight to his views. Rather, he simply asserts these views categorically, so as to make his even more sweeping first claim seem unquestionable.

Then, in volume 1 of *The Europeans in Australia*, Alan Atkinson several times states that in 1786-87, as the Pitt administration was mounting the expedition to establish a colony at Botany Bay, officials were not necessarily thinking that there would be a second one. 'To gentlemen in Downing Street it seemed likely to begin with that the First Fleet ... would also be the last to New South Wales', he says; and continues that it was 'doubtful' whether any more convicts might follow this first lot: 'There was no certain vision of a Second Fleet, a Third Fleet and so on indefinitely ... During the months of planning even Captain Phillip once seemed doubtful whether, as he put it, "ships may arrive in Botany Bay in future"'. And again: 'Nowhere was there any boasting about a permanent answer to the problem which had vexed the government and its critics for the last ten years. This was because there was no certainty at all that Botany Bay would be a permanent answer. Though expensive, it was a simple scheme with no clear future'. In her recent book, Emma Christopher has blithely endorsed these views.[2]

The idea that Botany Bay was likely to be a 'one-off' venture has lead traditional historians to various other suppositions. But what evidence is there that this is how ministers and officials were thinking in 1786-87? Atkinson offers only two pieces, which on close examination prove illusory. First, the relevant paragraph makes clear that when Phillip remarked that 'ships may arrive at Botany Bay in future' he meant trading vessels, for he continued: 'On account of the convicts, the orders of the port for no boats landing in particular places, coming on shore and returning to the ships at stated hours, must be strictly enforced.'[3] Atkinson's second supposed piece of evidence is that when the King announced the Botany Bay decision in his speech at the opening of parliament on 23 January 1787, he did not mention any future extension of it. As I showed in Chapter 1, this is an unwarranted construction.[4]

On the other hand, while it is true that there is no explicit statement from August 1786 to this effect, there is abundant evidence from the period 1785–88 that the Pitt administration did intend a new convict colony to be a permanent solution to the convict problem.

First, when he suggested that the convicts be sent to Cape Coast Castle, John Roberts said that 200 might be sent 'annually'. Then, in proposing Lemain Island as an alternative destination, John Barnes and his colleagues stated that, 'after the first year, the island would be of course in a more cultivated state, and would consequently grow more healthy, and a regular succession of convicts might be sent out annually', and that 'in a very few years they would become planters, and take those who might be sent out hereafter into their service'.[5]

And then, there is the overt evidence that the Pitt administration always intended such a colony to endure. First, we have Evan Nepean's statement that, by mid-1786, William Pitt had taken control of the convict business, and that he had decided that they should be used to establish a new settlement south of the equator.[6] As I explain in *Botany Bay: The Real Story*, the only possible context of this decision was the need for a base adjacent to the major shipping routes from Europe to the great world beyond.[7] This was the clear rationale for the administration's interest in Das Voltas Bay, on the southwest coast of Africa, which it had sent a ship to survey the previous September, a rationale that would not be realized if the colony were not a permanent one.

In mid-1786, as they waited for the *Nautilus* to return, the Prime Minister moved to placate two of parliament's most vocal critics of his administration's failure to resume transportation, writing to John Rolle:

> Though I am not at this moment able to state to you the place to which any number of the convicts will be sent, I am able to assure you that measures are taken for procuring the quantity of shipping necessary for conveying above a thousand of them. And I have every reason to suppose that all the steps necessary for the removal of at least that number may be completed in about a month. The plan

may, I am in hopes, afterwards be extended to whatever farther number may be found requisite.

PS: I will beg the favour of you to communicate the contents of this letter to Mr Bastard.[8]

The plan may, I am in hopes, afterwards be extended to whatever farther number may be found requisite! Yes, Pitt wrote this in the expectation that the convict colony would be established at Das Voltas Bay; but if we claim on this ground that the expectation was not then transferred to Botany Bay, we are postulating an abrupt chasm in official thinking, a sudden abandonment of an earlier view, a decision indeed taken in 'a fit of absence of mind'. This did not happen.

Then, there is William Richards's request to Pitt on 28 September 1786, when he had secured the First Fleet contract: 'As the convicts will, I suppose, go out annually, I hope that as I have been the first promoter of this plan of economy in transporting them, you will be kind enough to let this be secured to me in future'.[9]

From the time of his appointment, Arthur Phillip also clearly understood that the administration intended the colony to endure. There are his October 1786 comments that 'as I would not wish convicts to lay the foundations of an empire, I think they should ever remain separated from the garrison, and other settlers that may come from Europe, and not be allowed to mix with them, even after the seven or fourteen years for which they are transported may be expired'; and: 'the laws of this country will of course be introduced in [New] South Wales, and there is one that I would wish to take place from the moment His Majesty's forces take possession of the country – that there can be no slavery in a free land and consequently no slaves'.[10] Then, at the end of October, when he asked to be allowed a commodore's pennant, he told Nepean: 'I shall not, I hope, leave the colony till it is in such a state as to repay government the annual expense, as well as to be of the greatest consequence to this country. In such a state, I presume, it will be in every respect as advantageous to the officer who supercedes me, as the Newfoundland station is.' He repeated this point to Sydney a few days later:

By putting this service on the same footing as the Newfoundland station, the appointment will be adequate to the expenses, which no commanding officers will find so great hereafter, and as there's some *désagrément* thought to attend this particular service, it will then be effectually done away. To me, my Lord, the difference of the appointment is considerable, to the nation it cannot be an object, and still less as I presume, though the rough task is mine, no commanding officer will be sent out hereafter without the honourable distinction I solicit.

In April 1787, in telling Ralph Clark that he might not take his wife with him, Phillip said: 'When the settlement is made I make no doubt but government will provide for the passage of those officers' wives who wish to join the garrison'.[11] These statements contradict the view that in 1786–87 officials expected the colony's existence to be short.

Phillip repeated these sentiments in his early letters home from New South Wales, which, as he had then received no new despatches from England, could only reflect understandings he had been given before sailing. He told Lansdowne: 'Perhaps no country in the world affords less assistance to first settlers. Still, my Lord, I think that perseverance will answer every purpose proposed by government, and that this country will hereafter be a most valuable acquisition to Great Britain from its situation'. To Sydney he wrote: 'The additional force which I presume your Lordship will see it is necessary to send out, [and] a few families and proper people to superintend the convicts, will change the face of this country, a country that from its situation will, I doubt not, be hereafter a valuable acquisition to Great Britain'. And to Middleton: 'The rough survey [of Port Jackson] which I enclose will show that hereafter, when this colony is the seat of empire, there is room for ships of all nations'.[12]

In the mind of its first governor, then, the colony was to be no fly-by-night venture. Numbers of the administrative arrangements made for the colony reflect the same view. There is the Home Office's advice to the Admiralty that, in the first instance, the marines going out to the colony should be volunteers, encouraged to do so either by 'bounty, or promise of discharge should they desire it upon their return, or at the expiration of three years, to be computed from the time of their landing at the new intended settlement should they prefer the remaining in that country'.[13] Then, there are Phillip's comments that he needed to know:

> How far I may permit the seamen and marines of the garrison to cultivate spots of land when the duty of the day is over, and how far I can give them hopes that the grounds they cultivate will be secured to them hereafter; likewise how far I may permit any of the garrison to remain, when they are ordered home in consequence of a relief;

and that he envisaged rewarding well-behaved convicts by allowing them 'to work occasionally on the small lots of land set apart for them, and which they will be put in possession of at the expiration of the time for which they are transported'.[14]

Then, there is Phillip's comment, on a draft of his instructions, that he needed to have 'the tenor by which lands are to be granted, [to be] pointed out by the article which gives me the power of granting lands'; and the inclusion of precise advice in the amended instructions issued on 25 April 1787.[15] Then, there is the way in which, over the next two years, the administration reinforced the governor's ability to grant lands and to emancipate by legislation and through additional instructions.[16]

Now, of course it is true that only in the last of these documents are transportations other than that of the First Fleet alluded to; but together they show that, from the first, the administration intended that the colony should be a permanent one, not one to wither quickly. Why would the officials have gone to so much effort, if they thought that it would soon disappear, or that they would not be sending more criminals to it?

Moreover, with all the replacement women's clothing not having arrived before they sailed, and having learnt that the marines lacked sufficient supplies of ammunition, cartridge paper and sets of armourer's tools, Philip wrote to Sydney and Nepean from Tenerife, asking that these items 'be sent out by the first ship'. He repeated this request from Rio de Janeiro. Phillip understood that the first British ship sent into the Pacific Ocean after those of the First Fleet would be that sent to collect breadfruit (i.e., the *Bounty*). Nonetheless, his use of the term 'first' indicates that he expected more.[17]

The plain fact is that Arthur Phillip left England knowing that other convict voyages would follow. This was because the officials who sent him told him it would be so. Indeed, he had helped them plan for it. In mid-1787, echoing what Nepean had written to Sackville Hamilton the previous October, he had told the Home Office 'it certainly will not be advisable to send out any more convicts till my situation is known, and the strength of the garrison must always be in proportion to the numbers of convicts, *till the garrison is of a certain force*'.[18]

The administration pursued this sensible policy. In December 1787, after Newton Fowell's mother had asked about sending items out to him, Evan Nepean replied:

> There is not the least probability of our sending out to Botany Bay until we receive accounts of Governor Phillip of his arrival and the situation in which he finds matters to be with regard to the inhabitants and the probability of supplying the convicts already sent out.[19]

And in October 1788 Sydney advised the Treasury:

> Not having received any accounts of Governor Phillip's arrival in New South Wales, I am unwilling to recommend the sending any more convicts thither immediately, but if the advices which I imagine I shall shortly receive from him answer my expectations, I shall certainly propose that the female convicts [in Newgate] should be sent to the same place.[20]

Thinking to delay a second embarkation, however, is by no means the same thing as not having one in mind. There were a number of reports

Conclusion

in the press that it was always the government's intention to send out further shipments of convicts. For example, the *Reading Mercury and Oxford Gazette* reported in early November 1786 that 'ships are to proceed annually to Botany Bay with convicts from the several jails in the kingdom'. Then, at the beginning of April 1787, the *Hampshire Chronicle* reported:

> It is the intention of government, as soon as the settlement in Botany Bay is fully formed, and Commodore Phillips has sent home his despatches (which cannot however be expected for twelve months at least from the time of his sailing) to send out two ships every year with convicts for the complete peopling of the colony, and getting rid of a set of people whom this over-cloyed country vomits forth.

Given that, then as now, government and opposition politicians were wont to play out their antagonisms in the press, we should normally be wary of accepting such reports as accurate; but these so closely mirror the advice that Nepean gave Mrs Fowell in December 1787 and Sydney gave the Treasury in 1788 that we may be confident about their accuracy. Atkinson's claims fly in the face of a large body of evidence: the old newspapers knew better than the modern historian.[21]

*

If Atkinson's idea can be refuted on empirical grounds, it can also be denied on logical ones.

From the autumn of 1786 into the spring of 1787, as the First Fleet was mounting, there were several moments when an administration whose fundamental interest lay in getting the convicts out of England quickly and at the least possible cost might have clearly revealed these aims. In late August, the Navy Board advertised for 1500 tons of shipping. By November, the volume contracted for had risen to 2800 tons; and in December, when it had become clear that even this increased total would not accommodate all the people and goods being sent, it engaged another ship, so that the total exceeded 3100 tons. Doubling the tonnage meant doubling the expense of hiring it; but the administration never said: 'Enough is enough. We shall spend no more money. The convicts aren't worth it.'

Next, in March 1787, as the ships waited at Portsmouth, Phillip argued fiercely for fresh foods and more supplies, so that the venture might succeed. He had his way. The fresh foods given to the marines, crews and convicts in March and April, the medicine chests, surgeon's necessaries, anti-scorbutics and wine put on board the ships, the extra clothing and the supplies for the voyage all cost more money. But again the administration spent rather than cut corners.

So was it too with Phillip's request that he be allowed to provide the colonists with fresh foods at the ports *en route*. Once more, the administration accepted the cost of doing so.

Similarly, the administration would have saved significant effort and expense had it provided only a minimal governance structure for the new colony. But it did not; rather, it created an elaborate mechanism of government, one not to be justified for a one-off landing of 1000 people, but one, of course, eminently justified and prudent for a settlement it intended to develop into a fully fledged colony.

And then, when Phillip reported the colony's initial difficulties, the Pitt administration did not decide to abandon it. Rather, it sent out a Royal Navy frigate, the *Guardian*, carrying fifteen agricultural supervisors and twenty-five skilled convicts, and loaded 1003 tons of supplies which cost £70,000. Lieutenant Riou loaded more supplies at the Cape of Good Hope, including seven horses, eighteen cattle, twenty-two sheep, pigs, rabbits and poultry of all kinds. The plants and trees loaded in England and at the Cape numbered 150. The ship was within six weeks of reaching Sydney when it struck an iceberg.[22]

By the end of 1789, the colony had cost something over £250,000, or over £100 per convict per annum. This made it, as Blainey pointed out, a very expensive solution to a penal problem if the intention was only to dump the convicts.[23] Other objectives, however, might justify such expense.

*

Conclusion

In March 1787, Arthur Phillip became insistent that the people of the First Fleet had to be better fed and otherwise better provided for. First, he told Sydney: 'I fear, my Lord, that it may be said hereafter, the officer who took charge of the expedition should have known, that it was more than probable he lost half the garrison and convicts, crowded and victualled in such a manner, for so long a voyage'. Then, he told Nepean: '*At present* the evils complained of may be redressed, and the intentions of government by this expedition answered'.[24]

This latter statement is at once opaque and translucent. It conceals, because Phillip did not state explicitly what he understood the 'intentions of government' to be. But it also reveals that there were indeed intentions, intentions which he would be unable to realize if his colonists were reduced by poor diet, illness and death. Logic and the evidence I give in *Botany Bay: The Real Story* suggest that among these intentions were:

- A viable colony
- And therefore a place of future convict transportation
- A settlement able to defend itself
- A port able to resupply ships operating in the Pacific Ocean
- A source of naval materials.

*

As I have pointed out in *Botany Bay: The Real Story* and elsewhere, the striking innovation in Britain's transportation of convicts to New South Wales when compared to its earlier transportation of criminals to North America was that the central government became the provider for and regulator of the convicts and (in the first years) the employer of their labour.

With this salient difference in mind, it is worth considering how else the Botany Bay venture differed from earlier ones, both undertaken and proposed.

The labour of those convicts shipped across the Atlantic Ocean to Virginia and Maryland was sold to merchants and planters for a maximum period of seven years, with these private individuals becoming responsible for the convicts' maintenance during their servitude.

If they did not go enlisted in the Army or Navy, convicts sent to West Africa were simply landed, and left to their own devices. As the governor of Cape Coast Castle described it:

> Since that time I have paid a deal of attention to what I humbly conceive to be the views of government in sending those wretches to this country, and the evident defect there is in the mode of transporting them. One motive is no doubt to save their lives, of which I conclude the major part have been forfeited to the laws of their own country; but the grand consideration seems to be, *to get them out of Europe at all events;* without ever once adverting to the evil consequences that must attend this mode, a few of which I shall beg leave to lay before you.
>
> The governor and council are directed to receive a certain number of convicts. No provision whatever is made for them; neither are we directed to receive them as soldiers: from which it is natural to infer that government understands it is just simply landing these people in Africa, to let them shift for themselves, and get their bread in the best manner they can. In some other parts of the world they might by their industry maintain themselves, but here it is impossible. We have no employment for them but that of soldiers ... The natives have none. How then are they to be maintained? They are landed as it were naked and diseased on the sandy shore. The more hardy of them probably will plunder for a living for a few days until the climate stops their progress, and then, shocking to humanity, loaded with the additional diseases incident to the country, these poor wretches are to be seen dying upon the rocks, or upon the sandy beach, under the scorching heat of the sun, without the means of support or the least relief afforded them.[25]

This was a 'dumping of convicts' scheme, as was the proposal intended to supplant it, that of sending the convicts to the island of

Lemain, 400 miles up the River Gambia, where they were again to be left to their own devices, with whatever governance they themselves chose to establish. The slavers who proposed this scheme explained: 'It is natural to suppose that upon the first settlement a great many of the convicts would die from the change of climate ... After the first year, the island would be of course in a more cultivated state, and would consequently grow more healthy.'[26]

And when the Irish government resumed transportation to North America in the late 1780s, often those to whom it contracted the business simply 'dumped' the convicts in Newfoundland or Nova Scotia or thereabouts. Consider the voyage of the *Providence* towards the end of 1788. This ship loaded 103 men and twenty-three women convicts, forty-six of whom (36 per cent) died during the four weeks' passage. In view of the onset of winter, Captain Debenham elected simply to land his charges on the almost uninhabited northeast coast of Cape Breton Island, where snow had already fallen: 'the seamen were armed with pistols, cutlasses and swords, and when the boat reached the shore, they tumbled these people headlong from the boat into the surf among the rocks, and one man was killed by being thrown against a rock'.

These poor people were lightly clothed (some in rags only), seven had no shoes, and Debenham gave them no food. Through the night, local fishermen tried to succour them. They found between thirty and forty persons straggling about, without knowing which way to go'; six of the seven without shoes died of exposure. Eventually, a fisherman took the survivors to Sydney, the main settlement in Nova Scotia.[27]

The next year, there was another such disastrous voyage. In June, Richard Harrison took 113 men and boys convicts and fourteen women off from Dublin in the *Leinster*. He reached Newfoundland on 15 July, and landed the convicts at two points on the southeast coast. He gave some food to the first group, but 'the strongest beat the weak, and over a cask of rank butter or beef, there was for a time as severe fighting as if a kingdom had been at stake'. When a majority of the convicts reached St John's, they stole from shops and houses, and attempted to burn down the town. Sixty-three of the men, many of them ill with typhus fever, were held in a large house and fed by the town's inhabitants, while the women were left to prostitute themselves. The illness spread into the population – as the local priest wrote, 'we've had a most malignant jail fever imported to us by some unhappy convicts landed here ..., of which no less than 200 people already died in this harbour, which is as yet an entire hospital'. When Admiral Milbanke arrived for his annual patrol at the beginning of September, he commended the magistrates for their handling of the situation: 'I think you acted very prudently in complying with the desire of the inhabitants and thereby prevented many irregularities in the fishery, which would have been the consequence of suffering such a Banditti to go at large about the island'. Milbanke organized for the surviving convicts to be shipped back, but this well-intentioned action led to a very serious situation, as it put him and the master of the ship they went on in danger of prosecution for aiding felons to return illegally.[28]

*

Consider how very different was the Botany Bay venture.

As soon as the convicts came under the control of the agents of central government they were cleaned, clothed, fed and had their ailments treated.

The ships they were embarked in were, according to Navy Board official George Teer, '*completely fitted*, their provisions and accommodations are better than any set of transports I have ever had any directions in'.[29] For two months at Portsmouth, they and the marines were given fresh foods in abundance, and the surgeons obtained adequate medical supplies (at a cost of some £1200). The issuing of fresh food continued at the ports *en route*. While at sea, the colonists were fed superior standard provisions: 'I believe few marines or soldiers going out on a foreign service under government were ever better, if so well provided for as these convicts are', Smyth said; and Collins wrote of 'the excellent quality of the provisions with which we were supplied by Mr Richards Junior, the contractor'.[30] And when landed, the convicts lived within established social and legal structures, which reduced violence and gave them good prospects, not just of survival, but of eventual freedom and some prosperity.

*

This central point – that Botany Bay was *not* a 'dumping of convicts' scheme – is also to be made via another comparison.

The victory of the rebellious American colonists meant that large numbers of Loyalists were dispossessed and displaced – numbers are uncertain, but the best estimate seems to be 60–80,000. About 7000 of them fled to England, there to live in much reduced circumstances, if not in outright penury. Take the case of Mrs Magra. Her husband, Dr Magra, had been a very wealthy New Yorker, with large business and property holdings; but the family lost just about everything in the revolution. Their son James (Matra) later declared that, 'exclusive' of his father's property, he 'had out in that country £6275 [sterling]. This money was formally tendered to my agent, in Congress bills, and while a law existed which declared such a tender, if refused, a legal discharge of the debt' – in other words, he lost the lot.[31]

Recognizing the inevitability of the family's financial ruin, his aged mother emigrated to England at the end of 1779. In her memorial for compensation, she stated that she 'was an inhabitant of New York, and since the commencement of the rebellion in America, she has been deprived of her whole property, and reduced to a dependence on her two sons, who are in His Majesty's service; but they having also suffered from the same cause, her support is rendered painful and precarious'. She continued, that from 'her great distresses, and the difficulty and uncertainty of her support …, at a very advanced time of life', she had found it necessary 'to relinquish every hope of recovering the smallest part of her property, and come to England'. The commissioners appointed to investigate Loyalist claims granted her a pension of £60 per year.[32]

Or take the case of Thomas Danforth. His memorial to the commission reads in part:

Having devoted his whole life, at the age of near thirty, in preparing himself for future usefulness, ten useless years have [closed] the account; and he now finds himself near his fortieth year, banished under pain of death, to a distant country, where he has not the most remote family connection, nor scarcely an acquaintance, who is not in the same circumstances – cut off from his profession – from every hope of importance in life, and in a great degree from social enjoyments. And where, unknowing and unknown, he finds, that after having expended the little, he hopes to receive, as above related, that he shall be unable, while he may be said only to wait for death, to procure common comforts and conveniences, in a station much inferior to that of a menial servant, without the assistance of government.[33]

Large numbers of the Loyalists – perhaps as many 30,000 – chose instead to migrate north to the Canadian provinces, where they set about building new lives for themselves. And 'building' is the operative term – in a region notorious for the harshness of its winters, they had to start again from scratch, finding shelter, grafting livings as farmers or merchants or in their former professions or occupations.

Now, these were people – landowners, government officials, doctors and lawyers, merchants, and ordinary men and women (and their children) – who had supported their country and upheld its laws, and who as a consequence had fallen on very hard times. They had suffered the loss of family members in fighting, had lost their money and possessions, had had friendship and business networks shattered; so that, in middle or advanced age, they were faced with beginning again, in arduous circumstances and with slender means, for, apart from some assistance in the form of land, food and tools, the government was applying strict criteria in assessing claims for compensation, and paying only a proportion of losses.

By comparison, how were those men and women who had transgressed their country's laws being treated? These too were going into exile. However, the government was providing them with food; with shelter (yes, I know, tents at first, but no one was going to freeze to death

Conclusion

in Botany Bay's winter); with medical care; and with social controls. True, they would need to work in their new situation; but had they eschewed a life of crime, they would have needed to work in England too. In some ways, to be a convict at Botany Bay was to be better circumstanced than a displaced and dispossessed Loyalist. Given that late eighteenth-century British society did not share our belief in the need for social welfare and broad reform programs, it is striking just how well the Pitt administration provided for the convicts sent to form the new colony.

*

I do not claim that none of the arrangements which the administration made for the colony might have been better done. The First Fleet did sail without a three-years' supply of women's clothing; the marines also lacked some equipment; animals and plants perished in the heavy seas; and some seeds became barren in the course of the voyage. Also, experience soon showed that some antipodean circumstances (e.g., areas of thin soil overlaying stone and hardwoods) called for sturdier tools than those which sufficed in England. However, the wonder is, not that a few of the hundreds upon hundreds of arrangements were flawed, but that so many were in fact satisfactory.

It is also true that a number of other factors combined to hinder the New South Wales colony's progress once it was established about the shores of Port Jackson. There was first the marine officers' churlish refusal to supervise the convicts in their work; then there was the long, *el niño*-induced drought, from July 1790 until October 1791; then the losses of the *Guardian* and the *Sirius*. But as Phillip told Grenville in June 1790, 'from the day of our landing to the present hour, [the colony] has laboured under every possible disadvantage, and many obstacles have been met with which could not have been guarded against, as they never could have been expected', so that it was rather 'a matter of surprise that a regular settlement exists than that it is not in a more flourishing state'.[34]

Even so, however, when Phillip left Sydney at the end of 1792, it was clear that the colony would survive – but more than this, that it was beginning to flourish. That is, it was showing signs of the future that the Pitt administration always intended it should have.

*

Twenty years ago, in analysing the mounting of the First Fleet, Roger Knight rightly pointed out that 'it is doubtful that in the late 1780s any other European power could have achieved a similar level of success in an expedition of this nature'.[35]

In this business, the Pitt administration deployed Britain's superior administrative capability, and its accumulative experience of sending large expeditions into distant seas. It also drew on the nation's considerable financial resources. The First Fleet was a very expensive venture. But just as it spent to see that its plan to bring the breadfruit from the Pacific Ocean to the West Indies succeeded (when the first voyage failed, it mounted an even more expensive second one), so too did the Pitt administration spend largely to make the New South Wales colony succeed.

It did so because it saw that a colony in the southwest Pacific Ocean would be clearly in the nation's interest, not only because it would provide a solution to a troubling penal problem, *but also* because (as the Heads of a Plan indicated) it would achieve other objects – most immediately a base and a source of naval materials, and more generally as a point of interchange for an intended vast trading network.

A variety of circumstances combined to mean that these other objects were not immediately realized; but this does not mean that they were not envisaged. History, whether in its course or in its retelling, is rarely a straightforward business. But most of the historians of the decision to colonize New South Wales and of the mounting of the First Fleet have greatly distorted ours by attending only to the fact of the convicts in Britain, and by comprehensively misrepresenting the scale and competence of the preparations to send them to distant New South Wales. They have assessed intentions in the past according to outcomes known to us in the present – since the scheme to obtain naval materials from the islands of the southwestern Pacific Ocean came to nothing, they reason, it must always have been a harebrained fantasy; and therefore, in

Conclusion

founding the Botany Bay colony, the British wished only to dump their convicts as far away as possible.

With this premise established, they have assumed that they needed to take account only of the evidence that seemed to validate it – principally, the many complaints from country officials about the presence of transport convicts in their jails. Accordingly, they have not considered that they needed to establish the precise extent of the documentary record; as the matter was clear, this was unnecessary: looking further would not lead to new insights. Nor have they seen fit to relate the decision to other matters of national concern – specifically, the shortages of naval materials, the political situation in Europe and India, and trading ambitions in the East.

Lacking a proper understanding of the range of Pitt's concerns and the seriousness of his intent, and of his administration's very detailed preparations for the First Fleet, these historians have characterized the founding of the convict colony as a shambles – which of course has only helped to confirm the premise they started from. Later writers have accepted the assumptions of earlier ones, and repeated their mistakes.

The historians of the beginning of modern Australia have given us less than half a history. The real story is much more intricate – and much more interesting.

Acknowledgments

As before, I have received much help with this book from many people, prominent among whom have been my good friends Glyn Williams and Sarah Palmer, Bernard Bailyn, John Salmond, Inga Clendinnen and Roger Wales (who sadly died before he might see it). Geoffrey Blainey has encouraged me in my endeavour for decades. Michelle Novacco contributed to some last-minute research.

As I indicated in *Botany Bay: The Real Story*, Natasha Campo undertook the bulk of the laborious task of transcribing and editing the documents on which this analysis is based.

I wish also to acknowledge the great help I have had from Gary Sturgess, who also possesses very extensive knowledge of the documentary record, and who has freely shared his knowledge, both by extended conversations about meanings and significance, and by locating and providing materials I did not know about. Briony Sturgess has also helped in this last task. Advice from Gary Sturgess and Michael Flynn has enabled me to correct some mistakes in the first printing.

Again, too, I have to thank the editorial and production staff at Black Inc., in particular Denise O'Dea and Chris Feik.

*

All reasonable efforts have been made to locate copyright holders. Where they have held the copyright, the directors and/or governing bodies of the institutions listed in the bibliography have kindly given permission to cite and to quote from original sources.

I have specifically to acknowledge: the Trustees of the British Library, London; the UK Science and Technology Facilities Council and the Syndics of Cambridge University Library; the Trustees of the Royal Botanic Gardens, Kew; the Trustees of the Natural History Museum, London; the Archive and Manuscripts Manager, National Maritime Museum, London; the Keeper of Public Records, Public Records Office, National Archives, Kew; the Council of the Royal Society, London; the Director, William L. Clements Library, University of Michigan, Ann Arbor; the Director of the Sutro Library, the San Francisco branch of the California State Library; the Director, National Library of Australia, Canberra; the State Librarian and Chief Executive, State Library of New South Wales, Sydney; and the National Librarian, Alexander Turnbull Library, Wellington.

Two sections of this work have been published earlier in a somewhat different form. These are Chapter 10, Leaving the World, in *Arthur Phillip, 1738–1814: His Voyaging* (Oxford University Press, Melbourne, 1987) and Chapter 11, No Cheaper Mode, in *Botany Bay Mirages: Illusions of Australia's Convict Beginnings* (Melbourne University Press, Melbourne, 1995). These publishers have kindly agreed to my including them here.

Endnotes

ABBREVIATIONS

1. Archives and files

AHN: Archivo Historico Nacional (Madrid)
    Estado
AJCP: Australian Joint Copying Project
    Microfilms at the National Library of Australia and the State Library of New South Wales
ANTT: Arquivo Nacional da Torre do Tombo (Lisbon)
    MNE: Ministério dos Negócios Estrangeiros
BL: The British Library (London)
    Add. MS: Additional Manuscript
    Egerton: Egerton MS
    OIOC: Oriental and India Office Collections
        B: Minutes of the Court of Directors
        D: Committee of Correspondence
        E: General Correspondence
        F: Board of Control Records
        G: Factory Records
        H: Home Miscellaneous Series
        I: Europeans in India
        L/MAR: Marine Records
        L/PS: Political and Secret Department Records
Clements: William L. Clements Library, University of Michigan (Ann Arbor)
    Sydney: Sydney papers
CUL: Cambridge University Library (Cambridge)
    RGO: Records of the Royal Greenwich Observatory
Kew: Royal Botanic Gardens (Kew)
    KBP: Banks papers
Kingston: Kingston-upon-Thames Record Office
NHM: The Natural History Museum (London)
    DTC: Dawson Turner transcripts of Banks papers
NLA: National Library of Australia (Canberra)
    MS: Manuscript

NLNZ: National Library of New Zealand (Wellington)
    Turnbull: Alexander Turnbull MS
NMM: National Maritime Museum (London)
    ADM A, B, BP, C, OT: Navy Board papers
    MID: Middleton papers
    SAN: Sandwich papers
PRO: Public Record Office, The National Archives (London)
    ADM: Admiralty
    AO: Audit Office
    BT: Board of Trade
    CO: Colonial Office
    FO: Foreign Office
    HCA: High Court of Admiralty
    HO: Home Office
    PC: Privy Council
    PR: Patent Rolls
    PRO: Public Record Office
    SP: State Papers
    WO: War Office
RMM: Royal Marines Museum (Southsea)
    Archive
RS: The Royal Society (London)
SLNSW: State Library of New South Wales (Sydney)
    Bonwick: Bonwick transcripts
    Dixson: Dixson Library MS
    Mitchell: Mitchell Library MS
SRNSW: State Records of New South Wales (Sydney)
Sutro: Sutro Library, California State Library (San Franscisco)
    Banks: Banks papers
    EN: Entomology
USNA: National Archives of the United States (Washington, DC)
    Record Group: Miscellaneous records

2. Printed sources

Authentic Journal: [An Officer], *An Authentic Journal of the Expedition under Commodore Phillips to Botany Bay* (London, 1789).

Authentic Narrative: [An Officer], *An Authentic and Interesting Narrative of the late Expedition to Botany Bay* (Aberdeen, 1789).

Banks: *The Endeavour Journal of Joseph Banks*, ed. J.C. Beaglehole, 2 vols (Angus & Robertson, Sydney, 1963).

Clark: *The Journal and Letters of Lt Ralph Clark, 1787–1792*, eds Paul G. Fidlon and R.J. Ryan (Australian Documents Library, Sydney, 1981).

Collins: David Collins, *An Account of the English Colony in New South Wales* (1798), ed. B.H. Fletcher (A.H. and A.W. Reed, Sydney, 1975).

Colnett: James Colnett, *A Voyage to the South Atlantic and round Cape Horn into the Pacific Ocean* (London, 1798).

Cook: *The Journals of Captain James Cook on his Voyages of Discovery*, ed. J.C. Beaglehole, 3 vols in 4 parts (Hakluyt Society, Cambridge, 1955–68).

Easty: John Easty, *Memorandum of the Transactions of a Voyage from England to Botany Bay, 1787–1793* (Angus & Robertson, Sydney, 1965).

Fowell: Newton Fowell, *The Sirius Letters: The Complete Letters of Newton Fowell, midshipman and lieutenant aboard the* Sirius, ed. Nance Irvine (The Fairfax Library, Sydney, 1988).

Hawkesworth: John Hawkesworth, comp., *An Account of the Voyages undertaken by the Order of His Present Majesty for making Discoveries in the Southern Hemisphere, and successively performed by Commodore Byron, Captain Wallis, Captain Carteret, and Captain Cook*, 3 vols (London, 1773).

Howard: *Prisons and Lazarettos, vol. 1: The State of the Prisons in England and Wales*, ed. R.W. England (Patterson Smith, Montclair, NJ, 1973). (This is a reprint of the 4th edition of Howard's work.)

HRA: *Historical Records of Australia*, 4 series (Commonwealth Parliament, Sydney, 1914–1925).

HRNSW: *Historical Records of New South Wales*, 7 vols (Government Printer, Sydney, 1892–1901).

Hunter: John Hunter, *An Historical Journal, 1787–1792*, ed. John Bach (Angus & Robertson, Sydney, 1968).

JRAHS: *Journal of the Royal Australian Historical Society*

JHC: *Journals of the House of Commons*

King: *The Journal of Philip Gidley King: Lieutenant, RN, 1787–1790*, eds P.G. Fildon and R.J. Ryan (Australian Documents Library, Sydney, 1980).

Martin: *Letters and Papers of Admiral of the Fleet Sir Thomas Byam Martin*, ed. Sir Richard Vesey Hamilton (London, 1898–1903).

Nagle: *The Nagle Journal*, ed. J.C. Dann (Weidenfeld & Nicolson, New York, 1988).

Péron: M.F. Péron, *A Voyage of Discovery to the Southern Hemisphere* (London, 1809).

PH: *Parliamentary History*

Phillip: *The Voyage of Governor Phillip to Botany Bay* (1789), ed. J.J. Auchmuty (Angus & Robertson, Sydney, 1970).

PR: *Parliamentary Register*

Smyth (1): Arthur Bowes Smyth, Journal extracts, *HRNSW*, vol. 2, pp. 387–14.

Smyth (2): *The Journal of Arthur Bowes Smyth, Surgeon*, Lady Penrhyn, 1787–1789, eds P.G. Fildon and R.J. Ryan (Australian Documents Library, Sydney, 1979).

Statutes at Large: *Great Britain: Statutes at Large* (London, 1763–).

Tench: Watkin Tench, *A Narrative of the Expedition to Botany Bay* (1789), in *Sydney's First Four Years*, ed. L.F. Fitzhardinge (Library of Australian History, Sydney, 1979).

White: John White, *Journal of a Voyage to New South Wales* (1790), ed. A.H. Chisholm (Angus & Robertson, Sydney, 1962).

Wilberforce: *The Private Papers of William Wilberforce*, ed. A.W. Wilberforce (London, 1897).

Wordsworth: *Journals of Dorothy Wordsworth*, ed. Mary Moorman (Oxford University Press, Oxford, 1971).

Worgan: George Worgan, *Journal of a first Fleet Surgeon* (Library of Australian History, Sydney, 1978).

INTRODUCTION

1. Clark, p. 77.
2. Shaw (1966), p. 54.
3. King (1982), p. 31.
4. Mackay, p. 57.
5. Hughes, pp. 74–5.
6. Molony, p. 1.
7. Gillen (1989), pp. xxiii, xxxiii, xxxvi.
8. Wilson, p. 32.
9. Clark, p. 77.
10. Phillip to Nepean, 18 March 1787, CO 201/2, fo. 123.
11. Hughes, p. 70.
12. *Botany Bay: The Real Story* (Black Inc., Melbourne, 2011), pp. 55–76.
13. *Smyth (2)*, p. 47; *Tench*, p. 32; *Collins*, pp. 1–2.
14. Shaw (1966), pp. 53–4.
15. See Gillen (1989), p. 445. There is some uncertainty about these figures, as the number of seamen on the transport ships cannot be known accurately, which means that there may have been as many as 100 more.
16. 15,000 nautical miles; 17,500 miles; 28,000 kilometres.
17. *Collins*, p. 1.
18. Campbell, Testimony to the House of Commons Committee, [April 1778], *JHC*, vol. 36 (1776–8), p. 927.
19. Barnard Eldershaw, p. 34.
20. Frost (1980), p. 137. The error was repeated by Jonathan King (1982), p. 17, and by John Moore (1987), p. 24.

21. *King*, p. 19; Henderson and Stanbury, p. 39; Hill, p. 48.
22. Campbell, pp. 264-6.
23. Barnard Eldershaw, p. 25.
24. Clark, p. 73; *Phillip*, pp. 343-4; Moore, p. 25.
25. Hill, p. 37; Keneally, p. 42. (At least Keneally got Rose's position right.)
26. See Frost (1987), pp. 49-55.
27. See ibid, pp. 105-25, 129-33.
28. *Fowell*, pp. 23, 26.
29. Frost (1980), p. 218.
30. For example, the vast bulk of the Earl of Shelburne's papers went to the William L. Clements Library at the University of Michigan. Papers relating to Australia from the collections of Sir Joseph Banks and Lord Sydney came first to the remarkable collectors David Scott Mitchell and Sir William Dixson, and then to the State Library of New South Wales. Others found their way to the Sutro Library in San Francisco. Some of Pitt's and Dundas's papers went to the Duke University Library, others to the William L. Clements Library.
31. This very brief summary is based on the studies by Edward Hughes (1934) and Brewer.
32. Dorset to Carmarthen, 5 May and 9 June 1785, FO 27/16; Dalrymple to Carmarthen, 8 June 1785, BL, Egerton 3501, fo. 39.
33. For details, see Frost (1987), pp. 129-33.
34. Various intelligence reports sent to Nepean, and his ledgers, are in FO 95/7/3, 4.
35. Middleton to Nepean, 11 December 1786, and 20 March 1787, CO 201/2, fos 51-2, 243.

1. *Announcing the Decision*

1. The earliest version of this letter is in Nepean's hand, and is dated 21 August 1786, with 21 then cancelled and 18 substituted (HO 35/7).
2. This letter is another indication of the true date of the decision and the administrative steps that followed it.
3. Sydney to Treasury, 18 August 1786, T 1/639, no. 2176.
4. Though the titles are different, they were the joint heads of the Treasury Department, and therefore Nepean's equivalents.
5. Treasury, Minutes, 18 and 19 August and 26 October 1786, T 29/58, pp. 22-4, 28-9.
6. Sydney to Admiralty, 31 August 1786, ADM 1/4152, no. 25.
7. Sydney to Chairmen, EIC, 15 September 1786, BL, OIOC E/1/79, no. 187; Court of Directors, Minutes, 19 September 1786, OIOC B/103, p. 570, and 21 September 1786, D/1.

8. Richards to Pitt, 6 October 1786, PRO 30/8/171, fos 31–2; *Daily Universal Register*, 12 October 1786.
9. There had been earlier information, when the Navy Board had advertised for shipping and supplies at the beginning of September (e.g., in *Morning Herald* and *Whitehall Evening Post* on 1 September). However, these were specialist notices intended for ship-brokers and commercial firms.
10. *Public Advertiser*, 19 September 1786; *Hawkesworth*, vol. 3, pp. 495–506.
11. Other, briefer, descriptions of Botany Bay/New South Wales appeared in the *Morning Chronicle*, 30 September 1786, and the *Public Advertiser*, 30 September 1786.
12. *Daily Universal Register*, 27 September 1786.
13. *Birmingham Daily Gazette*, 25 September 1786.
14. *Morning Chronicle*, 13 October 1786; the *London Chronicle*, 14–17 October 1786. Since the quoting is so direct, the papers either had these details from Matra, or from the Home Office.
15. *London Chronicle*, 4 December 1786; and see *Botany Bay: The Real Story*, pp. 190–2.
16. *St James's Chronicle*, 5–7 December 1786; *Daily Universal Register*, 8 and 18 December 1786 and 4 January 1787.
17. *Morning Chronicle*, 3 October 1786.
18. *Public Advertiser*, 13 October 1786.
19. *St James's Chronicle*, 16 January 1787; *London Chronicle*, 16–18 January 1787.
20. *Daily Universal Register*, 21 and 23 November 1786.
21. *Daily Universal Register*, 4 December 1786.
22. *Gentleman's Magazine*, vol. 56 (1786), pp. 806–7.
23. *Bath Chronicle*, 11 January 1787.
24. Pinto de Souza to Mello e Castro, 19 September 1786, ANTT, MNE caixa 706, no. 705.
25. Robert J. King, p. 17 (citing Campo de Alange to Florida Blanca, 13 October 1786, AHN, Estado legajo 4250/1).
26. 'Mercator', in the *Public Advertiser*, 6 October 1786; *Hampshire Chronicle*, 16 October 1786; *Dublin Evening Herald*, 30 October 1786; *Reading Mercury and Oxford Gazette*, 30 October 1786; *Hampshire Chronicle*, 1 January 1787.
27. *Daily Universal Register*, 23 January 1787; *JHC*, vol. 42 (1787), pp. 3–4; *PH*, vol. 26 (1787), col. 214.
28. E.g., Clark cited this paragraph in the context of his assertion that 'everyone associated with the execution of the decision named the overcrowding in the jails as the only motive' (p. 69).
29. Camden to Sydney, 11 January 1787, Clements, Sydney vol. 14. In the event, the reference to troubles in Ireland was removed from the address.

Endnotes

2. *The Colony: Society, Law and Governance*

1. Camden to Pitt, 29 January 1787, PRO 30/8/119, fo. 131.
2. See *Botany Bay: The Real Story*, p. 201; and 'Our Original Aggression? New South Wales as *terra nullius*', in Frost (1994), pp. 176–89.
3. Matra, 'Supplement', 6 April 1784, CO 201/1, fos 64–5.
4. Pitt to Wilberforce, 23 September 1786, *Wilberforce*, pp. 16–17; quoted in Thomas, p. 19; Phillip to Sydney, July 1788, *HRNSW*, vol. 1, part 2, p. 179.
5. 'Phillip's Views on the Conduct of the Expedition and the Treatment of Convicts', *HRNSW*, vol. 1, part 2, pp. 50–4.
6. Phillip, Memorandum, [c. 1 October 1786], CO 201/2, fos 88–93. Phillip's reference to his ship as the *Berwick* fixes the latest date of composition of this document as 11 October, since it was renamed the *Sirius* the next day (Admiralty to Navy Board, 12 October 1786, ADM A/2816). As for the earliest date: while Phillip's appointment was mooted at the beginning of September (Howe to Sydney, 3 September 1786, CO 201/2, fo. 31), it was first publicly announced on 27 September (*Daily Universal Register*, 27 September 1786). It therefore seems likely that Phillip returned to London only about this time, a supposition reinforced by his afterwards remarking of the victualling contracts for the First Fleet which the Navy Board concluded on 12 September, that these 'were made before I ever saw the Navy Board on this business' (Phillip to Sydney, 12 March 1787, CO 201/2, fo. 120).
7. Phillip, Memorandum, [c. 1 October 1786], CO 201/2, fos 90–1.
8. Ibid; and Phillip to Sydney, 16 May 1788, *HRNSW*, vol. 1, part 2, p. 138.
9. Phillip, Memorandum, [c. 1 October 1786], CO 201/2, fo. 91.
10. Ibid.
11. Ibid, fos 90, 92.
12. Ibid, fo. 92.
13. [Home Office], Draft of Instructions, [c. 1 March 1787], CO 201/2, fos 29–40; Phillip, Comments on his Instructions, 11 April 1787, CO 201/2, fo. 130.
14. Privy Council, Amendments to draft Instructions, 25 April 1787, CO 201/1, fos 36–7, 38.
15. *Botany Bay: The Real Story*, pp. 155–6.
16. Matra, Testimony, 9 May 1785, HO 7/1.
17. Phillip, Memorandum, [c. 1 October 1786], CO 201/2, fo. 91.
18. Nepean to Hamilton, 24 October 1786, HO 100/18, fo. 372.
19. These commissions are printed in *HRNSW*, vol. 1, part 2, pp. 24–7. I have been unable to locate the originals.
20. Nepean to Sydney, 9 November 1786, SLNSW, Mitchell MS An 53/1.

21. [Sydney], ['Notes relative to Act to settle N. S. Wales'], [undated, but c. 9–27 November 1786], SLNSW, Dixson Add. MS Q 522. (It is not entirely clear that this title is a contemporary annotation, though.)
22. [Attorney-General or Solicitor-General] to [Sydney or Nepean], [undated, but c. 9–27 November 1786], HO 48/1B, p. 565.
23. *Daily Universal Register*, 27 November 1786; and cf. *Hampshire Chronicle*, 4 December 1786.
24. Camden to Pitt, 29 January 1787, PRO 30/8/119, fo. 131.
25. *JHC*, vol. 42 (for 1787: London, 1803), pp. 288, 305, 367, 376, 378, 381, 402, 404; 27 Geo. III, c. 2, *Statutes at Large* vol. 15 (London, 1789), pp. 254–5.
26. Privy Council, 'Charter for Establishing Courts of Civil and Criminal Jurisdiction on the Eastern Coast of New South Wales', 2 April 1787, PR, C 66/3834, part 5, no. 10.
27. Sydney to Admiralty, 26 March 1787, ADM 1/4152, no. 58; Admiralty, Minute, 27 March 1787, ADM 3/102, and to Privy Council, 27 March 1787, PC 1/62/16.
28. Privy Council, Order, 4 April 1787, PC 2/132, pp. 135–6, and to Admiralty, 12 April 1787, HCA 50/13, fos 136–7; Admiralty, Minute, 18 April 1787, ADM 3/103, and to Marriott, 18 April 1787, ADM 2/1062, pp. 314–5; HCA, Letters-Patent, 30 April 1787, HCA 50/13, fos 138–45, 146–9, 152–3; HCA, Letters-Patent, 5 May 1787, *HRNSW*, vol. 1, part 2, pp. 95–100.
29. Sydney to Lord President, 26 March 1787, HO 43/2, pp. 218–19; Privy Council, Minute, 4 April 1787, PC 2/132, p. 136; Board of Trade, Minute, 13 April 1787, BT 5/4, p. 239, and Report, BT 6/180, pp. 45–6; Privy Council, Order, 20 April 1787, PC 2/132, pp. 156–7, and Commission, 5 May 1787, HCA 50/13, fos 153–8; Phillip to Stephens, 10 May 1787, ADM 1/2308.
30. Privy Council, Commission, 26 March 1787, CO 202/5, fos 7–16. This is annotated: 'NB: The above commission passed the Great Seal the 2nd April 1787.'
31. For this precedent, see Macdonald to Nepean, 25 March 1787, HO 48/1B, fo. 119.
32. *Smyth (2)*, p. 68; cf. *Tench*, p. 42.
33. Privy Council, Minute, 23 June 1789, PC 2/134, pp. 125–6; Additional Instructions, draft, 23 June 1789, HO 31/1, and final version, 8 August 1789, PC 2/134, pp. 188–92; Grenville to Phillip, 24 August 1789, CO 201/4, fo. 28.
34. Macdonald to Nepean, 30 March 1790, HO 48/1B, p. 351; *JHC*, vol. 45 (for January–June 1790: London, 1803), pp. 410, 484, 486, 493, 496, 506, 522, 543; *Statutes at Large*, vol. 16 (London, 1794), p. 57; Attorney-General, Draft warrant, 8 November 1790, HO 48/1B, pp. 345–50; Grenville to Phillip, 13 and 15 November 1790, CO 201/5, fos 211, 218; Privy Council, Additional instructions, 15 November 1790, *HRNSW*, vol. 1, part 2, pp. 413–4.

Endnotes

35. Privy Council, Minute, 21 May 1790, PC 2/135, p. 76; Board of Trade, Minute, [c. 3 August 1790], BL, Add. MS 38392, fo. 122, and Report, 3 August 1790, BT 6/182, pp. 251–2; Privy Council, Minute, 4 August 1790, HO 31/1; Privy Council, Minute, 21 January 1791, PC 2/135, p. 378.
36. Phillip to Nepean, 28 September 1788, *HRNSW*, vol. 1, part 2, p. 183.
37. Phillip to Nepean, 28 October 1786, HO 42/9, fo. 84, and to Sydney, 15 May 1788, fos 6–7; to Lansdowne, 3 July 1788, SLNSW, Mitchell MS 7241; to Middleton, 6 July 1788, [privately owned].

3. The People 1: Officials and Officers

1. [Nepean], 'Staff Establishment for the Settlement at New South Wales', [c. 15 August 1786], T 1/639, no. 2176.
2. [Nepean], 'Estimate for defraying the Establishments in New South Wales from the 10 October 1786 to 10 October 1787', 10 October 1786, BT 6/263. (I have corrected the total, which Nepean incorrectly gave as £2705.)
3. For an extended account, see Frost (1987).
4. Phillip to Admiralty, 25 September 1769, ADM 106/2972.
5. Phillip to Sandwich, 17 January 1781, NMM, SAN F/26/23.
6. Phillip to Nepean, 28 October 1786, HO 42/9, fo. 83, and to Sydney, 3 December 1786, HO 42/10, fo. 304.
7. The editor wrote 'Buenos Aires', but as that was a Spanish town, whose authorities would scarcely have been willing to take charge of Portuguese criminals, it is much more likely that Phillip landed the convicts in Brazil.
8. *St James's Chronicle*, 2 February 1787.
9. Howe to Sydney, 3 September 1786, CO 201/2, fo. 31.
10. See Frost (1987), pp. 49–50, 225.
11. Edward Spain, Journal, SLNSW, Mitchell MS C 266, pp. 65–6.
12. King to Nepean, 14 February 1791, *HRNSW*, vol. 1, part 2, p. 455.
13. Privy Council, Ross's Commission, 24 October 1786, *HRNSW*, vol. 1, part 2, p. 26; Admiralty to Ross, 2 March 1787, ADM 2/1178, pp. 167–70.
14. Ross to Stephens, 10 July 1788, ADM 1/3824, fo. 52.
15. Admiralty to Collins, 29 November 1786, ADM 2/1178, p. 17; to Stewart, 23 December 1786, ADM 2/1178, pp. 64–5; Collins to Sydney, 7 February 1787, CO 201/2, fo. 211. (There is another puzzle concerning Collins's commissioning. The version of 24 October 1786 printed in *HRNSW* (vol. 1, part 2, pp. 26–7) is clearly a Privy Council document; however, the Admiralty subsequently said that he had been appointed 'by warrant from the Right Honourable the Lords Commissioners of His Majesty's Treasury dated 24 October last' – Admiralty to Steward, 6 March 1787, ADM 2/1178, p. 177.)
16. *Daily Universal Register*, 30 December 1786.
17. Phillip to Nepean, 20 May 1787, CO 201/2, fo. 156.

18. Edward Spain, Journal, SLNSW, Mitchell MS C 266, pp. 67–70.
19. Quoted in Thomas, p. 19.
20. Newton to Middleton, 30 October 1786, [privately owned].
21. Hamond to Nepean, 16 October 1786, CO 201/1, fo. 45.
22. White to Skill, 17 April 1790, *HRNSW*, vol. 1, part 2, p. 333.
23. Board of Trade, Report, 13 April 1787, BT 6/180, pp. 45–6; Commissions, 5 May 1787, HCA 50/13, fo. 154, and *HRNSW*, vol. 1, part 2, p. 96.
24. *Tench*, p. 66.
25. Banks to Masson, 3 June 1789, NHM, DTC vol. 5, pp. 173–4.
26. Phillip to Sydney, 3 December 1786, HO 42/10, fos 303–4.
27. Phillip to Nepean, 28 October 1786, HO 42/9, fos 83–4.
28. Ibid; Phillip to Nepean, [c. 28 October 1786], CO 201/2, fo. 84, and to Sydney, 1 November 1786, SLNSW, Dixson MS Q 162, pp. 1–2.
29. Sydney to Admiralty, 30 August 1786, ADM 1/4152, no. 25.
30. *Daily Universal Register*, 31 October 1786.
31. Phillip to Nepean, [c. 1 November 1786], CO 201/2, fo. 86.
32. Phillip, Comments on his Instructions, 11 April 1787, CO 201/2, fos 129–30; Sydney to Phillip, 20 April 1787, CO 201/2, fo. 27.
33. *Authentic Narrative*, p. v; and see the cover illustration.
34. Admiralty, Minute, 14 December 1786, ADM 3/102, and to Privy Council, 14 December 1786, PC 1/61/15; Order-in-Council, 15 December 1786, ADM 1/5177; Admiralty to Phillip, 18 December 1786, ADM 2/117, p. 269, and to Navy Board, 22 December 1786, ADM A/2816; Sydney to Phillip, 28 April 1787, CO 201/2, fo. 144. (The dormant commission has not been found.)
35. Stephens to Tench, 27 October 1786, ADM 2/1177, p. 525, to Collins, 14 December 1786, ADM 2/1178, p. 42.
36. Bayly to Banks, 8 [September] 1786, Kew, KBP vol. 1, no. 237; Stephens to Smith, ADM 2/1177, p. 521; Twiss to Watson, 29 October 1786, HO 42/10, fo. 394.
37. See below, Ch. 6, pp. 111–2.

4. *People 2: Ships' Crews, Marines, Convicts, Wives and Children*

1. Admiralty, Minute, 1 November 1786, ADM 3/102, and to Phillip and Ball, 1 November 1786, ADM 2/117, p. 213; to Navy Board, 1 November 1786, ADM 2/262, p. 495.
2. *King*, p. 40; Phillip to Nepean, 28 September 1788, *HRNSW*, vol. 1, part 2, p. 185.
3. The passes are recorded in ADM 7/104, 106. (I am grateful to Gary Sturgess for these references.) *King*, p. 6.
4. Stephens to Tupper and Hughes, 8 October 1786, ADM 2/1177, pp. 491–3.

5. *Tench*, p. 13.
6. Admiralty to Privy Council, 21 November 1786, ADM 2/1178, pp. 2–3.
7. Stephens to Ordnance Board and Generals Smith and Collins, 14 December, and Admiralty to Smith and Collins, 20 December 1786, ADM 2/1178, pp. 42, 43, 55–6.
8. See *Collins*, pp. 48–9, 66.
9. Admiralty to Sydney, 21 November 1786, CO 201/2, fo. 39.
10. Nepean to Rose, 22 December 1786, T 1/639, no. 2985; Thomas to Nepean, 24 December 1786, HO 28/61, fo. 120; Navy Board, Minute, 20 April 1787, ADM 106/2623; Phillip, 'State of the Garrison and Convicts ...', 10 June 1787, CO 201/2, fo. 172.
11. [   ] to Middleton, 13 October 1786, [privately owned].
12. Sydney to Treasury, 22 December 1786, T 1/639, no. 2984.
13. *Hampshire Chronicle*, 18 September 1786; *Reading Mercury and Oxford Gazette*, 2 October 1786.
14. *London Chronicle*, 17–19 October 1786.
15. Middleton to Nepean, 18 January 1787, CO 201/2, fo. 201; Teer to Navy Board, 29 January 1787, ADM 106/243.
16. We conducted this analysis during Professor Zebrow's time as a Fellow of the Institute for Advanced Study, La Trobe University. It has not been published.
17. Nepean to Campbell, 20 February 1787, HO 13/5, p. 58; Campbell to Erskine, [c. 20 February 1787], SLNSW, Mitchell MS ZA 3229, p. 270. As Nepean's list has evidently not survived, we cannot know what principle of selection Campbell followed.
18. *Tench*, p. 13.
19. *Clark*, pp. 2–6.
20. Gillen (1989), p. 446.
21. Phillip to Nepean, 11 January 1787, CO 201/2, fo. 105.
22. Campbell to Erskine, 30 January 1787, SLNSW, Mitchell MS ZA 3229, p. 262; Campbell's annotations to the list, 24 February 1787, HO 13/5, pp. 65–8.
23. [Campbell] to Erskine, 27 March 1787, SLNSW, Mitchell MS ZA 3229, p. 283.
24. Phillip to Sydney, 12 February 1790, and to Grenville, 17 July 1790, *HRNSW*, vol. 1, part 2, pp. 298, 361–2.
25. Nepean to Middleton, 8 March 1785, NMM, MID 1/131.
26. *Nagle*, p. 77.
27. Marshall to Stephens, 18 March 1787, ADM 1/989.
28. [Nepean], Heads of a Plan, [c. 15 August 1786], CO 201/2, fo. 11.
29. Hughes to Stephens, 14 October 1786, RMM, Archive 11/51/1, no. 345.
30. Ross, 'Artificers belonging to the Marine Detachment, employed from the 17th May to the 30th September 1788', *HRA*, series 1, vol. 1, p. 81; cf. Ross,

'Return of Artificers belonging to the Detachment, employed from the 30th of September 1788, to the 31st December 1789', CO 201/5, fo. 89.
31. *Authentic Narrative*, pp. v–vi.
32. *Daily Universal Register*, 30 November 1786.
33. Phillip to Nepean, 28 September 1788, *HRNSW*, vol. 1, part 2, p. 183.
34. Victualling Board to Phillip, 29 November 1786, and Minute, 6 December 1786, ADM 111/108.
35. Lochart to Phillip, [c. 21] and 22 December 1786, Phillip to Stephens, 23 December 1786, ADM 1/2308.
36. 'Humanitas', the *London Chronicle*, 2–5 December 1786.

5. The Ships

1. See Bateson, pp. 94–6, and Knight.
2. See Webb.
3. *Martin*, vol. 3, p. 381.
4. Navy Board, Minutes, 20 September 1786 and 2 January 1787, ADM 106/2622; Admiralty, Minute, 4 January 1787, ADM 3/102.
5. Steele to Navy Board, 26 August 1786, HO 35/7.
6. Admiralty, Minute, 6 September 1786, ADM 3/102, and to Navy Board, 6 September 1786, ADM 2/262, pp. 418–9.
7. See Introduction, p. 4.
8. *King*, p. 5.
9. Barnard Eldershaw, p. 34; Mackay, p. 59; Henderson and Stanbury, p. 61.
10. Deptford Officers to Navy Board, 12 November and 6 December 1781, ADM 106/3320, fos 30–31, 34.
11. *Hunter*, p. 1.
12. *King*, p. 5.
13. Admiralty to Navy Board, 23 August 1786, ADM 2/262, p. 393; Navy Board, Minute, 25 August 1786, ADM 106/2622.
14. Deptford Officers to Navy Board, 6 September 1786, ADM 106/3321, fo. 87.
15. Navy Board, Minute, 22 September 1786, ADM 106/2622, and to Stephens, 22 September 1786, ADM 106/2213, p. 432; Deptford Officers to Navy Board, 27 September 1786, ADM 106/3321, fos 84–5.
16. A 'tide' was an overtime unit of 1.5 hours.
17. Navy Board, Minutes, 9 and 11 October 1786, ADM 106/2622, and to Stephens, 9 October 1786, ADM 106/2213, p. 437; Deptford Officers to Navy Board, 11 October 1786, ADM 106/3321, fo. 91.
18. Admiralty, Minute, 12 October 1786, ADM 3/102, and to Navy Board, 12 October 1786, ADM A/2816; to Sydney, 12 October 1786, ADM 2/374, pp. 135–6, and to Richmond, 12 October 1786, ADM 2/262, pp. 468–9; *King*, p. 5.

Endnotes

19. Navy Board to Stephens, 25 October 1786, ADM 106/2213, p. 456; Admiralty to Navy Board, 25 October 1786, ADM 2/262, fos 485-6, and to Phillip, 25 October 1786, ADM 2/117; to Navy Board, 1 November 1786, ADM A/2816, and to Phillip and Ball, 1 November 1786, ADM 2/117, pp. 213-4; Navy Board to Victualling Board, 2 November 1786, ADM C/664.
20. Phillip to Stephens, 31 October 1786, ADM 1/2308; Admiralty to Richmond, 1 November 1786, ADM 2/262, pp. 496-7, and to Navy Board, 1 November 1786, ADM A/2816; Navy Board, Minute, 3 November 1786, ADM 106/2622.
21. Admiralty, Minute, 1 November 1786, ADM 3/102, and to Navy Board, 1 November 1786, ADM A/2816.
22. Deptford Officers to Navy Board, 13 November 1786, ADM 106/3364, fo. 80; Navy Board, Minute, 21 November 1786, ADM 106/2622; Parker to Phillip, 21 November 1786, CUL, RGO series 14, vol. 9, fo. 33.
23. Navy Board, Minutes, 12 September, 14, 15 and 16 November 1786, ADM 106/2622; Phillip to Admiralty, 27 October 1786, ADM 1/2308; Admiralty to Navy Board, 8 November 1786, ADM A/2816; Navy Board to Teer, 1 December 1786, ADM 106/2347, p. 166.
24. Victualling Board, Minutes, 1, 7, 8, 10, 14, 21, 22 and 28 November, 5 and 12 December 1786, ADM 111/108.
25. The bark of the cinchona tree, considered efficacious in treating fevers, neuralgia and debility.
26. Worgan to Phillip, 21 November 1786, Phillip to Stephens, 30 November 1786, ADM 1/2308.
27. Navy Board, Minutes, 1 and 3 January 1787, ADM 106/2623; Deptford Officers to Navy Board, 3 and 5 January 1787, ADM 106/3364, fo. 93.
28. Victualling Board, Minute, [c. 10 January 1787], ADM 111/108; Palmer to Navy Board, 20 January 1787, ADM 106/1291; Navy Board to Teer, 24 January 1787, ADM 106/2347, p. 188.
29. Deptford Officers to Navy Board, 9 September 1786, ADM 106/3321, fo. 87; Navy Board, Minute, 11 September 1786, ADM 106/2622; Deptford Officers to Navy Board, 12 September 1786, ADM 106/3321, fo. 89.
30. *Daily Universal Register*, 7 September 1786.
31. Navy Board, Minute, 22 September 1786, ADM 106/2622, and to Stephens, 22 September 1786, ADM 106/2213, p. 432; Deptford Officers to Navy Board, 27 and 28 September 1786, ADM 106/3321, fo. 85 and ADM 106/3364, fos 73-4.
32. Navy Board, Minute, 27 September 1786, ADM 106/2622, and to Stephens, [28] September 1786, ADM 106/2213, p. 435; Admiralty to Navy Board, 12 October 1786, ADM 2/262, pp. 469-70.
33. *Hunter*, pp. 1-2; *King*, pp. 5-6.
34. Deptford Officers to Navy Board, 18 October 1786, ADM 106/3321, fos 93-4.
35. Stephens to Navy Board, 20 October 1786, ADM 2/587, p. 98; Deptford

Officers to Navy Board, 24 October 1786, ADM 106/3321, fo. 96; Navy Board, Minute, 24 October 1786, ADM 106/2622, and to Stephens, 24 October 1786, ADM 106/2213, p. 454.
36. Stephens to Navy Board, 12 December 1786, ADM A/2816; Navy Board, Minute, 13 December 1786, ADM 106/2622, and to Stephens, 13 December 1786, ADM 106/2213, p. 506; Admiralty, Minute, 14 December 1786, ADM 3/102, to Richmond, 14 December 1786, ADM 2/262, p. 556, and to Navy Board, 14 December 1786, ADM A/2816; Navy Board, Minute, 16 December 1786, ADM 106/2622.
37. Admiralty to Navy Board, 27 October 1786, ADM 2/262, p. 490, and to Ball, 27 October 1786, ADM 2/117, pp. 210-11; Navy Board, Minute, 28 October 1786, ADM 106/2622.
38. Deptford Officers to Navy Board, 1 and 6 November 1786, ADM 106/3321, fos 97-9; Navy Board, Minute, 8 November 1786, ADM 106/2622; Deptford Officers to Navy Board, 15 November 1786, ADM 106/3321, fo. 99.
39. Ball to Navy Board, 11 November 1786, ADM 106/1286; Navy Board, Minute, 16 November 1786, ADM 106/2622; Victualling Board, Minutes, 14, 21, 22, 23, and 28 November, 5 and 12 December 1786, ADM 111/108; Ball to Navy Board, 2 and 6 December 1786, ADM 106/1286; Navy Board, Minutes, 5 and 8 December 1786, ADM 106/2622.
40. Navy Board, Minute, 29 August 1786, ADM 106/2622, and Draft advertisement, [29 August 1786], [privately owned]; *Morning Herald*, 1 September 1786; *Whitehall Evening Post*, 1, 4 and 8 September 1786.
41. Navy Board, Minute, 6 September 1786, ADM 106/2622.
42. Brough to Navy Board, 9 September 1786, ADM 106/1286; Navy Board to Brough, 11 September 1786, ADM 106/2347, p. 160.
43. Richards to Pitt, 9 and 28 September and 6 October 1786, PRO 30/8/171, fos 17, 29-30, 31-2.
44. Rose to Chairmen, EIC, 15 September 1786, BL, OIOC E/1/79, no. 184; Richards to EIC, 19 September, OIOC E/1/79, fo. 193; EIC, Minutes, 19 and 27 September 1786, OIOC B 103, pp. 570, 588-9.
45. Deptford Officers to Navy Board, 28, 29 and 30 September 1786, ADM 106/3364, fos 73-4.
46. See Deptford Officers to Navy Board, 12 October 2786, ADM 106/3321, fo. 92.
47. Deptford Officers to Navy Board, 2, 16, 18, 20 and 24 October, 3 and 10 November 1786, ADM 106/3321, fos 92-8.
48. Deptford Officers to Navy Board, 29 December 1786, ADM 106/3407, p. 34.
49. Deptford Officers to Navy Board, 1 November 1786, ADM 106/3321, fo. 97; Teer to Navy Board, 29 November 1786, ADM 106/243.
50. Johnston to Stephens, 18 December 1786, ADM OT; Stephens to Nepean, 18 December 1786, HO 28/5, p. 358; Nepean to Rose, 18 December 1786, T

1/639, no. 2927b; Rose to Navy Board, 18 December 1786, ADM OT; Navy Board, Minutes, 19 and 20 December 1786, ADM 106/2622.
51. Navy Board, Minutes, 9 November and 19 and 20 December 1786, ADM 106/2622; Teer to Navy Board, 13 December 1786, ADM 106/243.
52. Deptford Officers to Navy Board, 18 and 24 October 1786, ADM 106/3321, fos 94, 96.
53. Navy Board, Minute, 31 October 1786, ADM 106/2622.
54. See, e.g., Stephens to Stiles, 29 November 1786, ADM 2/587, p. 179. There are copies of the licences in ADM 7/104, 106. (I am grateful to Gary Sturgess for this information.)
55. Navy Board, Minute, 15 December 1786, ADM 106/2622, and Thomas to Morton, 15 December 1786, USNA, Record group 45/446.
56. Navy Board, Minute, 18 October 1786, ADM 106/2622.
57. Rose to Navy Board, 20 October 1786, ADM OT; Rose to Nepean, 21 October 1786, HO 35/7, and to Stephens, 21 October 1786, T 27/38, fo. 375; EIC to Canton Supercargoes, 13 December 1786, BL, OIOC R/10/33; Navy Board, Minutes, 15 and 28 December 1786, ADM 106/2622.
58. Deptford Officers to Navy Board, 8 November 1786, ADM 106/3321, fo. 98.

6. *Equipping the Colonists*

1. For the date, see Navy Board, Minute, 27 November 1786, ADM 106/2622.
2. See above, Introduction, pp. 2–3.
3. Steele to Navy Board, 26 August 1786, ADM OT.
4. Navy Board, Minute, 29 August 1786, ADM 106/2622, and to Steele, 29 August 1786, T 1/639, no. 2218; Steele to Nepean, 30 August 1786, HO 35/7; Nepean to Steele, 4 September 1786, T 1/639, no. 2269.
5. Steele to Navy Board, 9 September 1786, ADM A/2816.
6. Thomas to Watts, 12 and 14 September 1786, Watts to Thomas, 14 September 1786, ADM C/663.
7. *Morning Herald*, 18 and 23 September 1786.
8. Navy Board, Minute, 26 December 1786, ADM 106/2622; Thomas to Dawson and Atkinson, 26 December 1786, USNA, Record group 45/446.
9. Navy Board, Minute, 22 January 1787, ADM 106/2623.
10. Fell to Teer, 4 December 1786; Teer to Navy Board, 2 November 1786, ADM 106/243; Navy Board, Minute, 6 November 1786, ADM 106/2622; Navy Board to Teer, 13 November 1787, ADM 106/2347, p. 233; Teer to Navy Board, 14 and 28 November 1787, ADM 106/243.
11. Sydney to Treasury, 21/18 August 1786, T 1/639, no. 2176; Steele to Navy Board, 26 August 1786, ADM OT.
12. Rose to Nepean, 24 October 1786, HO 35/7, to Navy Board, 24 October 1786, ADM A/2816; Navy Board, Minute, 25 October 1786, ADM 106/2622.

13. Adair and White, List, [c. 14 November], and Nepean to Steele, 14 November 1786, T 1/639, no. 2643.
14. Steele to Navy Board, 20 November 1786, ADM OT; Navy Board to Steele, 21 November 1786, T 1/639, no. 2683.
15. Navy Board, Minute, 15 January 1787, ADM 106/2623.
16. See Lloyd and Coulter, pp. 92–3.
17. Nepean to Steele, 14 November 1786, T 1/639, no. 2643; Steele to Nepean, 18 December 1786, HO 35/7; Nepean to Phillip, 21 December 1786, HO 43/2, pp. 186–7.
18. See *St James's Chronicle*, 16 January 1787 and *London Chronicle*, 16–18 January 1787; *Smyth (1)*, p. 389.
19. Steele to Nepean, 31 August 1786, HO 35/7.
20. Banks, Instructions, [c. 1 March 1787], NHM, DTC vol. 5, p. 213; and see *Smyth (2)*, p. 16.
21. Phillip, Memorandum, [c. 1 October 1786], CO 201/2, fos 92–3, and to Nepean, [30 October 1786], HO 42/10, fo. 301.
22. Banks, 'Scheme of plants for Botany Bay', and List, [c. 28 November 1786], Sutro, Banks SS 1/48, 49.
23. Tony Courtis, Letter, 29 January 1987.
24. *Péron*, p. 273.
25. *Péron*, pp. 37, 271–6, 273–85, 293–5; and see Fletcher, p. 229.
26. For an extended discussion of this progress, see Frost (1994 (2)).
27. Nepean to Middleton, [c. 7 December 1786], ADM 106/243.
28. Steele to Navy Board, 26 August 1786, ADM OT; Navy Board, Minutes, 11 and 26 September 1786, ADM 106/2622.
29. Phillip to Nepean, [30 October 1786], HO 42/10, fo. 302; Nepean to Middleton, [c. 7 December 1786], ADM 106/243; Rose to Navy Board, 16 December 1786, ADM OT; Navy Board, Minute, 19 December 1786, ADM 106/2622, and to Rose, 19 December 1786, T 1/639, no. 2957; Ross, Memorandum, and to Phillip, 22 December 1786, CO 201/2, fos 71–3.
30. Stephens to Ross, 29 December 1786, ADM 2/1178, p. 78; Middleton to Nepean, 4 January 1787, CO 201/2, fo. 193; Navy Board, Minute, 4 January 1787, ADM 106/2623, and Thomas to Trotter, 4 January 1787, USNA, Record group 45/446; Navy Board, Minute, 25 January 1787, ADM 106/2623, and to Teer, 25 January 1787, ADM 106/2347, p. 189.
31. Navy Board, Minute, 8 November 1786, ADM 106/2622; Teer to Navy Board, 26 October 1786, ADM 106/243; Phillip to Sydney, 15 May 1788, CO 201/3, fo. 24.
32. 'Estimate of clothing to serve a male convict for one year', T 1/639, no. 2176.
33. Ibid.

Endnotes

34. Navy Board, Minute, 7 September 1786, *HRNSW*, vol. 2, pp. 367–8, and Minute, 26 December 1786, ADM 106/2622, and Thomas to Wadham, *et al.*, 26 December 1786, USNA, Record group 45/446.
35. This item is not included in the original list – or at least, in the transcription of it published in *HRNSW*. Later lists of women's clothing indicate that it should have been.
36. I.e., common/coarse shirts, trousers, frocks.
37. Navy Board to Darby, 2 November 1786, ADM 106/2347, fo. 82; Thomas to Stiles, 21 November 1786, USNA, Record group 45/446.
38. Nepean to Middleton, 21 December 1787, NMM, MID 1/131; Navy Board, Minute, 26 December 1786, ADM 106/2622, and Thomas to the various contractors, 26 December 1786, USNA, Record group 45/446.
39. Steele to Navy Board, 26 August 1786, ADM OT.
40. Thomas to Harrison, Gordon and Stanley, 13 September 1786, USNA, Record group 45/446; Middleton to Nepean, [c. 18 October 1786], CO 201/2, fo. 99.
41. Navy Board, Minute, 18 October 1786, ADM 106/2622, and Thomas to Harrison, Gordon and Stanley, 18 and 19 October 1786, USNA, Record group 45/446; Teer to Navy Board, 26 October 1786, ADM 106/243; Phillip to Nepean, [30 October 1786], HO 42/10, fos 301–2; Thomas to Harrison, Gordon and Stanley, 31 October 1786, USNA, Record group 45/446; Harrison, Gordon and Stanley to Navy Board, [c. 13 November 1786], CO 201/2, fo. 19; Navy Board, Minute, 13 November 1786, ADM 106/2622, and to Rose, 13 November 1786, T 1/639, no. 2624.
42. Thomas to Harrison, Gordon and Stanley, 29 December 1786 and 24 January 1787, USNA, Record group 45/446; Phillip to Nepean, 4 January 1787, CO 201/2, fo. 103.
43. See Frost (1987), pp. 55, 99; Phillip, Memorandum, [c. 1 October 1786], CO 201/2, fo. 90; Francis Wheatley, Captain Arthur Phillip, 1786 (SLNSW, Mitchell Library).
44. Phillip to Nepean, [30 October 1786], HO 42/10, fo. 301; Nepean to Sydney, 9 November 1786, SLNSW, Mitchell MS An 53/1; Richmond to Pitt, 3 December 1786, PRO 30/8/171, fo. 97; Rogers, 'Proportion of Ordnance, Ammunition and Stores demanded for the Equipment for Botany Bay', 21 December 1786, CO 201/2, fos 66–8.
45. Steele to Ordnance Board, 7 November 1786, T 27/38, p. 391; Stephens to Smith and Collins, 23 November 1786, ADM 2/1178, pp. 6–7.
46. Teer to Navy Board, 26 October 1786, ADM 106/243; Navy Board, Minute, 26 October 1786, ADM 106/2622; 'Articles sent by [the] First Fleet to Botany Bay', *HRNSW*, vol. 2, p. 388.
47. After agitation by domestic wool and silk manufacturers, parliament banned the printing of calicoes in England, but continued to permit that

of fustians with a warp of linen and a weft of cotton. Hence 'fustian' came to comprehend cloth that would earlier have been classified as calico.
48. Nepean to Sackville Hamilton, 24 October 1786 (draft), HO 100/18, fo. 372; Privy Council, Instructions to Phillip, 25 April 1787, CO 201/1, fo. 35.
49. Account of proceedings, 6 February 1783, *JHC*, vol. 39 (1782-4), pp. 157-8. (I am grateful to Ken Cozens for this information.)
50. Nepean to Sharrow, 27 October 1786, HO 43/2, p. 175; Sharrow to Nepean, 30 October 1786, HO 42/9, fo. 92, and [c. 5 November 1786], HO 42/8, fo. 12.
51. Phillip to Nepean, [30 October 1786], HO 42/10, fo. 301; Singleton to Nepean, 5 November 1786, HO 42/10, fo. 383.
52. Phillip to Banks, 2 September 1787, SLNSW, Mitchell MS C 213, p. 5; *King*, pp. 56, 106; Phillip to Nepean, 17 November 1788, CO 201/3, fo. 166.
53. 'Articles sent by [the] First Fleet to Botany Bay', *HRNSW*, vol. 2, p. 388; *Lady Penrhyn* Log, 25 March 1788, ADM 51/4376, fo. 38.
54. Steele to Navy Board, 27 January 1787, ADM A/2817.
55. Navy Board, Minute, 4 December 1786, ADM 106/2622, and Thomas to Harrison, Gordon and Stanley, 4 December 1786, USNA, Record group 45/446.
56. Phillip to Nepean, [30 October 1786], HO 42/10, fos 301-2; Nepean, 'Articles to be provided for the purchase of stock etc. for the intended settlement at Botany Bay', [c. 31 October 1786], CO 201/1, fo. 48, and to Rose, 31 October 1786, T 1/639, no. 2553; Steele to Rashleigh, 8 November 1786, T 27/38, p. 395; Rashleigh to Steele, 13 November 1786, T 1/639, no. 2621; Navy Board, Minute, 8 December 1786, ADM 106/2622, and Teer to Thomas, 8 December 1786, ADM 106/243; Navy Board to Teer, 8 December 1786, ADM 106/2347, p. 169; *London Chronicle*, 23-25 November 1786.
57. Stephens to Greenway, 20 November 1786, ADM 2/1177, p. 556, and to Prater, 5 and 22 December 1786 and 5 January 1787, ADM 2/1178, pp. 30, 62, 85.
58. Navy Board to Steele, 1 November 1786, T 1/639, no. 2558; Steele to Navy Board, 2 November 1786, ADM OT.
59. Steele to Navy Board, 8 November 1786, ADM OT; Cologan, Pollard and Cooper to Treasury, 17 October 1786, T 1/639, no. 2498; Navy Board to Steele, 13 November 1786, T 1/639, no. 2618.
60. Navy Board, Minute, 30 November 1786, ADM 106/2622; Phillip to Nepean, 2 December 1786, CO 201/2, fo. 45.
61. Dawes, 'List of Instruments proper for making astronomical Observations at Botany Bay', [c. 1 November 1786], RS, Misc. MS vol. 7, no. 56A; Board of Longitude, Minutes, 14 November 1786, CUL, RGO series 14, vol. 6, pp. 100-4.
62. Ibid; and Parker to Phillip, 21 November 1786, CUL, RGO series 14, vol. 9, fo. 33.

Endnotes

63. Dawes, Receipt, 8 March 1800, CUL, RGO series 14, vol. 14, fo. 204.
64. Society for the Propagation of the Gospel, Minutes, 14, 21 and 28 November 1786, SLNSW, Bonwick box 47, pp. 28–32.
65. [Banks and Dickson], '*Sirius* seeds continued', [c. 28 December 1786], T 1/639, fo. 253.
66. 'Proportion of each specie of Provisions', ADM 30/44; and Rodger, pp. 83, 90.
67. Colnett, p. 73; Yarwood, p. 176.

7. *Loading the Ships and Embarking the People*

1. Admiralty, Minute, 25 October 1785, ADM 3/102, and to Navy Board, 25 October 1786, ADM 2/262, fos 485–6.
2. Deptford Officers to Navy Board, 25 October 1786, ADM 106/3321, fo. 95; Phillip to Admiralty, 11 November 1786, ADM 1/2308; Deptford Officers to Navy Board, 22 November 1786, ADM 106/3321, fo. 103; Navy Board to Stephens, 25 October 1786, ADM 106/2213, fo. 241; *Bradley*, p. 2.
3. Admiralty, Minute, 27 October 1786, ADM 3/102, and to Navy Board, 27 October 1786, ADM A/2816.
4. Deptford Officers to Navy Board, 1 and 6 November 1786, ADM 106/3321, fos 97, 98.
5. Navy Board, Minute, 31 October 1786, ADM 106/2622.
6. *Lady Penrhyn* Log, ADM 51/4376, fo. 2.
7. Navy Board to Treasury, 20 November 1786, T 1/639, no. 2702; *Alexander* Log, ADM 51/4375, fo. 4.
8. Phillip to Nepean, 4 January 1787, CO 201/2, fo. 103.
9. Teer to Navy Board, 4 December 1786, ADM 106/243, and Navy Board to Teer, 4 December 1786, ADM 106/2347, p. 166.
10. Teer to Navy Board, 7 December 1786 (two letters), ADM 106/243.
11. The first sign of this decision is in a memorandum written by Nepean for Middleton about 7 December 1786, ADM 106/243.
12. Treasury, Minute, 18 August 1786, T 29/58, p. 23.
13. Nepean to Middleton, 9 December 1786, CO 201/2, fos 49–50; Middleton to Nepean, 11 December 1786, CO 201/2, fos 51–2.
14. Navy Board, Minute, 6 December 1786, ADM 106/2622; Rose to Nepean, 7 December 1786, HO 35/7.
15. Teer to Navy Board, 13 and 15 December 1786, ADM 106/243; Navy Board, Minute, 14 December 1786, ADM 106/2622; Stephens to Smith, 18 January 1787, ADM 2/1178, p. 107.
16. Navy Board, Minutes, 8 and 18 January 1787, ADM 106/2623, and to Richards, 8 January 1787, ADM 106/2347, p. 178.
17. Tench to Ross, 14 January 1787, ADM A/2816; Ross to Stephens, 17 January 1787, Stephens to Navy Board, 17 January 1787, ADM A/2817; Navy Board,

Minute, 18 January 1787, ADM 106/2623, and to Richards, 18 January 1787, ADM 106/2347, p. 183.
18. Stephens to Collins, 2 January, to Greenway and Pownoll, 13 January, to Lewis, 18 January, to Mackenzie, 20 January, to Prater, 26 January and to Smith, 27 January 1787, ADM 2/1178, pp. 82, 98–100, 107, 112, 117, 120.
19. Navy Board, Minute, 22 January 1787, ADM 106/2623, and to Shortland and Richards, 22 January 1787, ADM 106/2347, pp. 185, 187.
20. Phillip to Nepean, 12 December, Nepean to Rose, 13 December 1786, T 1/639, nos 2892 a and b; Rose to Navy Board, 19 December 1786, ADM OT; Navy Board, Minute, 27 December 1786, ADM 106/2622; Deptford Officers to Navy Board, 29 December 1786, ADM 106/3407, p. 34.
21. Ross to Phillip, 22 December 1786, CO 201/2, fos 71–3, and to Stephens, 11 January 1787, ADM 108/1D, fo. 192; Nepean to Rose, 17 January 1787, HO 36/5, pp. 235–6; Navy Board, Minutes, 17 January and 14 February 1787, ADM 106/2623.
22. Harrison, Gordon and Stanley to Navy Board, 6 November, and Navy Board to Treasury, 6 November 1786, T 1/639, no. 2575; Rose to Navy Board, 7 November 1786, T 27/38, p. 392; Navy Board, Minute, 29 November 1786, ADM 106/2622, and Thomas to Stiles, 29 November 1786, USNA, Record group 45/446. A 'cocket' was a certificate stating that goods had been entered in the Customs register, and the requisite duties paid upon them.
23. Navy Board, Minute, 28 November 1786, ADM 106/2622, and Thomas to Fisher, 28 November 1786, USNA, Record group 45/446; Navy Board to Treasury, 30 November 1786, T 1/639, no. 2791; Steele to Excise Board, 30 November 1786, T 27/38, p. 408; Jackson to Steele, 2 December 1786, T 1/639, no. 2702; Rose to Navy Board, 7 December 1786, ADM OT; Steele to Customs Board, 2 February 1787, T 11/34.
24. Phillip to Nepean, [c. 30 October 1786], HO 42/10, fo. 302; to Nepean, 15 November 1786, and Nepean to Steele, 15 November 1786, T 1/639, no. 2649; Rose to Customs Board, 22 November 1786, T 11/34; Stiles to Rose, 23 November 1786, T 1/639, no. 2746.
25. Sydney to Lord President, 1 December 1786, HO 43/2, pp. 180–1; Privy Council, Draft Order, [6 December 1786], HO 42/10, fos 296–9.
26. Privy Council, Orders-in-Council, 6 and 22 December 1786, PC 2/131, pp. 492–505, 505–19, 544–7, 540–3; 12 February and 20 April 1787, PC 2/132, pp. 36–9, 39–41, 158–60, 160–3.
27. See, e.g., Orders-in-Council, 12 and 14 March, HO 13/5, pp. 85–6, 86–7, 98.
28. Privy Council, Warrants, 3 and 20 January, 24 February, 5 and 10 March and 4 April 1787, HO 13/5, pp. 1–6, 31–2, 65–8, 74–5, 77, 129.
29. Nepean to Middleton, 9 December 1786, CO 201/2, fo. 50; Middleton to Nepean, 11 December 1786, CO 201/2, fos 51–2.

Endnotes

30. Nepean to Clerks, 13 December 1786, HO 13/4, p. 355; Sydney to Law Officers, 16 December 1786, HO 49/1, pp. 274-5; Law Officers to Sydney, 19 December 1786, HO 48/1A, p. 858.
31. Contract, 27 January 1787, Kingston, KE 2/4/6. (I am indebted to Gary Sturgess for this reference.)
32. Stephens to Johnston, 8 December 1786, ADM 2/1178, p. 35, and to Navy Board, 8 December 1786, ADM A/2816; Johnson to Stephens, 18 December 1786, ADM OT.
33. Campbell, Returns of convicts on the hulks, 13 January 1787, T 1/641; *Alexander* Log, ADM 51/4375, fos 5-6.
34. *Lady Penrhyn* Log, ADM 51/4376, fos 5-6, 8; *Smyth (2)*, p. 15.
35. Admiralty to Hood, Smith, Phillip and Ball, 11 January 1787, ADM 2/1178, pp. 93-5; *Bradley*, p. 9.
36. Smith to Stephens, 27 February 1787, ADM 1/3290; Marshall to Stephens, 27 February 1787, ADM 1/989; *Prince of Wales* Log, 7 March 1787, ADM 51/4376, fo. 8; *Lady Penrhyn* Log, 17 and 20 March 1787, ADM 51/4376, fo. 8.
37. Nepean to Campbell, 20 February 1787, HO 13/5, p. 58; Campbell to Erskine, [c. 20 February 1787], SLNSW, Mitchell MS ZA 3229, pp. 270-1; Privy Council, Warrant, 24 February 1787, HO 13/5, pp. 65-8.
38. Nepean to Thomas, 21 February 1787, [privately owned]; to Stephens, 23 February 1787, ADM 1/4152, no. 49; to Lewis, 25 February 1787, WO 1/685, pp. 85-6; Stephens to Martin, 26 February 1787, ADM 2/587, pp. 395-6; Marshall to Stephens, 4 March 1787, ADM 1/989.
39. Quoted in Thomas, p. 22.
40. Nepean to Stephens, 3 March 1787, ADM 1/4152, no. 52; Marshall to Stephens, 4 March 1787, ADM 1/987.
41. *Scarborough* Log, ADM 51/4376, fo. 9, which states that 185 convicts were embarked.
42. Sydney to Bradley, 5 March 1787, HO 13/5, pp. 74-5; *Friendship* Log, ADM 51/4376, fos 8-9; *Charlotte* Log, ADM 51/4375, fo. 9.
43. Privy Council, Warrant, 27 April 1787, HO 13/5, p. 172; John Townsend and William Badger, Accounts, 1 May, Sydney to Treasury, 14 May 1787, T 1/646, no. 1235; *Prince of Wales* Log, ADM 51/4376, fos 9, 10, 11; Richards to Nepean, 8 May 1787, CO 201/2, fo. 334.
44. Stephens to Long and Furzer, 21 February 1787, ADM 2/1178, pp. 145-6; Admiralty, Minute, 2 March 1787, ADM 3/102, and Minute, 30 April 1787, ADM 3/103; *Bradley*, p. 11.
45. Ross to Nepean, 18 April 1787, CO 201/2, fos 305-7; Richards to Nepean, 26 April 1787, CO 201/2, fos 315-6.
46. Richards to Nepean, 26 April 1787, CO 201/2, fos 315-6; Ross, Return, 6 May 1787, CO 201/2, fo. 333; and see O'Brien (1950), pp. 279-84.

47. This was John Irwin, who was acting as surgeon on the ship.
48. Phillip, 'State of the Garrison and Convicts that are on board the Transports, June 10th 1787', CO 201/2, fo. 172. (The slight variations in the numbers are due to the lack of precise details for those put on board in the week before the ships sailed, and to deaths and births between the beginning of May and arrival at Tenerife – for a detailed discussion, see O'Brien (1950)).

8. *At Portsmouth*

1. Navy Board to Treasury Secretaries, 5 September 1786, T 1/639, no. 2267; e.g., Sydney to Colqhitt, and to the mayor of Chester, 11 October 1786, HO 13/4, pp. 236–7.
2. Nepean, Memorandum, [c. 1 January 1787], SLNSW, Dixson MS Q 522. [The *Hampshire Chronicle*'s description of the route on 15 January 1787 was clearly based on this memorandum.]
3. *General Evening Post*, 27 February 1787; Collins, Entry, 7 March 1787, Orderly Book, RMM, Archive 11/51/5.
4. Fowell to John Fowell, 17 April 1787, *Fowell*, p. 36; Nepean to Middleton, 18 April 1787, CO 201/2, fo. 302.
5. Clark, p. 77; Shaw (1966), p. 54; Hughes, p. 70; Thomas, p. 14.
6. Rose to Nepean, 7 December 1786, HO 35/7; Nepean to Rose, 7 December 1786, T 1/639, no. 2850; Navy Board to Rose, 11 December 1786, T 1/639, no. 2876; Teer to Middleton, 15 December 1786, ADM 106/243.
7. The dates of the ships' departures and arrivals are mostly taken from their logs, ADM 51/4375–6, from reports to the Navy Board, and from the First Fleet journals. There are sometimes variations between one source and another; and whether the log or journal was kept according to land time or sea time can also give rise to differences.
8. Nepean to Rose, 8 January 1787, HO 36/5, pp. 229–30; Steele to Stephens, and to Navy Board, 10 January 1787, T 27/38, p. 458; Admiralty, Minutes, 16 January 1787, ADM 3/102, and to Phillip and Hunter, 16 January 1787, ADM 2/117, p. 280; Admiralty to Phillip, 2 March 1787, ADM 2/117, pp. 314–5, and to Navy Board, 2 March 1787, ADM 108/1D, fo. 203.
9. Phillip to Navy Board, 15 February 1787, ADM 106/1291; Navy Board, Minute, 15 February 1787, ADM 106/2623; Hunter to Marshall, 21 February 1787, ADM 1/989; Admiralty, Minute, 23 February 1787, ADM 3/102, and Stephens to Navy Board, 23 February 1787, ADM 2/587, p. 389; Phillip to Stephens, 24 February 1787, ADM 1/2308; Navy Board, Minute, 24 February 1787, ADM 106/2623; Hunter to Marshall, 24 February 1787, ADM 1/989; Phillip to Stephens, 30 March 1787, ADM 1/2308; Admiralty to Navy Board, 31 March 1787, ADM 2/263, p. 148.
10. Admiralty, Minute, 6 January 1787, ADM 3/102, and Stephens to Navy Board,

6 January 1787, ADM 2/587, pp. 284–5; Navy Board, Minute, 6 January 1787, ADM 106/2623, and to Ball, 6 January 1787, ADM 106/2347, p. 177; Thomas to Deptford Officers, 6 January 1787, USNA, Record group 45/446; Deptford Officers to Navy Board, 11 January 1787, ADM 106/3364, fo. 89; Admiralty, Minute, 24 February 1787, ADM 3/102, and Stephens to Marshall, 24 February 1787, ADM 2/587, p. 392; and Marshall to Stephens, 25 February 1787, ADM 1/989.

11. Admiralty, Minute, 26 February 1787, ADM 3/102, and Stephens to Marshall, 26 February 1787, ADM 2/587, pp. 397–8.
12. Navy Board, Minutes, 23 February and 5 March 1787, ADM 106/2623.
13. Phillip to Stephens, 22 March 1787, ADM 1/2308; Admiralty, Minute, 22 March 1787, ADM 3/102.
14. Navy Board, Minutes, 5, 19 and 22 March 1787, ADM 106/2623, and to Shortland, 5, 19 and 22 March, and to Martin, 28 March 1787, ADM 106/2347, pp. 187, 211, 214, 217, 219.
15. Thomas to Shortland, 2 January 1787, USNA, Record group 45/446; Phillip to Nepean, 4 January 1787, CO 201/2, fo. 103; Stephens to Navy Board, 25 January 1787, ADM 2/1178, p. 116; Navy Board to Laforey, 26 January and 3 February 1787, ADM 106/2347, pp. 189, 192; Meredith and Walton to Stephens, 21 February 1787, ADM 108/1D, fo. 200; Navy Board, Minute, 26 February 1787, ADM 106/2623, and to Laforey, 26 February 1787, ADM 106/2347, p. 206.
16. Navy Board, Minutes, 8 and 31 January 1787, ADM 106/2623, and to Teer, 31 January 1783, ADM 106/2347, p. 192.
17. Ross to Stephens, 13 April 1787, CO 201/2, fo. 298; Stephens to Navy Board, 16 April 1787, ADM 108/1D, fo. 212; Navy Board, Minutes, 16 and 19 April 1787, ADM 106/2623, and to Martin, 16 and 19 April 1787, ADM 106/2347, pp. 233–4; Hunter to Phillip, 18 April 1787, [privately owned].
18. Navy Board, Minute, 28 March 1787, ADM 106/2623, and to Martin, 28 March 1787, ADM 106/2347, p. 219; Navy Board, Minutes, 9 March and 5 April 1787, ADM 106/2623, and 2 May 1787, ADM 106/2624, and to Shortland, 2 May 1787, ADM 106/2347, p. 228.
19. Admiralty, Minute, 26 February 1787, ADM 3/102, and Stephens to Marshall, 26 February 1787, ADM 2/587, pp. 397–8; Navy Board, Minute, 27 February 1787, ADM 106/2623; Marshall to Stephens, 28 February 1787, ADM 1/989; Navy Board, Minutes, 28 February, 2 and 5 March 1787, ADM 106/2623; Navy Board to Phillip, 2 March 1787, ADM 106/2347, pp. 209–10; Phillip to Stephens, 20 and 22 March 1787, ADM 1/2308; Navy Board, Minute, 16 March 1787, ADM 106/2623, and to Shortland, 22 March 1787, ADM 106/2347, p. 217; e.g., Navy Board to Shortland and Richards, 13 March 1787, ADM 106/2347, p. 213.

20. Stephens to Greenway, 28 February and 10 March, to Collins, 13 March, to Ross, 16 March 1787, ADM 2/1178, pp. 158, 183, 191, 195; Stephens to Smith, 13 March, and to Pownoll, 16 March 1787, ADM 2/1178, pp. 190, 196–7; Navy Board, Minutes, 20 March and 20 April 1787, ADM 106/2623.
21. Ross to Stephens, 13 April 1787, CO 201/2, fo. 299; Nepean to Stephens, 18 April 1787, ADM 1/4152, no. 63; Navy Board, Minute, 20 April 1787, ADM 106/2623; Richards to Nepean, 5 April 1787, CO 201/2, fo. 294.
22. Phillip to Nepean, 11 April 1787, CO 201/2, fo. 126.
23. Phillip to Nepean, 18 March 1787, CO 201/2, fo. 123; Middleton to Nepean, 20 March 1787, CO 201/2, fo. 243; Navy Board, Minute, 27 March 1787, ADM 106/2623.
24. *Clark*, pp. 247, 249.
25. Navy Board, Minute, 16 March 1787, ADM 106/2623; Stephens to Navy Board, 20 March 1787, ADM A/2817; Hunter to Stephens, 28 March 1787, ADM A/2818; Admiralty, Minute, 31 March 1787, ADM 3/102; Stephens to Navy Board, 2 April 1787, ADM A/2818.
26. Ball to Marshall, 27 March 1787, ADM 1/989; Admiralty, Minute, 29 March 1787, ADM 3/102, and Stephens to Marshall, 29 March 1787, ADM 2/587, p. 498; Marshall to Stephens, 2 April 1787, ADM A/2818; Admiralty, Minute, 3 April 1787, ADM 3/103, and Stephens to Marshall and Navy Board, 3 April 1787, ADM 2/587, pp. 519, 521–2.
27. White to Nepean, 27 February 1787, CO 201/2, fo. 220.
28. Fowell to John Fowell, 17 April 1787, *Fowell*, p. 36.
29. Stephens to Smith, 6 and 26 March, to Morrison, 14 March 1787, ADM 2/1178, pp. 176, 194, 202–3.
30. Clark to Phillip, 3 and 16 April 1787, Phillip to Clark, 10, 13 and 17 April, Howe to Clark, 16 April 1787, *Clark*, pp. 241–5.
31. *Clark*, pp. 19, 65, 94, 97.
32. Hunter to Phillip, 18 April 1787, [privately owned]; Navy Board, Minute, 19 April 1787, ADM 106/2623.
33. Sydney to Admiralty, 31 August 1786, ADM 1/4152, no. 25; Stephens to Tupper and Hughes, 8 October 1786, ADM 1/1177, p. 492; Ross to Stephens, 8 May 1787, CO 201/2, fo. 338.
34. *Alexander* marines, Petition, 7 April, *Prince of Wales* marines, Petition, 4 May, *Charlotte* marines, Petition, 7 May, *Scarborough* marines, Petition, 7 May 1787, CO 201/2, fos 327, 340, 342, 344; Phillip to Nepean, 8 May, Ross to Stephens, 8 May, Stephens to Nepean, 9 May 1787, CO 201/2, fos 150, 336, 338.
35. Sydney to Middleton, Middleton to Thomas, Thomas to Middleton, 23 April 1787, NLA, MS 1399; Sydney to Phillip, 5 May, Phillip to Nepean, 11 May 1787, CO 201/2, fos 146, 154–5.

Endnotes

36. *Tench*, pp. 11–12.

9. *Preparing Bodies for the Voyage*

1. Clark, p. 77; Shaw (1966), pp. 53–4; Mackay, pp. 69–70; Hughes, pp. 70–1; Hill, p. 45.
2. Phillip to Nepean, 18 March 1788, CO 201/2, fos 122–3.
3. Navy Board to Rose, 11 December 1786, T 1/639, no. 2876; Sydney to Treasury, 22 December 1786, T 1/639, no. 2984; Navy Board, Minute, 26 December 1786, ADM 106/2622, and Thomas to Wadham, *et al.*, 26 December 1786, USNA, Record group 45/446.
4. Navy Board, Minutes, 20 and 22 January 1787, ADM 106/2623; Teer to Navy Board, 22 January 1787, ADM 106/243.
5. Navy Board, Minute, 16 March 1787, ADM 106/2623, and to Shortland, 16 March 1787, ADM 106/2347, p. 214; Phillip to Nepean, 18 March 1787, CO 201/2, fos 122–3; Nepean to Middleton, 18 April 1787, NMM, MID 1/131.
6. Navy Board, Minutes, 9, 19 and 20 April 1787, ADM 106/2623, and to Shortland, 9 and 20 April, and to Martin, 19 April 1787, ADM 106/2347, pp. 223–5.
7. Treasury to Navy Board, 10 May 1787, ADM/OT; Navy Board, Minutes, 7, 9, and 14 May 1787, ADM 106/2624, and to Shortland, 7 May, and to Martin, 11 May 1787, ADM 106/2347, p. 229; Steele to Navy Board, 10 May 1787, ADM OT; Thomas to Yerbury, *et al.*, 11 and 16 May 1787, USNA, Record group 45/446.
8. *Howard*, pp. 236–7, 266, 272, 275, 276, 290, 341.
9. Navy Board, Minute, 8 February 1787, ADM 106/2623; Sydney to Admiralty, 19 March 1787, ADM 1/4152, no. 56; Admiralty to Navy Board, 20 March 1787, ADM 108/1D, fo. 208; Navy Board, Minute, 20 March 1787, ADM 106/2623; *Alexander* Log, ADM 51/4375, fos 8–10; and see Watt (1989), p. 140.
10. *Nagle*, p. 106.
11. Watt (1981), p. 12; Gordon, pp. 155–66.
12. C. R. Markham, ed., *The Hawkins' Voyages* (Burt Franklin, New York, 1970), p. 163.
13. *Banks*, vol. 1, pp. 243–4, 251, vol. 2, pp. 74, 301.
14. Phillip, Memorandum, [c. 1 October 1786], and to Sydney, 12 March 1787, CO 201/2, fos 88, 121.
15. *Collins*, p. 1.
16. Balmain to Shortland, Shortland to Navy Board, 17 February 1787, T 1/643, no. 409; Navy Board, Minutes, 19 and 22 February 1787, ADM 106/2623, and to Treasury Secretaries, 19 February 1787, T 1/643, no. 409; Admiralty, Minute, 21 February 1787, ADM 3/102, and Stephens to Navy Board, 21 February 1787, ADM 2/587, p. 379; Steele to Navy Board, 21

February 1787, ADM OT; Navy Board, Minute, 22 February, ADM 106/2623, and to Shortland and Richards, 22 February 1787, ADM 106/2347, pp. 203-4.
17. Phillip to Sydney, Nepean to Middleton, and Middleton to Nepean, 28 February 1787, CO 201/2, fos 96-7, 112, and [privately owned].
18. Navy Board, Minute, 6 March 1787, ADM 106/2623, and to Shortland, 6 March 1787, ADM 106/2347, p. 211.
19. Phillip to Nepean, 18 March 1787, CO 201/2, fo. 122; Navy Board, Minutes, 19 and 21 March 1787, ADM 106/2623, and to Shortland and Richards, 21 March 1787, ADM 106/2347, pp. 216-17; *Tench*, p. 12.
20. Middleton to Nepean, 28 February 1787, CO 201/2, fo. 96. For the date of the contract, see Navy Board, Minute, 27 November 1786, ADM 106/2622.
21. Phillip to Sydney, 12 March 1787, CO 201/2, fos 120-1.
22. Phillip to Admiralty, 27 December 1786, ADM 1/2308; Admiralty to Phillip, 23 February 1787, CO 201/2, fos 118-9; Navy Board, Minutes, 28 February and 2 March 1787, ADM 106/2623; Middleton to Nepean, 28 February 1787, CO 201/2, fo. 96.
23. Phillip to Sydney, Nepean to Middleton and Middleton to Nepean, 28 February 1787, CO 201/2, fos 96-7, 112, and [privately owned]; Navy Board, Minute, 28 February 1787, ADM 106/2623, and to Phillip and Richards, 28 February 1787, ADM 106/2347, p. 208; Phillip to Nepean, 1 March 1787, CO 201/2, fos 114-5.
24. Phillip to Sydney, 12 March 1787, CO 201/2, fo. 120; Navy Board, Minute, 25 April 1787, ADM 106/2623, and to Phillip, 25 April 1787, ADM 106/2347, pp. 227-8.
25. Privy Council, Instructions to Phillip, 25 April 1787, CO 201/2, fos 30-1; Nepean to Richards, 25 April 1787, HO 13/5, pp. 165-6; Phillip to Nepean, 11 May 1787, CO 201/2, fo. 154.
26. Lloyd and Coulter, p. 92.
27. White to Phillip, and Phillip to Stephens, 7 February 1787, ADM 1/2308; Phillip to Nepean, 7 February 1787, CO 201/2, fo. 108; Stephens to Navy Board, 10 February 1787, ADM A/2187; Navy Board, Minute, 12 February 1787, ADM 106/2623, and to Phillip, Martin and Laforey, 12 February 1787, ADM 106/2347, pp. 196-7; Nepean to Middleton, 13 February 1787, [privately owned]; Middleton to Nepean, 13 February 1787, CO 201/2, fo. 214; Navy Board, Minute, 28 February 1787, ADM 106/2623, and to Cawthorne, 28 February 1787, ADM 106/2347, p. 207; Navy Board, Minute, 12 March 1787, ADM 106/2623, and to White, Shortland and Cawthorne, 12 March 1787, ADM 106/2347, pp. 212-3.
28. Phillip to Nepean, 18 March 1787, CO 201/2, fos 122-4; Navy Board,

Minutes, 19 and 21 March 1787, ADM 106/2623, and to Shortland and Richards, 21 March 1787, ADM 106/2347, pp. 216–7; Middleton to Nepean, 20 March 1787, CO 201/2, fo. 243.
29. Navy Board, Minute, 4 April 1787, ADM 106/2623, and to Cawthorne and Martin, 4 April 1787, ADM 106/2347, p. 222; Phillip to Nepean, 11 April 1787, CO 201/2, fo. 126; Nepean to Middleton, 18 April 1787, NMM MID 1/131; Navy Board, Minutes, 20 and 23 April 1787, ADM 106/2623, and to Shortland and Richards, 20 and 23 April 1787, ADM 106/2347, pp. 225–6; Phillip to Nepean, 11 May 1787, CO 201/2, fo. 154.
30. *Smyth (2)*, p. 47.
31. *Collins*, p. 1.
32. Navy Board, Minute, 28 February 1787, ADM 106/2623; Phillip to Nepean, 18 March 1787, CO 201/2, fo. 124.
33. *Bath Chronicle*, 5 April 1787.
34. White, Return, 15 November 1788, CO 201/3, fo. 160; *Collins*, p. 1.
35. Pemberton to Dundas, [September 1785], BL, OIOC G 9/1, pp. 18–25; Grimes to Grimes, 21 October 1792, *HRNSW*, vol. 1, part 2, p. 672; *Wordsworth*, p. 154.
36. Phillip to Sydney, 2 September 1787, CO 201/2, fo. 176; Collins to his father, 6 November 1787, SLNSW, Mitchell MS 700.
37. Watt (1989), p. 144; Phillip to Sydney, 2 September 1787, CO 201/2, fo. 176.
38. Knight, p. 131.

10. Leaving the World

1. See *Botany Bay: The Real Story*, pp. 117–8.
2. For details, see Frost (1987).
3. Phillip, Memorandum, [c. 1 October 1786], CO 201/2, fos 88–93; and other documents cited following.
4. Nepean, Memorandum, [c. 1 January 1787], SLNSW, Dixson Add. MS Q 522.
5. *Worgan*, p. 12.
6. Privy Council, Instructions to Phillip, 25 April 1787, CO 201/1, fos 30–2.
7. Nepean to Middleton, 4 May 1787, NMM MID 1/131; Middleton to Nepean, 4 May 1787, CO 201/2, fo. 329.
8. Sydney to Admiralty, 5 May 1787, CO 201/2, fo. 331; Admiralty, Minute, 7 May 1787, ADM 3/103, and to Phillip, 7 May 1787, ADM 2/117, p. 397.
9. *Smyth (2)*, pp. 44–5.
10. For more on the development of the chronometer, see Sobel.
11. Phillip to Sydney, 5 June, and to Nepean, 2 September 1787 CO 201/2, fos 162, 182.
12. *Bradley*, p. 12.
13. *Smyth (2)*, p. 16.

14. *Collins*, p. lvii; Phillip to Sydney, 5 June and 6 August 1787, CO 201/2, fos 162, 174.
15. Phillip to Nepean, 5 June 1787, CO 201/2, fo. 169.
16. Phillip to Sydney, 5 June, and to Nepean, 5 and 10 June 1787, CO 201/2, fos 162, 168, 170.
17. *Collins*, p. lxiii; *Tench*, p. 17; *White*, p. 54.
18. Phillip to Nepean, 2 September 1787, CO 201/2, fos 182-4; *Bradley*, p. 38.
19. *Smyth (2)*, pp. 29, 34; *Clark*, p. 36.
20. *Smyth (2)*, p. 29.
21. Phillip to Nepean, 2 September 1787, CO 201/2, fos 182-4; *Easty*, p. 30; *White*, p. 73; Phillip to Sydney, 2 September 1787, CO 201/2, fo. 176.
22. Phillip to Nepean, 2 September 1787, CO 201/2, fos 182-4.
23. Phillip to Banks, 31 August 1787, Sutro, Banks EN 1/29, and 2 September 1787, SLNSW, Mitchell MS C 213, pp. 3-5; *Collins*, p. lxxx.
24. Phillip to Stephens, 10 November 1787, ADM 1/2308; *King*, p. 21; *Collins*, p. lxxix; *White*, p. 90.
25. *White*, p. 90.
26. Southwell to Butler, 11 November 1787, BL, Add. MS 16381, fo. 25.
27. *Tench*, p. 26; *White*, p. 81 (of Rio de Janeiro).
28. Phillip to Nepean, 28 October 1786, HO 42/9, fo. 83; *Worgan*, p. 1; *Hunter*, p. 21; *Tench*, p. 28.
29. *Worgan*, p. 1; *Collins*, p. lxxx.
30. Southwell to his mother, 11 November 1787, BL, Add. MS 16381, fo. 23.
31. Cook to Walker, 20 November 1772, NLNZ Turnbull, MS Papers 0230-30; *Collins*, p. lxxxvi.
32. *White*, p. 101; *Tench*, p. 28.
33. *Worgan*, p. 1; Masson to Banks, 13 November 1787, Sutro, Banks EN 1/36.
34. *Tench*, p. 66.
35. *King*, pp. 24-31; Phillip to Middleton, 6 July 1788 [privately owned].
36. *Smyth (2)*, pp. 50-4.
37. *Tench*, p. 31.
38. Blackburn to his sister, 5 June 1787, AJCP, Reel M 970.
39. *Collins*, p. 1.
40. This summary is based on the journals of the First Fleet officers.

11. *No Cheaper Mode?*

1. Hancock, p. 11; Mackay, p. 51; Shaw (1984), p. 90, and cf. Shaw (1955), p. 43. Pitt's speech of 9 February 1791 is reported in *PH*, vol. 28 (1789-91), cols 1223-5.
2. Campbell was contracted to accommodate 250 convicts on the *Justitia* for £1818 per quarter, and 240 on the *Censor* for £1625 - i.e., 490 for a total of

Endnotes

£13,772 per annum, or £28 per person. In practice, the actual cost might vary a little, according to whether the hulks were over or under complement, and to what was paid surgeons and clergymen. Reflecting what I take to be information from the Home Office, the *Daily Universal Register* announced on 23 November 1786 that 'The expense of keeping the convicts on board the hulks, amounted *communibas annis*, to about £28 each man per annum. The transporting of them to Botany Bay will cost the public, it is computed, £32 each nearly.' It seems best to settle on £28 as the base figure.

3. Moloney, p. 22.
4. Coggan and Campbell, Testimony, 12 May 1785, HO 7/1.
5. Nepean's queries, and Campbell's replies [before 22 January 1786], HO 42/10, fos 426-7; Campbell's detailed accounts of the cost of the ship, and his lists of the food and tools that would be needed, are in HO 42/8, no. 9 and HO 42/10, fo. 427; and his letter to Nepean, 22 January 1786, HO 42/8, no. 8.
6. [ ], Estimate, [undated, but August 1786], HO 42/10, fo. 425. (In some of these lists, the figures for £s only are given. Generally I have followed this practice. I have also supplied totals when these are not in the originals.)
7. [Nepean], Estimate, [undated, but August 1786], HO 42/7, fo. 23. There are some discrepancies between the figures in this list and those in the next.
8. [Nepean], 'Staff Establishment for the Settlement at New South Wales', [undated, but August 1786], HO 35/1.
9. [Nepean], Estimate, [undated, but August 1786], HO 42/7, fo. 24.
10. Nepean to Middleton, 12 December 1786, CO 201/2, fo. 53; Middleton to Pitt, 13 December 1786, [privately owned]. (In this list and those following, I have not adjusted the figure to the nearest pound. Rather, I have simply left off all shillings and pence.)
11. I have derived these figures from:
    Ships and marines: Stephens to Nepean, 28 December 1786, CO 201/2, fo. 43.
    Civil establishment: Nepean, 'An Account of Expenses Incurred in Transporting and Maintaining the Convicts Sent to New South Wales', February 1790, CO 201/4, fo. 189, where he gives the annual cost as £2877.10.0.
    Ordnance: Rogers, 'Estimate of the Expense of Ordnance ...', [c. 21 December 1786], CO 201/2, fo. 69.
12. [Middleton], 'An Account of the Expenses incurred and that will probably attend the Botany Bay establishment', 18 April 1787, [privately owned].
13. This is a composite list, compiled from: Middleton, 'Calculations given to Mr. Nepean Feby 1790 concerning convicts and Botany Bay', [privately owned]; Nepean, Lists, [undated], CO 201/4, ff. 182-90, 191-9; and Navy Board, 'An Account of the Total Expense incurred in our department for the settlements in New South Wales ...', 5 June 1793, *HRNSW*, vol. 2, pp. 38-9.

I have also re-arranged the sequence of Middleton's items somewhat, so as to make the phases clearer.
14. This was the number of women first intended to be sent. In the event, 192 women convicts and convicts' wives sailed, so that the cost in the clause is significantly understated.
15. This item does not appear in Middleton's list. However, it is included in the yet fuller one dated 5 June 1793 – see *HRNSW*, vol. 2, p. 38.
16. Middleton gave the figures for the nine transports and store ships separately.
17. Middleton calculated this expense variously at £31,663 (December 1786), £34,375 (April 1787) and £39,209 (April 1787). I have therefore used the last figure.
18. From List, 5 June 1793, *HRNSW*, vol. 2, p. 39.
19. List, CO 201/4, fo. 195.
20. Ross to Nepean, 10 July 1788, *HRNSW*, vol. 1, part 2, p. 176; Blainey (1966), p. 17.
21. *PH*, vol. 28 (1789–91), cols 1221–5.
22. *Botany Bay: The Real Story*, pp. 152–4.
23. Memorandum, 14 February 1791, Court of Directors, Proposed terms, [c. 17 March 1790]; and 'Observations on the Paper returned from the Court of Directors', BT 6/227; 'Heads of the proposed New Bill', 28 March 1791, BL, Add. MS 38350, pp. 284–7.
24. Dundas to Phillip, 10 January 1792, *HRNSW*, vol. 1, part 2, p. 585.

Conclusion

1. Mackay, p. 57.
2. Atkinson, pp. 59–61; Christopher, p. 335.
3. Phillip, Memorandum, [c. 1 October 1786], CO 201/2, fo. 92.
4. Camden to Sydney, 11 January 1787, Clements, Sydney vol. 14.
5. Roberts to Ross, [c. January 1785], HO 42/5, fo. 466; Barnes and others, Memorandum, [4 February 1785], HO 35/1.
6. Nepean to Steele, 10 June 1786, T 1/632, no. 1407.
7. See *Botany Bay: The Real Story*, pp. 146–7.
8. Pitt to Rolle, 6 May 1786, PRO 30/8/195, fo. 31.
9. Richards to Pitt, 28 September 1786, PRO 30/8/171, fo. 17.
10. Phillip, Memorandum, [c. 1 October 1786], CO 201/2, fo. 92.
11. Phillip to Nepean, 28 October 1786, HO 42/9, fo. 84; to Sydney, 1 November 1786, SLNSW, Dixson MS Q 162, pp. 1–2; to Clark, 13 April 1787, *Clark*, p. 243.
12. Phillip to Lansdowne, 3 July 1788, SLNSW, Mitchell MS 7241; to Sydney, 6 July 1788, SLNSW, Dixson MS Q 162, pp. 9–10; to Middleton, 6 July 1788, [privately owned].

Endnotes

13. Sydney to Admiralty, 31 August 1786, ADM 1/4152, no. 25.
14. Phillip, Memorandum, [c. 1 October 1786], fos 90, 92.
15. Phillip to Nepean, 1 March 1787, CO 201/2, fo. 115; Privy Council, Instructions to Phillip, 25 April 1787, fos 38–9.
16. Privy Council, Draft Additional Instructions to Phillip, 23 June 1789, HO 31/1, which were approved by the Privy Council on 8 August 1789, PC 2/134, pp. 188–92; Attorney-General, 'Draft of a Warrant for a Commission authorizing the Governor of New South Wales to remit Sentences', 8 November 1790, HO 48/1B, pp. 345–50; 30 Geo. III, c. 47, *Statutes at Large*, vol. 16 (London, 1784), p. 57.
17. Phillip to Sydney, 5 June, and to Nepean, 6 June and 2 September 1787, CO 201/2, fos 162, 168–9, 182.
18. Phillip to Nepean, 11 April 1787, CO 201/2, fo. 128.
19. *Fowell*, p. 57.
20. Sydney to Treasury, 31 October 1788, HO 35/9.
21. *Reading Mercury and Oxford Gazette*, 6 November 1786; *Hampshire Chronicle*, 2 April 1787; and cf. *Bath Chronicle*, 5 April 1787.
22. See Frost (1994), pp. 144–58.
23. Blainey (1966), p. 17.
24. Phillip to Nepean, 18 March 1787, CO 201/2, fo. 123.
25. Miles to the African Committee, 1 February 1783, T 70/33, pp. 53–4.
26. John Barnes and others, Memorandum, [4 February 1785], HO 35/1.
27. Reece, pp. 155–65.
28. Ibid, pp. 166–90.
29. Teer to Navy Board, 7 December 1786, ADM 106/243.
30. *Smyth (2)*, p. 47; *Collins*, p. 2.
31. See Frost (1995), p. 84.
32. Elizabeth Magra, Memorial, 31 March 1780, AO 13/56; Commissioners, Decision, 20 May 1783, AO 12/99.
33. Danforth, Memorial, 8 September 1783, quoted in Norton, p. [vii].
34. Phillip to Grenville, 20 June 1790, *HRNSW*, vol. 1, part 2, p. 351.
35. Knight, p. 136.

Select Bibliography

Alan Atkinson, *The Europeans in Australia: A History*, vol. 1: *The Beginning* (Oxford University Press, Melbourne, 1997).

Charles Bateson, *The Convict Ships, 1787–1868*, 2nd ed. (A.H. and A.W. Reed, Sydney, 1974 [1969]).

Geoffrey Blainey, *The Tyranny of Distance: How Distance Shaped Australia's History* (Sun Books, Melbourne, 1966).

John Brewer, *The Sinews of Power: War, Money and the English State, 1688–1783* (Alfred A. Knopf, New York, 1989).

W.S. Campbell, 'Arthur Phillip', *JRAHS*, vol. 21 (1935), pp. 264–6.

A.K. Cavanagh, 'The Return of the First Fleet Ships', *The Great Circle*, vol. 11, no. 2 (1989), pp. 1–16.

Emma Christopher, *A Merciless Place: The Lost Story of Britain's Convict Disaster in Africa and How it Led to the Settlement of Australia* (Allen & Unwin, Sydney, 2010).

C.M.H. Clark, *A History of Australia*, vol. 1: *From the Earliest Times to the Age of Macquarie* (Melbourne University Press, Melbourne, 1962).

R.M. Crawford, *Australia* (Hutchinson, London, 1952).

Victor Crittenden, *A Bibliography of the First Fleet* (Australian National University Press, Canberra, 1981).

Victor Crittenden, *The Voyage of the First Fleet, 1787–1788: Taken from Contemporary Accounts* (Mulini Press, Canberra, c. 1981).

F.K. Crowley, 'The Foundation Years, 1788–1821', in *Australia: A Social and Political History*, ed. Gordon Greenwood (Angus & Robertson, Sydney, 1955), pp. 1–43.

M. Barnard Eldershaw, *Phillip of Australia: An Account of the Settlement of Sydney Cove, 1788–92* (Harrup, London, 1938).

B.H. Fletcher, *Landed Enterprise and Penal Society* (Sydney University Press, Sydney, 1976).

Alan Frost, *Convicts and Empire: A Naval Question, 1776–1811* (Oxford University Press, Melbourne, 1980).

Alan Frost, *Arthur Phillip, 1738–1814: His Voyaging* (Oxford University Press, Melbourne, 1987).

Select Bibliography

Alan Frost, *Sir Joseph Banks and the Transfer of Plants to and from the South Pacific, 1786-1798* (The Colony Press, Melbourne, 1993).

Alan Frost, *Botany Bay Mirages* (Melbourne University Press, Melbourne, 1994).

Alan Frost, 'The Planting of New South Wales: Sir Joseph Banks and the creation of an Antipodean Europe', in *Sir Joseph Banks: a Global Perspective*, eds R.E.R. Banks, *et al.* (Royal Botanic Gardens, Kew, London, 1994), pp. 133–47.

Alan Frost, *The Precarious Life of James Mario Matra: Voyager with Cook; American Loyalist; Servant of Empire* (The Miegunyah Press, Melbourne, 1995).

Alan Frost, *The Global Reach of Empire* (Melbourne University Publishing, Melbourne, 2003).

Alan Frost, *Botany Bay: The Real Story* (Black Inc., Melbourne, 2011).

Mollie Gillen, *The Founders of Australia: A Biographical Dictionary of the First Fleet* (Library of Australian History, Sydney, 1989).

Mollie Gillen, 'His Majesty's Mercy: The circumstances of the First Fleet', *The Push*, no. 29 (1991), pp. 47–109.

E.C. Gordon, 'Scurvy and Anson's Voyage Round the World, 1740-1744: An analysis of the Royal Navy's worst outbreak', *American Neptune*, vol. 44 (1984), pp. 155–66.

W.K. Hancock, *Australia* (Ernest Benn, London, 1930).

Graeme Henderson and Myra Stanbury, *The Sirius: Past and Present* (Collins Australia, Sydney, 1988).

David Hill, *1788: The Brutal Truth of the First Fleet* (Heinemann, Sydney, 2008).

Edward Hughes, *Studies in Administration and Finance, 1558–1825* (Porcupine Press, Philadelphia, 1980 [1934]).

Robert Hughes, *The Fatal Shore: A History of the Transportation of Convicts to Australia, 1787-1868* (Harvill Collins, London, 1987).

Thomas Keneally, *Australians, vol. 1: Origins to Eureka* (Allen & Unwin, Sydney, 2009).

Jonathan King, *The First Fleet: The Convict Voyage that Founded Australia, 1787-88* (Macmillan, Melbourne, 1982).

Robert J. King, 'George Vancouver and the contemplated settlement at Nootka Sound', *The Great Circle*, vol. 32, no. 1 (2010), pp. 6–34.

Roger Knight, 'The First Fleet: Its state and preparation, 1786–1787', in *Studies from Terra Australis to Australia*, eds John Hardy and Alan Frost (Australian Academy of the Humanities, Canberra, 1989), pp. 121–36, 256–62.

C. Lloyd and J.L.S. Coulter, *Medicine and the Navy, 1200–1900, vol. 3: 1714–1815* (Edinburgh, Livingstone, 1961).

Neil K. Macintosh, *Richard Johnson: Chaplain to the Colony of New South Wales* (Library of Australian History, Sydney, 1978).

David Mackay, *A Place of Exile: The European Settlement of New South Wales* (Oxford University Press, Melbourne, 1985).

John Molony, *The Penguin Bicentennial History of Australia: The Story of 200 Years* (Ringwood, Viking, 1987).

John Moore, *The First Fleet Marines, 1786-1792* (University of Queensland Press, St Lucia, 1987).

Mary Beth Norton, *The British-Americans: The Loyalist Exiles in England, 1774-1789* (Little, Brown and Company, Boston, 1972).

Eris O'Brien, *The Foundation of Australia (1786-1800): A Study of English Criminal Practice and Penal Colonization in the Eighteenth Century* (Sheed & Ward, London, 1937).

Eris O'Brien, *The Foundation of Australia (1786-1800): A Study of English Criminal Practice and Penal Colonization in the Eighteenth Century,* 2nd ed. (Angus & Robertson, Sydney, 1950).

Wilfrid Oldham, *Britain's Convicts to the Colonies*, ed. Hugh Oldham (Library of Australian History, Sydney, 1990).

Bob Reece, *The Origins of Irish Convict Transportation to New South Wales* (Palgrave, Basingstoke, 2001).

N.A.M. Rodger, *The Wooden World: An Anatomy of the Georgian Navy* (Naval Institute Press, Annapolis, 1986).

Owen Rutter, ed., *The First Fleet* (Golden Cockerel Press, [n.p.], 1937).

A.G.L. Shaw, *The Story of Australia* (Faber & Faber, London, 1955).

A.G.L. Shaw, *Convicts and the Colonies* (Faber, London, 1966).

A.G.L. Shaw, 'The Reasons for the Foundation of a British Settlement at Botany Bay in 1788', *ARTS*, vol. 12 (1984), pp. 83-91.

Babette Smith, *Australia's Birthstain* (Allen & Unwin, Sydney, 2008).

Dava Sobel, *Longitude: The True Story of a Lone Genius Who Solved the Greatest Scientific Problem of His Time* (Fourth Estate, London, 1996).

J.H. Thomas, *Portsmouth and the First Fleet, 1786-1787* (Portsmouth City Council, Portsmouth, 1987).

Sir James Watt *et al.*, eds, *Starving Sailors* (National Maritime Museum, London, 1981)

Sir James Watt, 'The Colony's Health', in *Studies from Terra Australis to Australia*, eds John Hardy and Alan Frost (Australian Academy of the Humanities, Canberra, 1989), pp. 137-51, 262-6.

P.L.C. Webb, 'The Rebuilding and Repair of the Fleet, 1783-1793', *Bulletin of the Institute of Historical Research*, vol. 50 (1977), pp. 194-209.

Charles Wilson, *Australia, 1788-1988: The Creation of a Nation* (Weidenfeld & Nicolson, London, 1987).

A.T. Yarwood, *Samuel Marsden: The Great Survivor* (Melbourne University Press, Melbourne, 1977).

Index

The following abbreviation is used in the index: BB = Botany Bay

1788 (Hill), 4, 6, 9

Aborigines *see* Indigenous Australians
accommodation, 102
Adair, Robert, 98
Admiralty
   approval of Shortland's appointment, 83
   fitting out of ships
      Sirius, 85–6
      Supply, 12, 89
   information needs, 10
   informed of BB decision, 20
   investigation of complaints, 136
   marine enlistment, 66
Alexander, George, 56
Alexander (ship), 91, 133
   changes to accommodation, 134
   chartered to East India Co., 93
   crew tally, 65
   embarkation of convicts, 123
   fitting out, 118
   illness, 144
   intended mutiny, 176
   joins First Fleet, 131
   outbreak of disease, 130
   receives stores, 115
   selection of convicts, 71
   tally of convicts, 125
Alexander (ship-of-the-line), 51
Alt, August, 58
Altree, Jonathan, 135
animals *see* provisions, livestock
Anson, George, Baron, 146
Ariadne (ship), 51, 56
Arndell, Thomas, 57
Atkinson, Alan, 205
   The Europeans in Australia, 199
Auchmuty, J.J., 6

Australian Aborigines *see* Indigenous Australians

Ball, Henry Lidgbird, 62
   appointed to command *Supply*, 89, 115
   complaints against him, 136
   and fitting out of *Supply*, 89–90
Balmain, William, 57–8
   requests fresh food, 148
Banks, Joseph, 30, 99
   and appointment of botanist, 59
   and provision of seeds, 100
   seeds for commerce, 112–13
Barnard Eldershaw, M., 4, 6
Barnes, John, 200
Basilisk (ship), 51, 56
Bateson, Charles, 9
Bath Chronicle, 154
   reports BB decision, 23–4
Bayley, William, 165
Beauchamp Committee, 182
Berwick (ship) *see Sirius* (ship)
Birmingham Daily Gazette, 21
Blainey, Geoffrey, 194, 206
Bloodworth, James, 106
Borrowdale (ship)
   acquired for First Fleet, 91, 92
   crew tally, 65
   joins First Fleet, 131, 132
   receives stores, 115
Botany Bay *see* New South Wales
Bradley, Henry, 121, 124
Bradley, William, 62, 87
Brewer, Henry, 72
bricks, 106
Brooks, Thomas, 72
Brough, Anthony, 90
Burton, David, 59

Cabell, Henry, 75–80
  marriage, 79
Camden, Charles Pratt, Earl, 37
Campbell, Duncan, 2, 70–1, 121
  charge for convicts in hulks, 181–2
  cost of transportation to NSW, 182–4
  death rate on convict voyages, 4
Campbell, James, 123
Campbell, W.S., 4–6
Canary Islands, 166–7
Cape Town, 170–4
Cavanagh, A.K., 9
Cawthorne, George, 153
Charlotte (ship), 79
  acquired for First Fleet, 91
  changes to accommodation, 133
  chartered to East India Co., 93
  crew tally, 65
  embarkation of convicts, 124
  fitting out, 118
  joins First Fleet, 132
  receives stores, 115
  tally of convicts, 125
Christopher, Emma, 199
chronometer, 86, 111–12, 165
civil establishment, 49–59
Clark, C.H. Manning, 130
  on condition of convicts, 1, 2, 140, 198
  on Phillip's appointment as governor, 6
Clark, Ralph, 70, 137, 168, 202
Clarke, Charles, 161
cloth manufacture, 106–9
clothing
  provisions, 103–4, 134
  women convicts, 2
Coggan, Charles, 161, 182
Collins, David, 55, 63, 80
  on convict health, 3
  embarkation, 125
  at proclamation of the colony, 177
  quality of provisions, 210
  on success of voyage, 3–4, 176
Collins, William, 123
Colnett, James, 113
commerce, provision for, 112–13
Considen, Dennis, 57
convicts
  behaviour on voyage, 166
  dumping, 208–10

emancipation, 33
embarkation, 120–6
health
  before departure, 143–9
  on the voyage, 154–5, 166, 169
instructions to Phillip, 33
opportunity for redemption, 29–30
Phillip's intentions, 30–1
profile, 67–9
property holding, 28–9
remission of sentences, 41–2
selection, 69–71
wives and children, 69
see also women convicts
Cook, James, 161, 173
cotton, 109
courts, 37–9
Crittenden, Victor, 9
currency, 42–4

Daily Universal Register
  reports BB decision, 21, 22, 23
  selection of ships' crews, 72
Danforth, James, 211–12
Dawes, William, 62–3, 111–12
  in Rio de Janeiro, 170
Denison, Charlott, 50–1
Dickson, James, 100
Dodd, Henry, 64–5
Dundas, Henry, 196

East India Company
  informed of BB decision, 20–1
  ships licensed to, 93
Egmont (ship), 51
Eldershaw, M. Barnard *see* Barnard Eldershaw, M.
embarkation, 120–6
  legal steps, 120–2
Europe (ship), 51, 56, 73, 74
Europeans in Australia, The (Atkinson), 199

female convicts *see* women convicts
First Fleet
  delayed, 130–9
  health record, 154
  historiography, 8–13, 198–9
  precedents for the voyage, 161
  preparations, 18–21
  the voyage, 165–76

Index

Fishburn (ship)
  acquired for First Fleet, 92
  crew tally, 65
  joins First Fleet, 131, 132
  livestock losses, 175
  receives stores, 115
flax, 107-8
food *see* provisions, food
Fowell, Newton, 7-8, 129, 136
Fraser, William, 10
freedom of religion, 33-4
fresh food
  availability in Rio de Janeiro, 168-9
  purchases in Tenerife, 167
  requests in Portsmouth, 148-52
Friendship (ship), 79, 80
  acquired for First Fleet, 91
  changes to accommodation, 133
  crew tally, 65
  embarkation of convicts, 124
  fitting out, 118
  joins First Fleet, 132
  profile of convicts, 70
  receives stores, 115
  tally of convicts, 125
Furzer, James, 62, 125

Gentleman's Magazine
  reports BB decision, 23
Gillen, Mollie, 1-2
Golden Grove (ship)
  acquired for First Fleet, 91, 92
  crew tally, 65
  joins First Fleet, 131, 132
  livestock losses, 175
  receives stores, 115
Gorgon (ship), 59
government record-keeping, 9-12
Grantham (ship), 88
Great Seal, 42
Gregory, Thomas, 18, 90
Grimes, Charles, 155
Guardian (ship), 193, 194, 206, 213

Hamilton, Sackville, 204
Hamond, Andrew Snape, 57
Hampshire Chronicle
  BB decision, 24
  plans for future sailings, 205
  reports number of convicts, 68
Hancock, Keith, 181

Harrison, Richard, 209
Hawkesbury, Charles Jenkinson, Baron, 196
Hawkins, Sir John, 146
Hill, David, 141
1788, 4, 6, 9
historiography, 8-13, 181, 198-9
Holmes, Christopher, 136
Holmes, Susanna, 75-80
  marriage, 79
hospital ship, 154
Howard, John, 143-4
Howe, Richard Howe, Earl, 81, 82
  and military law, 35-6
  opposes broad pennant for Phillip, 60-1
  on Phillip's appointment, 53
Hughes, Robert, 1, 2, 130-1, 141
Hunter, John, 55, 59-61, 72, 174
  fitting out of *Sirius*, 87
  investigates complaint against Ball, 136
  on *Supply* (ship), 88
Hyaena (ship), 165, 166

illness
  in jails, 143-4
  on transports at Portsmouth, 144
Indigenous Australians
  instructions to Phillip, 32-3
  Phillip's intentions, 30-1

jail conditions, 143-4
Johnson, Richard, 29-30, 56-7, 112, 136
Johnston, George, 92, 123

Kable, Henry *see* Cabell, Henry
Kent (ship), 173
kilns, 106
King, Jonathan, 1, 9
King, Philip Gidley, 62, 72
  on *Sirius* (ship), 84
  on *Supply* (ship), 88
  tally of transport crews, 65
Knight, Roger, 9, 214

Lady Juliana (ship), 59, 193
Lady Penrhyn (ship), 2, 91
  chartered to East India Co., 93
  crew tally, 65
  embarkation of convicts, 123

illness, 144
joins First Fleet, 131, 132
livestock losses, 175
receives stores, 115
tally of convicts, 125
land grants, 41
law, 34–7
see also courts
Leinster (ship), 209
Lemain Island, 200
Lochart, James, 72, 73–5
London Chronicle
reports BB decision, 22, 23
Long, John, 62, 125
Loyalists, 211–12

Macaulay, George Mackenzie, 18, 90
Mackay, David, 1, 141, 181, 198–9
marines, 65–6
camp equipment, 102
decision to withhold liquor in NSW, 138–9
embarkation, 122–5
equipment, 110–11, 118
officers, 62–3
selection, 72
wives and children, 67
Marsden, Samuel, 101
Marshall, Samuel, 136
Maskelyne, Neville, 63, 111
Masson, Francis, 58–9, 173
Matra, James, 22, 28–9, 34, 211
medical supplies, 97–8
Middleton, Sir Charles, 57
estimate of transportation costs, 189–90
government service, 10
naval career, 81–2
at Navy Board, 82–3
preparations for First Fleet, 12–13, 82–3
receives letter re number of women convicts, 67
preparations for the voyage
arrangement of shipboard accommodation, 117
decision on food allowance, 149–50
and Phillip's request for fresh food, 151
returns on costs of NSW venture, 191–3

military law, 34–5
Miller, Andrew, 55–6, 109, 125
Mitchell, Mary, 122
Molony, John, 1, 182
money *see* currency
Moore, John, 6
Morley, Roger *see* Murley, Roger
Morning Chronicle
reports BB decision, 22
Morrison, James, 137
Murley, Roger, 65

Nautilus (ship), 58
Navy Board, 81
estimate of transportation costs, 184–5
information needs, 10–11
provisions for First Fleet, 95–7
Nepean, Evan, 10
communicates BB decision to Treasury, 17–18
and cultivation of cotton, 109
expected departure of First Fleet, 129
on flax plant, 107
correspondence with Sharrow, 108
future of NSW settlement, 204
informs Admiralty of BB decision, 20
investigates transportation costs, 182–4, 186–8
Newton Fowell's appointment, 7–8
on Pitt's control of convict policy, 200
preparations for First Fleet, 12–13, 19–20, 82
expectation re law in NSW, 35–6, 44
list of clothing requirements, 103
selection of marines, 72
preparations for the voyage
advice on provisions, 96
advises need for extra ship, 119
arrangement of shipboard accommodation, 117
arrangements to escort convicts, 123
on condition of women convicts, 142
contracts for transport of convicts, 121–2
plan for the voyage, 162–3
receives requests for fresh food, 151, 153

Index

on profile of convicts, 71
provision for civil establishment, 49–50
record keeping, 11
returns on costs of NSW venture, 191–3
New South Wales
  agricultural progress, 101
  civil establishment, 49–59
  commissions subsequent to settlement, 41–2
  courts, 37–9
  decision, 17–26
    in King's speech, 25–6
    news received in Europe, 24–5
  government intentions
    permanent settlement, 200–7
    purpose of settlement, 207
  law, 34–7
  social development plans, 28–34
  unique characteristics, 27, 207–13
Newton, John, 56–7
Norfolk Island, 22

ordnance, 105–6

Palmer, John, 87
Pemberton, Henry, 154–5
Péron, François, 101
Phillip, Arthur, 80
  accommodation requirements, 102
  appointed to command *Sirius*, 85, 114
  appointment as governor, 5–8
    announced, 21
  biographical sketch, 50–4
  civil commission, 40–1
  and cultivation of cotton, 109
  and decision to withhold liquor in NSW, 138–9
  early difficulties in NSW, 213
  expectation re law in NSW, 34–5, 44
  experience of scurvy, 146–7
  formally establishes colony, 177–8
  government instructions, 32–4
    on flax, 107
    on the voyage, 164
  intentions, 30–2
  linguistic ability, 52
  need for military law, 34–5
  plans for NSW, 44–5
  prefers Port Jackson to BB, 177
  preparations for the voyage
    condemns condition of women convicts, 141, 142
    embarkation, 125
    fitting out of *Sirius*, 86–7
    friction with Teer, 116
    loading of ships, 116–17
    need for supply of fresh food, 150–2
    need for trade goods, 110
    provision for defence of colony, 105–6
    requests fresh food, 148–9
    role, 13, 82–3
    suggests extra ship, 119
    supply of medical and surgical needs, 152–3
  purchase of provisions in
    Cape Town, 171, 172, 173
    Rio de Janeiro, 169–70
    Tenerife, 167
  qualifications for command of First Fleet, 53
  report on convict deaths, 71
  understands BB a permanent settlement, 201–4
  voyage
    decision to go ahead in *Supply*, 174
    planned route, 162
    purchase of provisions, 167, 169–70, 171–3
    reception in Rio de Janeiro, 168
  on women convicts, 2
pirates, 39
Pitt, William, 29
  on cost of transportation, 195–6
  planned trading innovation, 196–7
  on transportation policy, 200–1
plants *see* provisions, plants and seeds
Polynesian women, 32, 33
Portsmouth, 129–56
Preparations for the voyage
  medical preparations, 149–55
  pre-departure health, 143–9
Prince of Wales (ship), 87
  acquired for First Fleet, 91
  changes to accommodation, 133
  chartered to East India Co., 93
  crew tally, 65
  embarkation of convicts, 124
  embarkation of marines, 124

257

fitting out, 119
joins First Fleet, 132
livestock losses, 175
tally of convicts, 125
Providence (ship), 209
provisions
food, 95-7, 134, 135
availability in Rio de Janeiro, 168-9
fresh meat and vegetables, 148-9
purchases in Cape Town, 171
purchases in Rio de Janeiro, 169-70
purchases in Tenerife, 167
livestock, 99
losses on voyage, 175
purchases in Cape Town, 172
plants and seeds, 99-101
purchases in Cape Town, 173
quality, 3, 210
Public Advertiser
anticipates opposition from France and Holland, 24
reports BB decision, 21, 22
purchasing, 43
purser's necessaries, 152-4

Reading Mercury and Oxford Gazette
plans for annual sailings, 205
reports number of women convicts, 68
remission of sentences, 41-2
Richards, William, 2-3, 93
complains of obstruction from East India Co., 21
contracts for transport of convicts, 122
hopes for future contracts, 201
provisions, 95
wins contract to provide ships, 90-1
Rio de Janeiro, 168-70
Riou, Edward, 206
Roberts, John, 200
Rolle, John, 200
Rose, George, 10, 82
and appointment of Phillip, 5-8
minutes BB decision, 18-20
requests medical and surgical supplies, 97-8
Ross, Robert, 54-5, 62, 66, 174
camp equipment requirements, 102

on cost of NSW venture, 194
and decision to withhold liquor in NSW, 138
embarkation, 125
lack of camp utensils, 118
requests changes to marine accommodation, 133-4
Royal Navy crews, 64-5
Royal Navy ships, 84-90
crew selection, 71-2

St James's Chronicle
reports BB decision, 23
Santa Cruz, 167
Scarborough (ship), 90, 91
chartered to East India Co., 93
crew tally, 65
embarkation of convicts, 123
intended mutiny, 166, 176
joins First Fleet, 131, 132
receives stores, 115
selection of convicts, 70, 71
tally of convicts, 125
scientific equipment, 111-12
scurvy, 145-9
sea routes, 160-1
seeds *see* provisions, plants and seeds
Sever, William, 122
Sharrow, George, 108
Sharrow, William, 108
Shaw, A.G.L.
quality of planning, 1, 2, 130, 140-1
quotes Pitt on cost of transportation, 181, 195
shelter, 102
ships, 81-94
loading, 114-20
legal requirements, 119-20
see also embarkation
see also names of individual ships, e.g. *Sirius*
ships' crews
Royal Navy, 64-5
selection, 71-2
transports, 65
selection, 72-3
Shortland, John, 58, 118, 133
appointed agent for transports, 83
and clothing for women convicts, 142, 143
requests fresh food, 148

Index

Simpson, John, 75–9
Sinclair, Duncan, 122
Singleton, John, 108, 109
Sirius (ship), 4, 64–5, 84–7, 94
   command arrangements, 59–61
   crew selection, 71–2
   embarkation of marines, 123
   fitting out, 85–7, 114–15, 118
   junior officers, 62
   loss, 213
   outbreak of scurvy, 145
   purser, 73–5
   repairs, 132
slavery, 31
Smyth, Arthur Bowes
   criticism of Phillip, 164–5
   on Phillip's civil commission, 40
   purchase of fruit and vegetables in Rio, 169
   quality of provisions, 3, 210
Steele, Thomas, 10, 82
   advises Navy Board of BB decision, 83–4
   minutes BB decision, 18–20
   provisions and equipment, 95–6, 102, 104
Stephens, Philip, 10, 82
storeships, 92–3
   see also names of individual ships, e.g. *Borrowdale*
Supply (ship), 64, 87–90, 94
   embarkation of marines, 123
   fitting out, 12, 86, 89–90, 115
   repairs, 132–3
surgical supplies, 97–8, 152–4
Sydney, Thomas Townshend, Viscount
   and BB decision, 17–18
   contracts for transport of convicts, 122
   intervenes on behalf of Susanna Holmes, 77–8
   and law in NSW, 36
   plans for future fleets, 204

Tasman, Abel, 161
Teer, George, 13, 83, 92
   friction with Phillip, 116
   and loading of ships, 115–16
   and quality of provisions, 97, 210
Tench, Watkin, 62, 66
   on absence of botanist, 58–9
   on adequacy of provisions, 3
   inspection of convicts' letters, 139
   lack of camp utensils, 118
   on leaving Cape Town, 174
Tenerife, 167
Thomas, James, 131
Thomas, Joshua, 13, 83
tools, 104–5
trade goods, 109–10
Transportation Act, 1784, 120
transportation costs, 182–94
   Campbell's estimates, 182–4
   Middleton's estimates, 189–90
   Navy Board estimates, 184–5
   Nepean and Middleton's 1790 returns, 191–3
   Nepean's estimates, 186–8
transports, 90–2
   changes to accommodation, 133
   crew selection, 65, 72–3
   tally of convicts, 125
   see also names of individual ships, e.g. *Friendship*
Turnbull, John, 18, 90

United Empire Loyalists, 211–12

Vice-admiralty court, 39

Watson, Brook, 63
White, John, 57, 136, 171
   oversees embarkation of convicts, 124
   in Rio de Janeiro, 170
   supply of medical and surgical needs, 98, 134, 152, 153
White, Peter, 72
Wilberforce, William, 29, 57
Wilson, Charles, 2, 198
women convicts
   clothing, 2, 140–3
   number, 67–8
   Phillip's intentions, 31
   provision for, 18
   selection, 70
Worgan, George, 87, 163

yeoman-farmers, 32